# PRAISE FOR
# BEYOND FRAGILITY

"Well-intentioned White people often fear saying or doing something wrong across race, leaving them immobilized and ineffective. This accessible guidebook goes beyond the 'what' of anti-racist allyship and provides the 'how.' Through exercises, reflection questions, and familiar scenarios, *Beyond Fragility* supports potential White allies in developing the skills and agency to break through immobilization and stay true to the ongoing commitment of anti-racism allyship."

—**Robin DiAngelo, PhD,** #1 *New York Times* bestselling
author of *White Fragility* and *Nice Racism*

"*Beyond Fragility* is a powerfully instructive guide that reduces the defensiveness, uncertainty, and discomfort that many White people experience when it comes to confronting racial inequality. Its scientifically informed skills are drawn from the foundational principles of dialectical behavior therapy, making it a must-read for anyone who is devoted to embracing anti-racist allyship and actually *doing* the work."

—**Rheeda Walker, PhD,** author of *The Unapologetic Guide to Black
Mental Health* and *No Racial Elephants in the Therapy Room*

"*Beyond Fragility* is a groundbreaking guide that transcends rhetoric, providing a practical roadmap for effective anti-racist allyship. What sets this book apart is its hands-on approach, providing concrete activities that cultivate awareness and empower allies with tangible tools. Rooted in skills development, *Beyond Fragility* navigates the journey to adopting an anti-racist identity, emphasizing the crucial alignment of values and identity with the principles of anti-racism. The narrative dives into the messiness of this transformation, incorporating case studies, assessments, and reflection prompts throughout, transforming the material into a living, breathing guide. This meticulously crafted resource identifies and offers insights to overcome barriers to effective allyship, ensuring that readers emerge equipped to build anti-racist skills in the real world. *Beyond Fragility* is not just a book; it's an indispensable companion for those committed to genuine change."

—**Helen A. Neville, PhD,** professor at the University of Illinois Urbana-Champaign and
past president of the Society for the Psychological Study of Culture, Ethnicity and Race

"I am completely blown away by *Beyond Fragility*. Ultimately, I agree with the authors that this is a book for White people that doesn't center Whiteness. It does not center our comfort, our ignorance, or our fear of consequences—we are compelled to show up in more effective ways. As a therapist, I was immediately struck by the idea that we, as White allies, cannot do effective anti-racist work outside of our window of tolerance. That is part of why this book is so unique and powerful—the authors acknowledge that as allies, we cannot solely educate ourselves into anti-racism. We must use our emotional regulation skills, and these emotional regulation skills *are* anti-racist skills. The authors also perfectly balance compassion and conviction by tapping into the deeply human nature of the anti-racism process. They neither coddle nor condemn; while reading, I felt as though I was speaking to a longtime trusted therapist. Even as someone who has been on the anti-racism journey for many years, *Beyond Fragility* clarified my own thinking and I look forward to coming back to it again and again."

**—KC Davis, LPC,** author of *How to Keep House While Drowning* and creator of @strugglecare

"If you're a White person in the United States and you want to be a better ally or social justice advocate, then *Beyond Fragility* is the book for you. Through digestible definitions and easy-to-follow worksheets, the authors have gifted readers with an opportunity to explore their racial biases, to challenge the problematic messages they have been socialized with, and to develop and practice the skill sets needed to fight against racism in their everyday lives. What I appreciate most about the book is that it acknowledges the cognitive, emotional, and behavioral difficulties that White people may face when confronting racism, while reminding them that they must work consciously and intentionally hard to transform our society into one that is equitable and anti-racist."

**—Kevin Nadal, PhD,** distinguished professor, past president of the Asian American Psychological Association, and author of *Microaggressions and Traumatic Stress*

"As an expert in the field of racial trauma, I have devoted my career to helping youth and adults of color heal from the pernicious and traumatic effects of chronic structural racism. Healing work is critical, and at the same time, the burden *cannot* be on communities of color to figure out how to deal with ongoing racial trauma—as a society, we must work to end structural racism, which requires the willing collaboration of effective White allies. Without the powerful engagement of White allies encouraged in *Beyond Fragility*, it is difficult to imagine an end to the myriad racist experiences reported time and again by my clients."

**—Steven D. Kniffley Jr., PsyD, MPA, ABPP, HSP,** professor and senior associate dean for DEI at the University of Cincinnati and founder of Kniffley Racial Trauma Therapy & Training

"*Beyond Fragility* is an indispensable guide in our ongoing challenges to lean into true diversity and inclusion. Racism has long been a tool of division that has impacted every ethnic community across the globe. The eradication of this weapon is critical for us to truly move forward as a people versus repeating the trauma of racism endlessly, as has been evidenced through the course of time. I'm so grateful for the tools and strategies that are taught and illuminated in this wonderful book."

**—Eboni Webb, PsyD, HSP,** CEO of The Village of Kairos, international speaker and trainer

"This book is an essential guide for navigating the complexities of anti-racist allyship in our current era. It addresses core challenges with a comprehensive skills-based and compassionate approach, offering practical exercises and reflections that are invaluable in the fight against racism. *Beyond Fragility* is both empowering and transformative, making it a crucial read for those serious about making a sustainable difference."

**—Kate Truitt, PhD, MBA,** author of *Healing in Your Hands* and *Keep Breathing*

"For White would-be allies, it is easy to let the fear of 'getting it wrong' prevent you from speaking out against racism. *Beyond Fragility* is essential reading for anyone looking to break through these barriers and develop the fundamental skills needed to engage in anti-racism work with conviction and clarity."

**—Amanda White, LCPC,** author of *Not Drinking Tonight* and founder of @therapyforwomen

"With its masterfully clever use of assessments, affirmations, and acronyms, *Beyond Fragility* is an essential text that provides readers with actionable approaches to anti-racist allyship that will create sustainable change. The skills are broadly applicable to many contexts; for example, they can be used within families (e.g., talking to your children about race), friendships (e.g., gently calling out a friend), and at work (e.g., doing an equity audit). Whether you are a teacher, lawyer, academic professional, or doctor—or do any work with BIPOC—this book is for you and will take your anti-racist allyship to the next level!"

**—Sara Bufferd, PhD,** associate professor of psychology at the University of Louisville

"*Beyond Fragility* is a great resource for anyone who genuinely wants to be a better anti-racist ally but doesn't know how to overcome the fears that get in the way of doing so consistently. While some cross-cultural resources aim for breadth, this book hunkers down on one very crucial cultural factor—anti-racism—and explores it in more depth. With powerfully empathetic insights on the internal and external barriers that hinder allyship efforts, *Beyond Fragility* provides practical and nonjudgmental strategies for increasing your understanding of cultural experiences and the resulting allyship support opportunities around you, while helping you increase your confidence and efficacy within the personal and professional cross-cultural relationships you are able to cultivate."

**—Lambers Fisher, MS, LMFT, MDiv,** author of *Diversity in Clinical Practice*

"I cannot speak highly enough of this book. Yara Mekawi, Natalie Watson-Singleton, and Danyelle Dawson have created a resource that not only provides education around the importance of anti-racism work, but also has action items that are clear and relatable to today's world. This book is a must-have for individuals who have made the commitment to becoming active anti-racists, to being intentional and effective advocates and accomplices to Black people, Indigenous people, and other people of the global majority."

**—Portia Burch,** activist, abolitionist, justice strategist, and podcast host (@portia.noir)

"*Beyond Fragility* offers a step-by-step practical guide for White people who want to become more effective anti-racist allies. Based on psychological principles, the authors use everyday language and helpful examples to describe the concrete ways White people can grow as anti-racist allies. Whether someone is just starting or has already been working on anti-racist allyship, this book is a valuable resource for learning more and developing new skills."

**—Nathan Todd, PhD,** professor of psychology at the University of Illinois Urbana-Champaign

"*Beyond Fragility* is an essential read for organizational leaders, therapists, educators, and anyone ready to embark on, or expand, their work as anti-racism allies. The authors address key factors that stymie our efforts to live as good allies, including our fears, distorted thoughts, and desires to belong and avoid conflict. They guide the reader through research-based, concrete skills for engaging in effective and sustained allyship with examples and strategies that can create more equitable relationships and institutions. *Beyond Fragility* is an excellent resource for anyone ready to take on the 'good trouble' of anti-racism allyship."

**—NiCole Buchanan, PhD,** professor of psychology at Michigan State University

"*Beyond Fragility* is brimming with anti-racist terminology, illustrative examples, comprehensive case studies, and engaging activities. These elements, enriched with memorable acronyms, rigorously researched definitions, and therapeutic tools, guide White allies from mere theoretical comprehension of anti-racism to tangible, proactive steps. Engaging with the concepts presented in this book has the potential to catalyze profound learning experiences, mend damaged racial relationships, and cultivate a climate of safety within communities and for individuals who have suffered due to racist acts and systemic oppression."

**—Monica F. Cox, PhD, CEO,** www.drmonicacox.com

"Becoming genuinely anti-racist goes beyond good intentions; it demands interpersonal skills, emotional awareness, and a dedication to continuous learning and application. Mekawi, Watson-Singleton, and Dawson have created a user-friendly, evidence-based manual packed with scenarios and exercises to empower White allies with the psychological skills necessary to confront passivity, fear, and guardedness in anti-racist efforts. *Beyond Fragility* is essential for anyone looking to elevate from good intentions to transformative anti-racist action."

**—Robyn L. Gobin, PhD,** associate professor at the University of Illinois-Urbana Champaign and author of *The Self-Care Prescription*

"In the most supportive and nonjudgmental way, *Beyond Fragility* invites White people to take a good look at the thoughts and feelings that get in our way of being effective racial justice allies. This accessible workbook, grounded in psychological science, offers case examples for developing real-world, sustainable allyship skills. I have been waiting for a powerful, practical guide like *Beyond Fragility*; it is a must-read for any White person who wants to do better."

**—Lisa Spanierman, PhD,** professor and associate dean at Arizona State University College of Integrative Sciences and Arts

# BEYOND FRAGILITY

## A Skills-Based Guide to Effective Anti-Racist Allyship

YARA MEKAWI, PhD

NATALIE WATSON-SINGLETON, PhD

DANYELLE DAWSON, MA

Published by
Bridge City Books, an imprint of PESI Publishing, Inc.
3839 White Ave
Eau Claire, WI 54703

Cover and interior design by Emily Dyer
Editing by Jenessa Jackson, PhD

Library of Congress Cataloging-in-Publication Data
Description: Eau Claire, WI: Bridge City Books, [2024] | Includes bibliographical references.
Identifier: LCCN 2023058446
Subjects: LCSH: Anti-racism. | Race relations. | Allyship.
Classification: LCC HT1563.M44 2024 | DDC 305.8--dc23/eng/20240126
LC record available at https://lccn.loc.gov/2023058446

ISBN 9781962305068 (print)
ISBN 9781962305082 (ePDF)
ISBN 9781962305075 (ePUB)

**Bridge City** Books

# TABLE OF CONTENTS

■ ■ ■ ■ ■

# ACKNOWLEDGMENTS

• • • • •

Anti-racism has existed for as long as racism has existed. Although this fight is anything but new, a huge body of work and labor has allowed us to develop new strategies to resist racism and create a racially just world. We are grateful for our ancestors' wisdom and resilience. We are grateful for the scholar activists of color who paved the way for us to be able to do this work. We are grateful for the work of many researchers and clinicians, on which our skills are built. We are also grateful for *you* for picking up this book and making a choice to grow and redefine what it means for you to be an effective anti-racist ally.

# INTRODUCTION:
## Before You Dive In

. . . . .

Engaging in anti-racist work is complicated. As society is faced with the task of moving from "not racist" to "anti-racist," an increasing number of White allies are trying to do more and listen more and, in that process, have become exposed to a variety of ideas about what they can do to support Black, Indigenous, and other people of color (BIPOC). If this has been part of your own journey, you've probably discovered that meaningful anti-racist allyship is not an innate essence; it is not something you were born knowing how to do. Rather, moving from not racist to actively anti-racist requires a lot of skills—skills you likely were not exposed to in your home, school, or workplace environments. We know not having these skills can leave you feeling distressed, stuck, frustrated, or afraid of getting it wrong.

We also recognize that the skills needed to do anti-racism work cannot be reduced to a single checklist of "dos" and "don'ts" that applies in all situations. Committing to being an anti-racist ally is a lifelong process of learning, unlearning, and acting in ways consistent with anti-racist values. For this reason, anti-racism requires deep psychological work and a unique set of skills. You've got to be willing to learn how to cope with the discomfort and uncertainty associated with anti-racist work and learn how to prioritize action over stagnation and complacency. This requires an openness to building your capacity and stamina to engage with the cognitive, emotional, and interpersonal complexities inherent in anti-racist work.

As three women of color psychologists who have offered many anti-racism workshops and trainings to universities, corporations, and community members, we realize that most people engaging in anti-racist allyship genuinely want to be more effective allies. However, the vast majority of allyship efforts emphasize *educating* allies about anti-racism without teaching them how to actually *do* anti-racism work. Since combining education with skill-building leads to bigger change than providing education alone (Bezrukova et al., 2016), our workbook focuses on blending increased awareness with concrete skills so White allies can develop the skills needed to engage in effective and sustainable anti-racist action.

In particular, this workbook will provide you with the skills to (1) overcome common barriers to approaching anti-racism (e.g., misunderstanding what racism is, not knowing how to recognize racism, not having a clear anti-racist identity), (2) cope with intense emotions (e.g., guilt, fear) that arise when discussing racism and privilege, and (3) navigate complex interpersonal dynamics related to anti-racism (e.g., validating the experiences of BIPOC peers, engaging in intercultural dialogue without defensiveness, recovering from a racist misstep, speaking out against racist comments).

## What Is in This Book?

This book is organized into five overarching sections that are designed to help you overcome the main barriers to anti-racist allyship: cognitive, emotional, and inter-personal barriers.

In section I, we focus on building a foundation for effective anti-racist allyship by providing you with an overview of key concepts and terms relevant to anti-racism and allyship. These introductory chapters will explore key concepts central to understanding racism (e.g., systemic racism, cultural racism, individual racism) and anti-racism (e.g., effective allyship, White fragility), as well as common misconceptions about these concepts. We will also explore the benefits of using a structured skills-based approach for understanding and recognizing racism.

In section II, we focus on cognitive barriers to effective allyship, which can include interfering worldviews, inflexible thinking, lack of clarity about values, and difficulty overcoming ambivalence. All of these cognitive barriers can hinder your ability to engage in anti-racist work in a successful and ongoing way. For instance, in terms of interfering worldviews, White allies may find themselves operating from a worldview in which BIPOC are the only ones who "have a race" and White individuals are viewed as non-racialized beings. This worldview can get in the way of anti-racism because if BIPOC are seen as the only people who have a race, it may follow that BIPOC are the only ones impacted by racism and thus the ones ultimately responsible for ending racism. In addition, we highlight how inflexible, black-and-white thinking can stagnate efforts, and we introduce alternative approaches that allow for more flexible thinking.

In section III, we unpack emotional barriers to effective allyship. Engaging in anti-racist work entails confronting countless unpleasant emotions, such as fear, anxiety, overwhelm, guilt, hopelessness, powerlessness, and anger. And to be clear, the problem is not that you will experience these unpleasant emotions, but barriers can arise when you are unable to effectively manage these emotions in real time. These unpleasant emotional states can arise across different situations, such as when you are asked to consider your Whiteness and its privileges or when you are called out for a racist mishap. The topics covered in this section are aimed at helping you not only understand your emotions, but also develop the necessary skills to evaluate, tolerate, and overcome difficult emotions.

Section IV focuses on interpersonal barriers to allyship, which can arise when members of different racialized and cultural groups engage in challenging conversations with each other. For instance, you may find yourself in a work meeting where only the ideas of your White colleagues are emphasized and where your BIPOC colleagues do not feel comfortable to speak at all. In addition, you may find yourself saying the wrong thing and being called out by peers. Whether or not these conversations are explicitly about racial issues, we explore several reasons why these conversations can go awry and examine how you can validate the experiences of your BIPOC peers, successfully recover from a racist misstep, and speak out against racist comments.

Finally, section V is all about taking steps to make sure that your anti-racist work is sustainable and as impactful as possible. This is where we move beyond the barriers identified in previous sections and teach you how to implement these skills in the "real world" to make meaningful change. In this last section, we focus on putting the pieces together so that you can see how the skills are part of a larger, interdependent system. This means that the skills can work together in nuanced situations to make a big impact that overcomes numerous cognitive, emotional, and interpersonal barriers.

The chapters in each section are designed to provide you with education, case examples, guided reflections, and skill-building exercises necessary to overcome these barriers to effective allyship. To get the most out of the guided reflections and exercises, we encourage you to actually write out your responses and answers in the book! We promise it will help you process the information more deeply and learn to use the skills in your daily life. The skills we introduce are informed by scientifically supported therapeutic strategies from dialectical behavioral therapy (DBT), mindfulness-based stress reduction (MBSR), acceptance and commitment therapy (ACT), motivational interviewing (MI), and cognitive behavioral therapy (CBT)—strategies that have been found to produce long-term positive change.

Reading and practicing the skills outlined in this book will allow you to jumpstart your anti-racist endeavors so you can:

- Become more knowledgeable about the different elements of racism and anti-racism
- Feel more confident and less anxious using your voice as an anti-racism ally
- Increase your endurance in and commitment to anti-racism
- Learn to speak up without talking over BIPOC
- Call out racism in a way that is more likely to lead to change rather than tension
- Work toward ending the processes that reproduce systems of oppression

# How Do I Use This Book?

This book is designed to be used flexibly and to support your anti-racist journey for many years. We encourage you to read the chapters in order and to practice your skills along the way. It may also be helpful to read this book in an anti-racism reading group with colleagues or friends. You can read a chapter weekly and discuss progress with the group. We also encourage you to continue to use this book as a reference when you encounter a situation that calls for a particular skill (e.g., the need to engage in a specific anti-racist behavior). To support you in continuing to review and practice the skills even after you have finished reading this book, we have included in the appendix a summary of each skill outlining the key points and questions you should consider in that scenario.

# Whom Is This Book For?

This book is for any White ally who desires to take their allyship to the next level. It is relevant to anyone who has been racialized as White as well as anyone who has lighter skin, who has ancestral roots that trace back to Europe, and who does not have observable or known connections to Black, Asian, or Indigenous ancestry and heritage (Haeny et al., 2021). Our workbook is appropriate and helpful for people with a wide range of educational levels, personal and professional competencies, and exposure to anti-racism concepts. We encourage you to use these skills with friends or in your workplace and to use them regardless of whether you have limited organizational power or are the company's CEO.

As psychologists ourselves, we also encourage you to use this book if you are a mental health professional, as it can be a vital resource in providing effective anti-racist care to White and BIPOC clients alike. If you work with White clients, you can incorporate the skills from this book into your sessions to support clients in becoming effective anti-racist allies in their personal and professional lives. If you are a White mental health professional, you can also benefit from using these skills to recover from or to prevent missteps that occur in sessions with BIPOC clients.

We also want to note that since these skills were designed in the context of the United States, you may need to make some adjustments when generalizing to other parts of the world. For example, when we discuss certain racial groups or use certain terms such as *BIPOC*, we recognize that this language may not translate to other contexts. For example, some countries may not have a racial classification system at all, while other countries may have a classification system that bears no overlap to the one currently used in the US. Furthermore, although racism and colorism exist in every corner of the world, each country has its own historical context that may have led to present-day inequities. Thus, although this book represents the fundamentals of engaging in effective anti-racist work, we recognize that our content was designed within a US context.

Lastly, if you have made some missteps along your anti-racism journey, today is a new day. You *can* learn new skills. We invite you to begin again equipped with new ways of showing up and contributing to an anti-racist society.

# SECTION I

· · · · ·

# BUILDING A FOUNDATION FOR EFFECTIVE ANTI-RACIST ALLYSHIP

# CHAPTER 1

# Defining Racism:
# From Misunderstanding to Mastery

Effectively engaging in anti-racist work requires a solid grasp of what racism is and why it is still a problem (Bryant & Arrington, 2022). In this chapter, we help you move from misunderstanding to mastery by providing a primer on what racism really is and giving you a structured tool to help you identify the complexities of racism in *any* context. This will allow you to turn the concept of racism from something "fuzzy" into something you can concretely pinpoint within yourself or within your contexts.

## What Is Racism?

Although people often misunderstand racism as simply the expression of outward prejudice and discrimination, racism goes beyond negative attitudes and beliefs. Racism encompasses mutually reinforcing subsystems of power, privilege, and oppression designed to privilege White people and disadvantage and harm BIPOC. Racism manifests across different levels of society to maintain a racial hierarchy wherein White individuals have more access to resources and power than BIPOC (i.e., White supremacy). These levels of racism impact our everyday lives and create conditions in which racism is the norm, not the exception.

## What Is Systemic Racism?

The broadest level of racism is *systemic*, which is also known as institutional racism. Systemic racism refers to legalized and informal policies and practices that give White people greater access to material conditions (e.g., quality education), information (e.g., their own history and heritage), resources (e.g., wealth), and representation (e.g., voting rights, control of the media) compared to BIPOC. An example of systemic racism is the creation of voting laws, such as the addition of rigid ID requirements, that legislators know will disproportionately reduce access to voting. Even if the law does not explicitly say that BIPOC are not allowed to vote, the effect of the law is to disproportionately lower BIPOC access to being able to exercise voting rights.

## What Is Cultural Racism?

*Cultural racism* encompasses the belief that some cultures are superior to others, and it occurs when one group holds the power to define the cultural values of the society at large. In the US, you can see cultural racism at play in the degree to which White-centric cultural values are prioritized over the cultural values of BIPOC communities. One way this overreliance on White-centric cultural values has manifested is through standards of beauty and professionalism. For example, White hair norms have been accepted as the standard in both beauty and professional arenas, whereas Black hair norms, such as braids, locs, or hairstyles that celebrate the natural beauty of Black hair, are often seen as unprofessional. Only recently did the US military begin allowing Black service members to wear their hair in braids or in its natural state despite the fact that White service members have been able to wear their hair in its natural texture since the military's inception.

## What Is Individual Racism?

Finally, *individual racism* includes the persistence and internalization of racial prejudice that can manifest in unintentional and intentional ways. This type of racism is perhaps most readily identifiable because it occurs between individuals and can also be experienced personally and vicariously. Individual racism includes acts of commission (e.g., making a prejudiced comment) as well as acts of omission (e.g., not speaking up when someone else makes a prejudiced comment). Although comments that intentionally denigrate BIPOC are often easily understood as acts of racism, *unintentional* comments or behaviors that reinforce racist ideologies or White-centric cultural values are also manifestations of individual racism. Notably, individual racism can be both blatant and intentionally harmful (e.g., the use of racial slurs), or it can involve more subtle, brief, and commonplace behaviors or comments that are insulting to BIPOC, which are known as "racial microaggressions" (Sue et al., 2007). For example, perceiving someone of Asian descent to be "from somewhere else" or "not American" is a manifestation of individual racism because it privileges White Americans as "typical Americans" and subjugates Asian Americans as "others."

Given that racism is a multilevel system of mutually reinforcing subsystems of power, privilege, and oppression that harm BIPOC, limiting definitions of racism to outward expressions of discrimination is inadequate. We hope our definition highlights that committing racial slurs or overt acts of racism are not the only ways to perpetrate racism toward BIPOC—that racism can occur and "count" even if it is not conscious, intentional, or overt. We also hope this definition underscores why terms like "reverse racism" and "racism toward White people" are misinterpretations of the reality of racism. Racism involves a clear directionality in which society affords White people more access to power and privilege relative to BIPOC.

## Centering Anti-Black Racism

While racism negatively impacts *all* BIPOC, anti-Black racism is a specific kind of racial prejudice directed toward Black people or those perceived to be Black. Anti-Black racism amplifies and prioritizes proximity to Whiteness, which means that the closer to Whiteness (and further away from Blackness) individuals are, the more privilege and power they have in society. Like racism more generally, anti-Black racism occurs across all levels, and it systematically marginalizes Black people and devalues Blackness in all contexts. Anti-Black racism is also closely related to anti-darkness/colorism, which is the unequal treatment of and discrimination against individuals based on their skin tone and physical features. For this reason, anti-Black racist attitudes can also be evident *within* BIPOC communities, such that BIPOC individuals with darker skin and more Afrocentric physical features experience less privilege than BIPOC individuals with lighter skin and more Eurocentric physical features. Thus, anti-Blackness should also be distinctly attended to in efforts to dismantle all levels of racism.

# Intersecting Systems of Oppression

Although the focus of this book is racism, systems of oppression are interconnected, meaning that racism also intersects with experiences of classism, ableism, sexism, heterosexism, genderism, and weight-based discrimination (Combahee River Collective, 1978). As a result, people may have different experiences of racism depending on their other identities (Crenshaw, 2017). For example, a Black woman's experiences of racism may differ from those of a Black man and from those of a Black nonbinary or genderqueer person (Lewis & Neville, 2015; Nadal, 2023). This means it is impossible to fully separate racism from other oppressive systems that interact with racism to oppress individuals with multiple marginalized identities. Incorporating this into your understanding provides necessary context and nuance to your identification of racism.

# But What *Is* Racism?

While it can be easy to read about racism, rarely are discussions held about how to notice the existence of racism on an individual, cultural, and systemic level. For this reason, it can be challenging to recognize racism and its various forms in practice. One way to better understand racism and engage in anti-racist work is through the use of analogies, which help make complex and abstract ideas more concrete by drawing on your understanding of more familiar concepts. As a neutral story, it can also reduce your defenses and allow you to operate from a blank slate. With that in mind, let's consider a story about a T-shirt company.

## Case Study: The T-Shirt Company

As a teenager, Jim Sr. knew he was destined for greatness and had a knack for managing others. Growing up, he worked at a garment factory owned by a family friend named Charles. Jim Sr. worked long hours for free just to prove to Charles that he had "what it takes" to be a good leader who motivated workers to produce clothes faster. After some years, Jim Sr. became an apprentice at the factory, continuing to work for free. Because Jim Sr.'s parents did not need the money, they supported his apprenticeship and always cheered him on. After several years, Charles became ill and passed away. Because Charles did not have any heirs, he left the company to Jim Sr. Upon inheriting the factory, Jim Sr. turned it into a thriving T-shirt company.

Jim Sr. believed he was biologically cut out to be CEO due to his intellectual skills; he also believed that the workers were more suitable for manual labor—which, to him, required no intellect. As CEO of the T-shirt company, Jim Sr. took the largest share of profits while continuing to pay the factory workers barely enough to cover their bills. To build up his leadership team, he employed family members and friends as managers while prohibiting pathways to promotion for workers. In fact, applications for promotion were kept in a safe that could only be accessed by upper management. Individuals considered for managerial positions were required to attend invite-only trainings led by Jim Sr. himself.

To keep workers in line and prevent them from speaking out, Jim Sr. used abusive strategies, such as physical punishment (e.g., striking workers with a belt) and verbal reprimands. Jim Sr. also commissioned "artwork" for the factory, such that the walls were plastered with cartoonish drawings of workers depicted as children, and when the company started to use videos for their training, the videos stereotyped the workers as lazy and emphasized how important it was to stay in line. While management was served food prepared by a private chef, workers were only allowed five-minute lunch breaks at their workstations.

To really drive home the power differential, Jim Sr. created a color-coded badge system in which he wore a blue badge labeled "CEO," the board members wore a green badge labeled "manager," and everyone else wore a red badge labeled "factory worker." Workers who "caused trouble" got a black dot on their red badge, which made it even easier to poke fun at and disrespect the workers.

After a while, the factory workers became disgruntled and started to speak up regarding their concerns and share ideas about how to run the company. This confused and upset Jim Sr. because, in his mind, workers were not cut out for intellectual work. Therefore, in an attempt to maintain the hierarchy within the company, he implemented even more rules barring factory workers from speaking up or providing any input. If any employees dissented, they were met with threats of termination and warnings that Jim Sr. would spread the word to his well-connected colleagues that they were disruptive workers.

Jim Sr. continued to rule with an iron fist for decades until he, too, became ill and passed away, leading his son, Jim Jr., to take over the company. In an attempt to remedy his father's wrongdoings, Jim Jr. declared that he would do things differently and address the long-standing power differentials between upper management and the workers. However, Jim Jr. believed that the root of the continued inequality in the company was the badge system—despite the many other problematic power differences present.

In turn, he decided to get rid of the badges, proclaiming that now there was no way to tell management from workers, and therefore there were no differences between them. He held a ceremony where employees threw their badges into a large bonfire, and everyone watched as the blue, green, and red vestiges of the past went up in flames. To make his commitment to equality even clearer, he commissioned a plaque for his office door that stated, "Badges are not welcome here." After this event, Jim Jr. showed up to work the next day feeling like a revolutionary who had solved the problem of inequality in his company.

## REFLECTION

Has Jim Jr. correctly identified the source of the problem of inequality in the T-shirt company? Why or why not?

_____

_____

_____

_____

_____

_____

_____

_____

If your answer to this question was no, then you are right! This fictional example highlights how historical inequality can permeate different levels of a setting in a multitude of ways across time and generations. Even when the current members of an organization did not directly play a role in its problematic past, the historical permeation of inequality functions to benefit those with more privilege (the managers) and disadvantage those with less privilege (the workers). This permeation also makes it so that simple solutions, like getting rid of the badges, don't target core, long-standing problems. There are many oppressive practices at this company, occurring at all levels: individual (e.g., managers making fun of the workers), cultural (e.g., the training materials depicting workers as incompetent), and systemic (e.g., making the coursework and applications for promotion inaccessible to most workers). Jim Jr. has done nothing to change these practices; therefore, his action of burning the badges is purely symbolic.

Now, let's apply this relatively simple T-shirt company analogy to the more complex problem of racism.

# BASICS of Racism: A Skill for Understanding and Recognizing Racism

In order to understand and recognize racism within a given setting, we offer a structured, linear skill called BASICS, which is designed to guide you in considering the multifaceted forces that contribute to racism and enable it to persist in a particular context.

## "B" Is for Background

The first step in sufficiently understanding racism is to consider the historical background of a given context. This step is key to overcoming the historical ignorance that often perpetuates the lack of understanding and denial of racism. This step may require you to use the internet or your local libraries, and your analysis can be guided by questions such as "How were BIPOC historically treated in this particular context or setting?" and "What do we know about the history of segregation and rights within this context?"

For example, members of a local school board may start by investigating the history of racism in education and eventually the history of racism in their school district. This might involve examining the history of segregation more broadly and the process of desegregation in this local context specifically. They may summarize their findings in a report that is then shared with members of the larger community. This step helps the school board members and the community at large to think about the bigger context in which their schools exist.

## "A" Is for Application

The second step is to apply this background knowledge to the current context. This step counters the ahistorical fallacy, which is the dismissal of accurate historical information. Many people engage in the ahistorical fallacy when it comes to acknowledging the legacies of racism in this country, including slavery, the mass genocide of Indigenous peoples by European colonizers, racial segregation, forced sterilizations and harmful science experiments conducted on BIPOC, and media stereotypes that portray Asians, Blacks, and Hispanics in a negative light (Desmond & Emirbayer, 2009). By applying historical information to the current context, you directly challenge this fallacy and make connections between the past and the present. To do so, you might ask, "In what ways does this historical background inform the current situation?" and "How are BIPOC currently treated in this particular context as a result of historical racism?"

For example, a local OB-GYN office may consider the ways in which historical racism in medicine (e.g., abuses in medical research, forced sterilization of women of color) may contribute to current health care disparities, like the higher rates of maternal mortality for Black women and child mortality for Black infants. They might then analyze their own client data to determine whether there are disparities in pregnancy outcomes based on the race of their clients. They may even examine whether a provider's race influences how they engage with BIPOC patients (e.g., time spent with patients, likelihood of prescribing pain medication). To further apply their new knowledge about the history of racism in this context, they may then administer a survey specifically designed to assess patients' experiences in this space, including the degree to which patients feel listened to, validated, and treated with genuine care. Doing so allows the OB-GYN office to have a comprehensive understanding of how the vestiges of historical racism remain alive today.

## "S" Is for Systems of Oppression

The third step of the BASICS skill is to incorporate knowledge about other forms of oppression into your analysis of racism within a context. This step involves thinking holistically about systems of oppression and remembering that there are meaningful differences between and within groups. Toward this end, you might ask, "How do other systems of oppression, such as ableism, classism, sexism, heterosexism, genderism, and weight-based discrimination, worsen experiences of racism for BIPOC in this context?"

For example, a group of civilian review board members overseeing a police department may be tasked with identifying the role of racism in the extrajudicial shootings of Black people. This third step of BASICS would encourage the board members to consider how other intersecting systems of oppression affect certain marginalized communities within the larger Black community. For example, they might investigate the roles of intersecting racism and sexism (e.g., How are Black women treated by the police?) or intersecting racism and ableism (e.g., How are Black disabled people treated by the police?). Understanding the intersecting systems of oppression in police shootings can allow the civilian review board members to have a more comprehensive and accurate understanding of the problem.

## "I" Is for Individual Racism

The fourth step of the BASICS skill involves identifying the role of individual racism, such as implicit biases, explicit racist attitudes, and microaggressions, in maintaining inequities. This step could involve having intentional meetings where organizational members ask questions such as: "How often does discrimination occur in our organization?" and "What types of racial discrimination do our BIPOC members experience?" This is also an opportunity to identify whether there have been any particularly harmful incidents in the organization that need further resolution and repair.

Importantly, when group members are interrogating their own biases, it may be useful to do so in the context of race-based affinity groups, which are groups in which same-race individuals meet regularly to discuss, understand, and strategize about racism within their particular setting (Blitz & Kohl, 2012). Although the structure of how these groups are led may depend on a variety of factors, we encourage leaders of White-led spaces to focus on creating a space that is open and honest, does not reinforce stereotypes, and focuses on accountability. The purpose here is not to promote segregation, but to provide a space where White allies are able to explore their own biases without harming their BIPOC colleagues. To ensure these groups are maximally effective, we encourage that they be led by paid BIPOC consultants with expertise in anti-racism.

For example, a graduate student organization at a local university may implement the use of affinity groups wherein White individuals are asked to critically examine their own biases and the ways they may have internalized racism. Part of these discussions may include an acknowledgment of the harm done to BIPOC and, with guidance from BIPOC consultants, problem-solving to help White members repair the harm that has been done. This process could help members recognize and actively challenge their internalized bias, therefore reducing the potential for direct harm to their BIPOC colleagues.

## "C" Is for Cultural Racism

The fifth step of the BASICS skill is to identify the role of cultural racism in maintaining inequities. This requires you to be aware of and understand White supremacy culture, including how the values held by an organization compare to those inherent in White supremacy culture (more information about White supremacy values can be found in chapter 3). You might ask questions such as: "How does White supremacy culture implicitly or explicitly affect the way we run this organization and view members' behavior?" "What values do we prioritize?" and "What worldviews influence our assumptions and organizational processes?"

For example, members of a nonprofit organization serving displaced women in Yemen might compare their organizational mission with the tenets of White supremacy. They may note, for example, that although they report empowerment of Yemeni women as a strong value, many of their policies and practices actually are paternalistic and do not involve power sharing. This process can allow them to uncover the ways in which the norms and assumptions of their organization directly conflict with the empowerment and liberation of the population they are trying to serve.

## "S" Is for S̲ystemic Racism

The last step of the BASICS skill is to identify the specific policies, procedures, and laws that give rise to the outcomes and the processes identified in the previous steps. The questions to ask are: "What procedures might intentionally or unintentionally lead to the marginalization of BIPOC in this space?" "Who holds positions of power?" and "How does power sharing occur in ways that amplify BIPOC voices?"

For example, faculty members in a graduate program may use this step to "zoom out" on the results of all the previous steps and identify the policies that allow disparities between White and BIPOC students to remain. In doing so, faculty may realize that certain policies—such as those governing admission (e.g., requiring the GRE despite research showing that it reflects racial bias); funding (e.g., requiring students to pay for conference travel out of pocket before being reimbursed, which assumes that all students have the same access to disposable income); handling of Diversity, Equity, and Inclusion (DEI) concerns (e.g., encouraging students to report DEI concerns without a system that protects them from retaliation); and decision-making (e.g., excluding graduate students from meetings)—work together to maintain a system that harms BIPOC graduate students, especially those who experience other forms of oppression. The faculty members could then work to end these practices and change these policies to dismantle racism in impactful ways.

# Putting the BASICS Together: Operation SAVE

To bring it all together, let's consider how a particular organization could apply the BASICS skill to ensure that their organization is aligned with anti-racism. This example focuses on SAVE, a community mental health clinic that provides free mental health services to Black adolescents. The structure of the organization includes two White managers, five White board members, and ten Black providers. All of the Black providers are unpaid trainees who receive an evaluation grade at the end of the year. Consistent with its anti-racism values, SAVE decides to confront racism within their organization using the BASICS skill.

## Background

As a first step, the staff at SAVE decide to examine how Black youth have been treated both in the overarching mental health care system and within SAVE specifically. The organization's leaders, including the managers and board members, research how mental health has been understood and treated historically in Black populations, and they discover that there is a history of overdiagnosing certain mental health disorders, like psychotic disorders, and underdiagnosing other disorders, like depression. They also note that SAVE specifically has never had Black managers or board members. As a result of this process, they learn about the various biases that impact how Black youth are diagnosed and treated within mental health care systems. They also identify a new problem that warrants additional investigation: "What factors have hindered Black people from being represented in the core leadership at SAVE?"

## Application

During the first step, SAVE learned that there are various long-standing biases that impact how Black youth are diagnosed and treated for mental health symptoms, so for this step, they decide to ask the following questions: "What is the process of assessing the symptoms of Black youth in our organization? How do implicit and explicit biases influence how Black youth are diagnosed and treated in our organization currently?" In addition, given the lack of Black leadership within the organization, SAVE attempts to consider how Black clients and trainees feel about the all-White leadership within the organization. They ask questions like: "What types of experiences are our clients and trainees reporting with White managers and board members? How many attempts has SAVE made to successfully hire Black managers in the past few years?"

## Systems of Oppression

At this step, SAVE endeavors to identify the ways in which their services may be differentially experienced by Black youth who identify as LGBTQ+, who are low income, or who have learning disabilities. Engaging in this step involves reading about these interlocking systems of oppression and using this knowledge to identify, and eventually prioritize, those who experience multiple forms of marginalization. This might lead SAVE to evaluate which clients are more or less likely to receive adequate care within the organization, as well as to evaluate current services offered to meet the unique, intersecting needs of these groups. As a result, SAVE may decide to create a group specifically for queer Black youth or provide transportation resources for youth from low-income families.

## Individual Racism

Aligned with the fourth step of BASICS, SAVE endeavors to uncover the individual racism that may exist within the organization by conducting a self-assessment of various biases and prejudices held by White members. To do so, SAVE uses an implicit association test (a type of assessment designed to measure attitudes and beliefs that occur outside of explicit awareness) and supplements it with introspective reflection questions designed to help White members explore their internalized beliefs about Black youth and families. This step might allow SAVE members to identify ways they may be unintentionally harming Black youth and families by making biased assumptions about them. Affinity groups may be formed to further discuss the revelations uncovered in this step.

## Cultural Racism

To engage in the fifth step of this skill, SAVE's members critically examine their mission statement and reported values. They familiarize themselves with qualities of White supremacy culture and identify the ways in which their clinic's culture may be shaping patterns of cultural racism in the organization. They might note that even though their stated organizational value is "openness," many White members actually become defensive when concerns about cultural incompetence are raised by Black trainees and clients. Additionally, when these concerns are raised, staff meetings often prioritize the emotional reactions of White staff who feel targeted by complaints, rather than looking at ways to remedy the complaints. Therefore, the implicit culture of the organization often emphasizes the needs of White members over Black clients and trainees.

## Systemic Racism

In the final step, the members evaluate SAVE's organizational structure by conducting a formal assessment on how the organization is run. In turn, they find that major decisions are made primarily by White leaders with little input from Black clients or trainees. They also discover that their reliance on Black trainees results in a system where White leaders are paid for their efforts and Black staff are unpaid, perpetuating racialized inequities akin to plantations. Additionally, given that the trainees have less power within the organizational structure, they end up disproportionately burdened with more inconsequential tasks, such as making coffee, and have less opportunity to engage in meaningful tasks, such as creating policies that guide the organization.

After completing the BASICS skill, SAVE's members may choose to document this process in a formal report and make a plan to act on their findings.

# Practice Using the BASICS Skill

Now that you have a greater understanding of the BASICS skill, take a moment to apply your learning to the T-shirt company story we shared earlier. What might it look like for Jim Jr. to conduct the BASICS skill? Write down your answers as you walk through each step of the skill.

In terms of historical **background**, what history of inequality might Jim Jr. discover about the company?

_____

_____

_____

_____

_____

_____

How can Jim Jr. **apply** this background knowledge to see how the company's history informs current inequality in the company?

_____

_____

_____

_____

_____

How do other **systems of oppression** marginalize specific people in the company?

_____

_____

_____

_____

_____

How is **individual racism** maintained in the company?

_____

_____

_____

_____

_____

How is **cultural racism** maintained in the company?

_____

_____

_____

_____

_____

How is **systemic racism** maintained in the company?

_____

_____

_____

_____

_____

In our T-shirt company example, the historical **background** starts with Jim Sr.'s rise to power. Due to his family's financial resources, Jim Sr. was able to work without pay and impress Charles. He also benefited from intergenerational wealth, as the company was passed down to him. Then, as CEO, Jim Sr. made a series of changes that drastically widened the power differential between the company leadership and workers, including taking a larger share of the profits, hiring his friends and family members as managers while making the path to promotion inaccessible for most workers, and of course initiating corporal punishment of workers.

As he **applies** the background knowledge of his father's actions, Jim Jr. can see that many of the effects are ongoing. Although Jim Jr. has destroyed the badges that marked who is a manager and who is a worker, this does not mean that they are not still managers and workers. He has not taken any steps to address the physical abuse, pay inequality, barriers to advancement, and other forms of oppression that the workers are still experiencing.

Next, Jim Jr. considers the other intersecting **systems of oppression** at the company. All the workers have been mistreated, but some workers were also given a black dot on their badge, which encouraged the managers to treat them even more harshly. Again, simply removing the physical badge does not erase the harm that has been caused, nor will it necessarily prevent the managers from continuing to target those workers.

Jim Jr. continues his assessment by identifying how the oppression has manifested at all levels: **individual** (e.g., physical punishment, microaggressions in the form of jabs and sneers about the workers' intellectual capacity), **cultural** (e.g., training materials depicting the workers as incompetent, the practice of serving lunch to managers but not workers), and **systemic** (e.g., making the prerequisite coursework for promotion inaccessible for most workers, subjecting workers to inhumane working conditions, harshly punishing workers for expressing disagreement).

You can see how using the BASICS skill here differs from the reactive, quick approach originally taken by Jim Jr. Our hope is that you can see how assessing the elements of the BASICS skill can help Jim Jr. make a plan that goes beyond simply burning badges to making changes to create a more equitable T-shirt company.

## Why Use the BASICS Skill?

When the problem of inequality is not sufficiently understood (e.g., when Jim Jr. thought the problem was about badges), the corresponding solutions developed are fundamentally flawed. The inequality in the T-shirt company did not start and continue because badges were used—*in the same way* that racism in the US did not start and continue because race was simply acknowledged. In both cases, inequality was started and maintained by explicit and intentional endeavors by those with more power to oppress people with less power.

Practicing the BASICS will serve as a fundamental building block on which to build your anti-racism plans and to work toward meaningful change. However, this is only the first step in building a foundation for sustained anti-racism engagement. The next step is to truly understand what it means to be anti-racist and explore what is required to be an effective ally. In the following chapter, we briefly discuss anti-racism, clarify what it means to be an anti-racist ally, and examine the true meaning of *effective* allyship.

### CHAPTER SUMMARY

In this chapter, we provided an overview of racism and introduced the BASICS skill to help you move from misunderstanding to mastery on your anti-racism journey. If you feel intimidated by this skill, please know that this is a completely normal experience. You will get more comfortable using this skill as you begin identifying and dismantling the barriers to anti-racist work in the chapters that follow.

## CHAPTER 2

# Clarifying Anti-Racism: From Aimlessness to Direction

*Ally* is more than just a label. It is a particular way of showing up in the world. Whereas some types of allyship are performative, or rooted in centering your own personal gratification over a true commitment to social change, this chapter seeks to describe anti-racist allyship and clarify what it means to be an *effective* ally. We also briefly introduce the main barriers to allyship. We conclude with a skill to help you remember the attributes of an effective ally and to help you affirm these attributes as part of your ally identity.

## What Is Anti-Racism?

The pathway to anti-racism can feel winding and confusing for a number of reasons, including the fact that even defining it can be hard! For some, being anti-racist requires six characteristics (Spanierman & Smith, 2017):

1. A nuanced understanding of systemic racism and White privilege
2. Continual self-reflection of one's own participation in racism
3. A commitment to using one's racial privilege to promote equity
4. Engagement in actions that interrupt and challenge racism

5. Active participation in coalition building with people of color
6. Perseverance in the face of attempts to silence White allies

Similarly, for us, anti-racism involves a commitment to actively identifying and fighting against policies, behaviors, beliefs, and perceptions that perpetuate racist ideas and actions. Therefore, *any* action that takes a step toward ending racial inequality is considered anti-racist.

Anti-racist actions can look different, depending on your level of investment, the particular setting involved, and the scope of your efforts. For instance, anti-racism actions that are low-level investments may entail anonymously calling out racist language on social media, whereas high-level investments may involve completely restructuring your organization (e.g., workplace, church, school) to be more equitable. The way you engage in anti-racist efforts can also vary across different settings, such as in private family discussions versus in public town hall meetings. Anti-racist efforts can differ in scope as well, such as challenging an individual person who holds a racist worldview versus protesting against entire systems. Anti-racist efforts can also have different purposes, such as engaging in an action that is aimed to repair harm to BIPOC versus creating new equitable systems.

Given the limitless number of anti-racist actions out there that vary across all these dimensions, our intention is not to provide you with an exhaustive list of every single anti-racism effort you can engage in. Instead, our goal is to help you develop a new *framework* for approaching anti-racism in a way that is sustainable, is impactful, and provides a clear direction for moving forward. One particular way to obtain this sense of direction is to focus on *effective* anti-racist allyship.

## What Is *Effective* Anti-Racist Allyship?

Recently, there has been growing controversy about the term *ally*, and some anti-racist scholars have proposed using terms like *accomplice* or *co-conspirator* instead. For some, the term *ally* is preferred because it is more familiar and commonly used within the anti-racism conversation, whereas others feel that the term is too passive and does not reflect the hard work needed from White people to undo racism. Throughout this book, we use the term *ally* because of its familiarity, but we are not attached to it and support you in using whatever term best works for you. What is most important to us is clearly describing the skills needed to engage in meaningful, measurable anti-racist behavior. So regardless of the term you use, our aim is to focus on what it means to do anti-racist work *effectively*. Therefore, it doesn't really matter what you call yourself on this journey; what matters is what anti-racism work you do and how you do it as an anti-racist ally/accomplice/co-conspirator.

In terms of how you do anti-racism work, we believe that this work must be effective. Our use of the word *effective* is informed by dialectical behavioral therapy (DBT), an evidence-based psychotherapy approach that blends cognitive behavioral therapy (CBT) with mindfulness and acceptance strategies. From a DBT perspective, acting effectively is about moving away from a focus on what seems fair versus unfair (or who is right versus wrong), and instead moving toward a focus on *what works*. This is a powerful shift because it is easy to become overly attached to the way you think things "should" be or how you would like things to be, especially on your anti-racism journey. Perhaps you find yourself becoming overly attached to the desire for a foolproof checklist that lays out easy steps on how to be an anti-racist ally. Or maybe you believe you need to be a "perfect" ally before you take the risk of engaging in anti-racist actions. However, acting effectively means letting go of an attachment to a particular way of doing things or to a particular outcome and focusing instead on actions that will get you closer to your goals.

According to DBT, acting effectively requires:

- Paying attention to your thoughts and feelings in the moment
- Avoiding unhelpful self-judgments
- Choosing actions that are designed to move you closer to your goals
- Doing your best in a given moment

To drive this point home, imagine you have been hired as the head of an academic department at a university. Within a few months of starting your new job, you begin to learn about long-standing issues of racial inequality in the department. Suddenly, you receive a lengthy, strongly worded letter co-signed by BIPOC students calling out racism in the department and charging you with the task of addressing their concerns. You may initially be distraught by this and find yourself thinking, "But I am not the one who caused these inequities! Why are they mad at *me*?" In this case, you are 100 percent correct—you are not the one who created the harmful policies, nor did the inequity start with you. This intense discomfort and defensiveness in response to learning about racial injustice is referred to as White fragility (DiAngelo, 2018). In this scenario, giving in to White fragility and doing what *feels* "right" or "fair" might entail defending yourself by reminding the students that *you* did not create the harmful policies and by restating the anti-racism efforts *you* have taken in the department so far. Although it might feel good to get this out of your system, this response prioritizes your own emotions and your need to be perceived as the "good ally." The students' concerns take a back seat while your hurt emotions take the steering wheel, both of which do nothing to advance anti-racism in your department.

In contrast, doing *what works* could involve asking, "What responses will help me advance our department's anti-racist mission?" This might mean sitting down and processing the feelings you're having *and* also taking the time to really consider the issues brought up by students. You can then build on this by asking more questions, setting up meetings with students, and using this new knowledge to implement changes. To shift your focus toward what works, the question "What is the most effective thing to do?" should always be your North Star, guiding you to impactful anti-racist allyship.

Although focusing on what works may seem easy, it often requires doing things that are uncomfortable or unpleasant in the moment. When it comes to being an effective anti-racist ally, it requires recognizing how you may be participating in and benefiting from racism, attending to the unpleasant thoughts and feelings that accompany this awareness, and doing your best to learn and try new anti-racism skills to eliminate racism—no matter how uncomfortable using these skills may be.

## REFLECTION

What does it mean to be an effective anti-racism ally? Write your own personal definition of effective anti-racism allyship.

_____

_____

_____

_____

_____

_____

_____

# What Are Common Barriers to Allyship?

Unfortunately, there are many barriers that can disrupt your work as a White ally. Anything that blocks or gets in the way of your ability to successfully engage in anti-racist work is a barrier. To reflect on the barriers you may have experienced in your attempts to engage in anti-racism work, ask yourself the following questions.

In terms of cognitive barriers, have you ever:

- ❑ Wondered why people kept harping on racism given that racism was a thing of the past?
- ❑ Perceived the world as fair and just?
- ❑ Viewed your success as the sole result of hard work rather than influenced by the privileges of being White?
- ❑ Believed that "not seeing race" was the best way to overcome racial prejudice?
- ❑ Gotten stuck trying to figure out the "right way" to be an ally?
- ❑ Felt your willingness to engage in anti-racist work waver, such that one day you feel really "into it" and the next, it didn't feel like a priority?

In terms of emotional barriers, have you ever experienced:

- ❑ Fear of being perceived as a "bad" ally?
- ❑ Unbearable guilt about having unearned privileges?
- ❑ Anxiety that you may say or do something to make the situation worse?
- ❑ Powerlessness about your ability to truly make a difference?
- ❑ Frustration that your anti-racism efforts have gone unnoticed?
- ❑ Irritation that everything seems to be about race?

In terms of interpersonal barriers, have you ever felt:

- ❑ Unsure about what to say to your BIPOC peers following a racist incident?
- ❑ Hesitant to call out a racist remark enacted by a colleague or family member?
- ❑ Uncertain about how to apologize after making a racist misstep?
- ❑ Insecure about how to speak out against racism without centering your perspectives and ideas?
- ❑ Unskilled in how to ask BIPOC to support anti-racism efforts without burdening them?

In terms of other barriers, have you ever:

- ❏ Struggled to understand what racism is?
- ❏ Not understood what people mean by "systemic" racism or how racial inequities came to be?
- ❏ Felt unclear about what it takes to be an ally?
- ❏ Been unsure about how to set anti-racist goals?

## REFLECTION

Jot down any other barriers that have gotten in the way of your anti-racism allyship. You can also use this space to further reflect on the barriers you've experienced.

_____

_____

_____

_____

_____

_____

_____

_____

_____

_____

_____

_____

In our work with White allies, we have heard countless sentiments like these that speak to how hard it can be to step up as an anti-racist ally. If not overcome, these barriers can lead you to unintentionally maintain and perpetuate racism. In the chapters that follow, we will examine these barriers in greater detail and provide you with the tools needed to push past these roadblocks and continue working to become an effective ally.

# DEAR ALLY: The Qualities of Effective Anti-Racist Allyship

Being an effective ally requires having clarity about the attributes of successful anti-racist allyship. This can help you embody true allyship and persevere in the face of the challenges and barriers you will come up against. For each of these qualities, we offer an affirmation to repeat to yourself when you need encouragement and direction along your allyship journey.

## "D" Is for Dauntless

Effective anti-racist work requires you to be dauntless, or to embody a sense of fearlessness in the face of opposition. Being dauntless means having civic courage to engage in meaningful advocacy and social change (Williams et al., 2023). It also means being determined to fight against all types of resistance to change, whether that resistance is internal (e.g., your personal discomfort with speaking out against racism) or external (e.g., colleagues' resistance to changing racist policies in your organization). Throughout this book, we'll review various skills designed to help you overcome several types of internal and external resistance so that you can engage in the bold work of mitigating racism and its many consequences.

> **AFFIRMATION: "I am dauntless in the face of resistance, and my consistent, courageous actions create change."**

## "E" Is for Engaged

Engaged allies are active and do not merely wait for opportunities to come to them. Nor do they passively acknowledge that racism exists. Being engaged means taking action, building relationships with other anti-racist allies and BIPOC communities, and holding yourself accountable for change. This is why it is critical to use the BASICS skill from chapter 1 to make sure that you are getting a comprehensive understanding of racism in a particular context and that the anti-racist work you are doing is thoughtful and intentional.

> **AFFIRMATION: "I am an engaged anti-racist ally and I take intentional actions to disrupt White supremacy."**

## "A" Is for <u>A</u>ttentive

Being attentive to the needs of BIPOC is key to anti-racist allyship for several reasons. Being able to fully understand the factors that keep racism going has to be informed by the perspectives, lived experiences, and needs of BIPOC communities that are directly impacted by racism. BIPOC are also active agents of their own liberation and are not passively experiencing racism without a fight. Being attuned to their needs allows you to be part of how they want to fight anti-racism. Without attuning to the needs of BIPOC, it is very easy for anti-racist work to become about other issues (e.g., your own advancement or recognition), which can lead to superficial work that doesn't make an impact. Being attuned to BIPOC's needs makes sure that they are centered in your anti-racist work.

> **AFFIRMATION: "I am attentive to the needs of BIPOC and use their guidance as my North Star for anti-racist work."**

## "R" Is for <u>R</u>eflexive

Being reflexive refers to a willingness to engage in self-critique and critical reflection about your own biases, assumptions, and behaviors that may—even without intention—maintain racism. Reflexivity allows you to be aware of biases and ineffective behaviors, which is critical for change to occur. Even as experts in the field of racism, we acknowledge that future iterations of this book will have even more knowledge and improved skills based on new experiences that we reflect on. This openness can even boost your capacity to overcome missteps; if missteps are made, there is a clear path to repair because of how open you are to self-critique.

> **AFFIRMATION: "My reflexive attitude makes me open to learning and being challenged."**

## "A" Is for <u>A</u>daptable

As we discussed in chapter 1, racism has so many levels. Because of this, the nature of racism can change over time and the urgency with which a response is needed can vary. Thus, being adaptable allows you to be responsive to the changing needs and concerns of BIPOC communities and to adjust your anti-racist work according to those needs. Although some forms of racism occur over a long period of time (e.g., policies or laws that maintain racism), other forms (e.g., an extrajudicial police shooting of a BIPOC) can be sudden and require a quick response. Being adaptable means that you can engage in long-term anti-racist work while also being able to respond to unexpected and immediate needs from BIPOC communities. It also means that you are willing to change course when something isn't working and to shift to another strategy, which can involve using different *Beyond Fragility* skills as needed.

**AFFIRMATION: "I am adaptable and can meet the changing demands of anti-racism work."**

## "L" Is for Lasting

Given how painfully pervasive racism is in our society, anti-racism work must keep going until racism is over. Lasting efforts are necessary to undo the ways in which racism is baked into the fabric of our society. Making sure that your work is consistent means taking part in long-term efforts to change policies that maintain inequity and creating long-term partnerships with BIPOC rather than participating in "one and done" types of events. This means being part of BIPOC-led activist organizations rather than just attending a single event. While attending a single protest is definitely valuable, your anti-racist work must reflect a consistent pattern of behavior rather than a few isolated efforts. Lasting anti-racist work is absolutely critical for creating sustainable change that will make a big difference beyond singular actions or initiatives.

**AFFIRMATION: "I participate in lasting anti-racism efforts that range from small, everyday actions to large, big-picture actions."**

## "L" Is for Liberatory

Anti-racist work must be liberatory. Doing anti-racist work in a liberatory way means letting go of the need to hold on to your power and, instead, ensuring that BIPOC communities experience freedom from the burdens of racism, marginalization, and unequal access to resources and power. It's important to recognize that liberation of a single group can liberate others. For example, economic policies that tackle the racial wealth gap are likely to be helpful for many communities and can create a more equitable society. Focusing on liberation also requires seeking feedback from BIPOC communities and adjusting your strategies to be most effective in terms of leading to increased freedom from oppression.

**AFFIRMATION: "When I release my attachment to White supremacy and privilege, I allow for collective liberation to occur."**

## "Y" Is for Yearslong

As noted in chapter 1, racism is ongoing. It is not only a problem after a single racist incident. It is not only relevant during Asian American and Pacific Islander Heritage Month, Indigenous Peoples' Day, or Juneteenth. Therefore, anti-racist allyship requires a yearslong commitment that is not constrained to designated days or months. While it is still valuable to respond to and participate in such celebrations or activities, the point here is that these one-off efforts are insufficient for lasting change. If you only attend a protest after a racist incident or only speak out against racism during Black History Month, but do not also engage in sustained efforts to create policy change (e.g., reaching out to lawmakers, educating others about racism), it is not possible for change to occur. Furthermore, to embody some of the other qualities in DEAR ALLY such as "lasting" and "adaptable," it is necessary for your efforts to be yearslong. Remember that anti-racist work is a lifelong commitment. We encourage you to view this work as a journey, rather than a task that can be checked off a to-do list.

**AFFIRMATION: "My anti-racist journey is yearslong and not confined to arbitrary dates and holidays."**

# Why Use the DEAR ALLY Skill?

Throughout this book, we repeatedly invite you to go outside of your comfort zone and really try to do things differently even when it's hard. One way to persist when this work gets hard is through the use of affirmations like the ones in DEAR ALLY. Affirmations allow you to replace negative or anxious thoughts with positive and encouraging statements, which can help calm your mind and body. Also, research indicates that affirming yourself can boost your ability to cope with uncertainty and improve your self-worth (Gu et al., 2019). This coping ability is especially important given that any effective anti-racism journey will be fraught with uncertainty. We are also confident that using the DEAR ALLY affirmations can bolster your stamina to overcome the various barriers you will encounter along this journey. In fact, studies show that positive thoughts and affirmations can lead to successful action (Cascio et al., 2016), so we encourage you to draw on these affirmations as often as needed as you intentionally commit to the lifelong work of undoing racism.

# CHAPTER SUMMARY

In this chapter, we introduced you to the idea of effective allyship—a type of allyship that goes beyond a trendy label or vague aspiration and that requires a particular way of embodying the worldviews and emotional and interpersonal skills vital to anti-racism. We also introduced you to DEAR ALLY, which described the qualities of effective anti-racist allyship. We hope this newfound definition of allyship provides direction in what can feel like an aimless, winding road of changing and competing expectations. With this much-needed direction, we are also hopeful that allies, like you, will be even more equipped to overcome the barriers to effective allyship. With this foundational knowledge now in hand, you are ready to deepen your anti-racism work and skills in the chapters to come.

# SECTION II

. . . . .

# OVERCOMING COGNITIVE BARRIERS TO EFFECTIVE ANTI-RACIST ALLYSHIP

## CHAPTER 3

# Identifying Your Role in Anti-Racism: From Denial to Acceptance

To work toward dismantling racism as a White ally, you must first be willing and able to see racism for what it is and confront the horrible realities that support its existence. In the previous section, we helped you understand and identify some external factors that maintain racism in a given context. But as we noted before, ending racism is not just about dismantling *external* systems; it also requires identifying *internal* factors that contribute to racism. In this chapter, we will guide you in assessing your worldviews, explore why you might be tempted to deny racism, and discuss what you can do about it.

## Assessing Worldviews

How you make sense of the world can be deeply complicated and personal. Your worldviews (a set of core beliefs, values, and attitudes about the nature of humanity, the nature of society, your place in the world, and how you should live your life) shape your experiences and inform how you interpret reality. These worldviews and assumptions are rarely things you explicitly put into words, which can make them harder to assess and critically reflect upon.

Taking the time to reflect on your worldviews is crucial, as some common worldviews are actually indicative of a denial of racism. In fact, allyship requires ongoing reflection on your worldviews and the ways they may be undermining your anti-racist efforts. Otherwise, you can fall into the trap of denial, which is ultimately a distortion of reality and an attempt to reshape reality into what you want it to be, rather than what it is. Denial is a common response when you are faced with a truth that is too uncomfortable to accept. Rather than confronting reality, denial allows you to reject the truth, even when there is overwhelming evidence in support of it. However, White allies must be willing to accept the reality of racism to meaningfully engage in anti-racist work.

In the following activity, we ask you to reflect on your own worldviews as they pertain to common beliefs and assumptions that many Americans hold. Later in the chapter, you will have the chance to critically reflect on how these worldviews impact your anti-racism journey.

## ACTIVITY

# Worldview Assessment

Reflecting on American society, rate the degree to which you personally agree or disagree with each statement. Please be honest when providing your answers.

| 0 | 1 | 2 | 3 | 4 |
|---|---|---|---|---|
| Strongly disagree | Somewhat disagree | Neither agree nor disagree | Somewhat agree | Strongly agree |

| | | |
|---|---|---|
| **A** | Our society works best when some groups are on top and others are on the bottom. | |
| | It is unfair to take away privileges of one group to give to another. | |
| | Prioritizing diversity in admissions or hiring harms other qualified applicants. | |
| **B** | Anti-racism efforts are designed to make White people feel bad about themselves. | |
| | Highlighting White people's role in racism unfairly stereotypes White people as prejudiced. | |
| | Discussions about White privilege cast White people in a negative light. | |

| C | I feel that people generally earn the rewards and punishments they get in life. | |
| | People are generally fair and unbiased in their evaluation of others. | |
| | To do well in life you just need to treat people well and be a good person. | |
| D | Regardless of race, anyone who puts in the work has an equal chance to become successful. | |
| | BIPOC and White people have the same opportunities in the US. | |
| | Everyone struggles sometimes and so people need to pull themselves up by their bootstraps to overcome it. | |
| E | People in the US need to start referring to themselves as simply American rather than making more divisions (e.g., African American, Asian American). | |
| | Immigrants should try to fit into American culture and adopt the values of the US. | |
| | I see people for who they are, not the color of their skin. | |
| F | Racism rarely happens in the US anymore. | |
| | Talking about racism creates division and hinders present progress. | |
| | Racism is an issue, but It doesn't impact people's opportunities as much as it did in the past. | |
| G | Policies like affirmative action are unfair because they discriminate against White people. | |
| | White privilege is only a thing for rich White people. | |
| | My race as a White person has not afforded me any benefits or opportunities. | |
| H | It's easier for me to empathize with others who look like me. | |
| | As a White person, I have a hard time understanding what experiencing racism might be like. | |
| | It's a lot easier for me to empathize with experiences I've had personally. | |

# Why Might You Be Tempted to Deny Racism?

Despite more and more conversations about racial inequality in the US, there still remains a denial of the underlying systemic issues that allow racism to persist. After the killing of George Floyd in the summer of 2020, a survey released later that year found that the proportion of White Americans who acknowledged racism as a major problem had declined from 45 to 33 percent (Tesler, 2020). This phenomenon is consistent with what has been named "White denial," or the defensive response that manifests as the denial or minimization of racial inequality. Individuals who deny or downplay racism often claim that racism does not exist. They may also hold related beliefs, such as the belief that slavery was not "that bad" or even had positive effects on Black Americans. Others who deny or downplay racism may believe that BIPOC would be more successful "if they only tried harder," thus blaming BIPOC, rather than racist systems, for inequalities.

For most people, the denial of racism is not the result of negative *personal* characteristics, inadequacies, or failings. Rather, this denial is often due to multiple, interacting factors that we discuss in greater detail in the following paragraphs, such as an inaccurate understanding of history, the reality of Whiteness and White privilege, the socialization of racial color-blindness, beliefs in a just world, the myth of meritocracy, the empathy bias, a social dominance orientation, and the activation of social identity threat.

## Inaccurate Understanding of History

American society encourages White people to idealize the history of their ancestors and the development of the US (Bryant & Arrington, 2022). However, this idealization leads to a distorted historical record that maintains an ignorance of the harsh realities of racism. This ignorance has been found to contribute to the denial of racism, as well as to the limited ability to recognize racism in the modern world, which is why we believe the BASICS skill from chapter 1 is so fundamental.

Take, for instance, the teachings on Manifest Destiny in many American K–12 educational systems. Manifest Destiny was the belief held by many American settlers in the nineteenth century that they were "destined" to expand the US. As a result, Manifest Destiny is often lifted up within American history as an expression of true patriotism, self-determination, and democracy—that through striving, anyone can achieve and create their own destiny. Yet, in reality, this "expansion" was not the result of a trailblazing and individualist spirit; it was the result of governmental assistance in which the US government distributed 270 million acres of Indigenous peoples' land to 1.5 million White families. This effort also led to the violent dispossession of and genocide against Indigenous peoples—actions that still negatively impact Indigenous peoples to this day. However, these consequences of Manifest Destiny are often not taught or emphasized in American history.

Understanding American history is to reckon with the history of White supremacy and its atrocities toward BIPOC. These atrocities include, but are not limited to, the legacy of African American enslavement, the Tulsa Race Massacre, the creation of Japanese American internment camps during World War II, the centuries-long displacement of Indigenous peoples, and the illegal deportations of Mexican American citizens since the late 1800s. As a White ally, if you found yourself unaware of many of these historical realities, a great place to start is by reading accurate historical accounts from academic sources (e.g., historians) about how BIPOC have been treated in the US and globally.

## Reality of Whiteness and White Privilege

Whiteness represents a particular worldview that captures how White people view themselves, others, and the world. Whiteness is not simply about having white skin, but about obvious and subtle ways that our legal systems, institutions, and cultural practices favor White individuals over other racial groups (Helms, 2017; McIntosh, 2020). Thus, Whiteness as a worldview encompasses many social and cultural practices that go unnoticed to White people.

As a worldview, Whiteness creates a lens in which White people move throughout the world without thinking of themselves as racialized beings. As a result, White people hardly think about how their race affects their life experiences or their biases and assumptions. For instance, because many White people do not see themselves as having a race, they lack an awareness of White privilege (the unearned advantages and benefits they receive simply due to being White). Similarly, when White people do not see how race affects their own lives, it is hard for them to understand how someone *else* (i.e., a person of color) could have a life shaped by race. This can contribute to the denial-based belief, "If *I* don't see racism, it must not exist."

Whiteness also encompasses the belief that White people—and their ideas, views, and beliefs—are superior to others. White people who unconsciously accept this belief assert a level of superiority about topics they have a limited understanding about, such as racism. Even though White people have not been socialized as racialized beings and thus have an inadequate understanding of racism, they nonetheless elevate their personal thoughts and beliefs about racism over and above the lived experiences of BIPOC who *have* lived with racism. This can manifest as the denial-based belief, "If *I* do not think racism exists, it must not exist."

Whiteness also presumes that White people are entitled to emotional comfort and cognitive ease at all times. As a result, facts about race and racism that bring about emotional discomfort or cognitive unease are outright denied to prevent White people from feeling distressed or challenged. Attempts to deny racism can manifest as White people questioning the validity of claims regarding racist policies or writing off facts about racism as "wrong" simply because they do not agree. Unfortunately, prioritizing emotional comfort and cognitive ease at all costs ensures that racism will neither be faced nor upended.

## Socialization of Racial Color-Blindness

Another reason White people may deny racism is because they have been socialized to be color-blind when it comes to race. Many White people grow up being taught that they should "not see race" and that this approach is the best way to end racism and racial discrimination. However, dismissing a person's race, culture, or ethnicity ends up being more harmful in the long run, with racial color-blindness being associated with greater engagement in racially insensitive behavior and anti-Black attitudes (Yi et al., 2022).

Racial color-blindness includes two interrelated dimensions: color evasion and power evasion. Color evasion refers to any attempts to downplay or minimize the existence of racial differences (Frankenberg, 1993; Neville et al., 2013; Mekawi et al., 2020). Color evasion can manifest as attempts to avoid acknowledging race altogether ("I don't see race") and an overemphasis on similarities rather than differences ("Everyone is a part of the human race"). Color evasion also functions as a way for White people to avoid the discomfort of possibly appearing prejudiced, as they believe that by not talking about race, they can circumvent accusations of being racist. However, the reality is that people who are more concerned about appearing prejudiced tend to make more harmful color-blind statements during interracial encounters (Goff et al., 2013).

Power evasion is the belief that everyone has access to the same opportunities for success, meaning that BIPOC are to blame if they don't achieve this success (Frankenberg, 1993). It often manifests as the denial of historical and continued institutional racism, as well as rigid support for legislation and rules that appear to, on the surface, "level the playing field" while ultimately allowing racism to continue. For instance, someone who endorses power evasion may desire to eliminate affirmative action because they view it as perpetuating unfair advantages. Yet removing affirmative action dismisses the reality of a racial hierarchy that perpetuates inequalities that make affirmative action necessary in the first place. Notably, power evasion uniquely harms Black individuals compared to non-Black people of color (Yi et al., 2022). This highlights the importance of centering anti-Black racism and attending to the unique implications of racist ideologies for Black individuals within anti-racism work.

Overall, racial color-blindness denies or minimizes racial inequalities and the institutional and structural forces that maintain these inequalities. Thus, racial color-blindness is unrealistic and antithetical to anti-racism allyship.

## Belief in a Fair and Just World

Whiteness also perpetuates the belief that the world is orderly, just, and fair. In psychology, this is referred to as the "just-world phenomenon," or the tendency to believe that the world is just and that people get what they deserve. Because of this belief, many White people find themselves explaining away instances of injustice by blaming the person who experienced the wrongdoing—even if the situation was outside of that person's control. This commonly occurs whenever a Black person is killed by the police. In most instances, the killing is explained away by looking for some action the victim did (or didn't do) to cause the shooting. Responses like "He wouldn't have been killed if only he had complied" end up taking over the social narrative, showcasing how eager people can be for explanations that undermine any evidence that our society devalues Black life.

Acknowledging racism requires you to accept that there *are* multiple systems working together to unjustly shape the lives of BIPOC relative to White people. It requires a willingness to let go of the belief that the world is just and fair, which can cause anxiety and fear of not being in control. Given this, many people deny racism in order to make sense of or cope with injustices.

## The Myth of Meritocracy

Related to the just-world phenomenon is the belief in meritocracy, which presumes that an individual's rewards—university admissions, high-paying jobs, professional accomplishments, and so forth—are directly and solely attributed to their skill and effort. Meritocracy fuels people's desire to achieve the American Dream by "pulling themselves up by their bootstraps." It perpetuates the notion that anyone who works hard can become prosperous and that unsuccessful people struggle due to their own incompetence and shortcomings.

The problem with this ideology is that it promotes the view that people who get ahead do so based solely on their own merit rather than forces outside of themselves. Take, for example, the link between parental social class and academic achievement. Although a child can work hard in the classroom to get good grades, their ability to excel is also influenced by whether or not their parents can afford tutors and private lessons or live in a neighborhood with high-quality schools. Therefore, people's success is undoubtedly influenced by the extent to which they have access to resources that either foster or diminish opportunities for success.

Relatedly, meritocracy promotes the myth that inequalities are the result of personal failings rather than policies that marginalize and disproportionately punish BIPOC relative to their White peers. For example, in a 2016 report, the net worth of a typical White family ($171,000) was nearly ten times greater than that of a Black family ($17,150) (McIntosh et al., 2020). Meritocracy reduces these inequities to differences in work ethic and personal effort, despite the fact that economists have shown that these gaps in wealth are the result of discrimination that can be traced back to the start of the US. For example, consider the disbursement of the GI Bill, which provided $190 billion in federal loans for nearly 2.4 million veterans returning from World War II. Unfortunately, Black veterans were largely excluded from these loans, whereas the White middle class grew as a result of this financial assistance. Governmental acts like these have allowed White families to pass on much larger inheritances than Black families, another factor that has fueled this racial wealth gap.

Overall, the belief in meritocracy is rooted in American idealism and fantasy. Subscribing to the myth of meritocracy maintains a denial of racism because it ignores the role of systems in creating and maintaining racial inequities. Therefore, letting go of the belief in meritocracy is key to moving toward an acceptance of the reality of racism.

## Empathy Bias

Empathy is the ability to understand and feel alongside someone else's experiences. Cultivating empathy for people from historically disenfranchised ethnic and racial groups can be a useful strategy for dismantling racism. However, a common barrier that prevents many people from doing so is empathy bias, or a lack of compassion, care, understanding, and perspective-taking for individuals who belong to a different social group.

Empathy bias can start young. Although infants and toddlers demonstrate remarkable empathy toward others, empathy levels begin to change by early to mid-childhood, especially for others of different races. There are several reasons that have been put forth to explain this bias. First, as children get older, they are exposed to more and more factors that strengthen empathy bias over time, such as learning inaccurate information about history, picking up on stereotypes about different groups, and being exposed to beliefs in a just world and meritocracy. Second, some brain imaging studies suggest that we feel greater empathy for the pain of others when their pain is similar to ours (Han, 2018), meaning that we may feel less emotionally connected to individuals who are different from us or whose pain is different from ours. Third, some recent findings suggest that people, including doctors and physicians, assume Black people feel less pain than White people because they "have thicker skin" as a result of the hardships they have endured (Trawalter et al., 2016). Regardless of the reasons, empathy bias can be a significant barrier to undoing racism.

The problem with empathy bias is that it often leads people to disregard the suffering of entire cultural groups. This can result in the lack of support for policies designed to address that group's suffering. For instance, a 2001 report completed by the Associated Press revealed that approximately 24,000 acres of Black-owned land—valued at tens of millions of dollars—had been stolen from Black families since the antebellum period (Lewan & Barclay, 2001). In light of this, various policies were put forth to remedy this injustice, such as reparations. However, these policies have often been met with derision, which highlights the fact that many people do not believe that Black people *really* experienced unspeakable theft and harm.

Empathy bias also increases the likelihood that White people will hold prejudicial or stereotypical views toward BIPOC. Building on the previous example of reparations, these policies are often referred to as "handouts." This use of language invokes the stereotype that Black people are lazy and do not want to work hard to get ahead. The underlying message here is that governmental policies intended to fix the wealth gap are going to people who are undeserving, rather than to people who have been harmed or who have experienced unjust treatment by the government. This empathy bias likely maintains a denial of racism (Mekawi et al., 2017).

## Social Dominance Orientation

Social dominance orientation refers to the extent to which you believe that your group is superior and should dominate over other groups (Pratto et al., 1994). This orientation exists on a continuum—people can endorse low, moderate, or high levels of social dominance orientation—with high levels being most associated with the denial of racism. People high on social dominance orientation generally support the hierarchy of their group and believe that social groups do and should differ in value.

Related to the denial of racism, people high on social dominance orientation tend to oppose social programs that promote equality between groups (Ho et al., 2012; Jost & Thompson, 2000). In the US specifically, people who highly endorse social dominance orientation also tend to strongly endorse the myth of meritocracy, just-world beliefs, and the belief that equal opportunities already exist within society (Pratto et al., 1994).

A good illustration of social dominance orientation is Donald Trump and his 2016 US presidential campaign. During his campaign (and presidency), Trump regularly espoused ideas about reinstating the superiority of America over other countries (e.g., saying at a 2015 campaign launch rally: "Our country is in serious trouble. We don't have victories anymore. We used to have victories but [now] we don't have them. When was the last time anybody saw us beating, let's say, China, in a trade deal?"). He also regularly made comments opposing social programs that eliminate inequities (e.g., tweeting in 2020 that the Affirmatively Furthering Fair Housing mandate was "not fair to homeowners" and "having a devastating impact on these once thriving suburban areas"). He was known, and still is, for his desire to attain and maintain power and dominance, other facets that have been associated with social dominance orientation. Therefore, it is not surprising that individuals who backed Trump during the Republican primaries and the general election in 2016 were more likely to exhibit group-based dominance, a component of social dominance orientation, than individuals who supported other Republican candidates (Womick et al., 2019).

## Activation of Social Identity Threat

According to social identity theory (Tajfel, 1974), a person's social group reflects back on their identity and self-esteem. Because of this, people are motivated to regard their social group positively, and any time the group's image is threatened by negative stereotypes or stigmatization, people experience social identity threat.

In today's society, increasing discussions around White privilege and White supremacy have activated White people's fears that their racial group has been stereotyped as prejudiced (Marshburn & Knowles, 2018). Because individuals may respond to social identity threat by striving to preserve a positive sense of self, they often engage in cognitive and behavioral strategies designed to neutralize the threat. This can involve avoiding or disengaging from any conversations, situations, or cues that evoke these stereotypes. In fact, White people may deny the existence of racism altogether in an attempt to circumvent identity threat and preserve their positive self and group image. In other words, they deny racism not because it does not exist, but because accepting that it *does* exist could threaten their group's image.

# What Do Your Worldviews Mean?

Depending on where you are in your allyship journey, acknowledging the sources of your denial of racism may feel relatively easy or frustratingly overwhelming. While you may be able to acknowledge that distorted worldviews are commonplace, it may be harder to see how your own worldviews deny racism. It can certainly be uncomfortable to confront the fact that your worldviews may be misaligned with your anti-racist values. However, anti-racist allyship requires you to continually reflect on your worldviews and their potential congruence and incongruence with the reality of racism.

Our intention with the worldview assessment at the start of the chapter was to help you begin this reflective journey. The following is a brief scoring tool intended to assess your responses to that questionnaire. After using the scoring tool, reflect on the guided prompts that follow to critically examine how you make sense of the world, consider potential reasons why you may deny racism, and highlight areas for growth.

## SCORING INSTRUCTIONS

Start by adding up your responses within each section to obtain domain-specific scores. Then add up all your responses to obtain an overall score.

| Domain-Specific Scores | |
| --- | --- |
| Endorsement of social dominance orientation (*add section A items*) | |
| Sensitivity to social identity threat (*add section B items*) | |
| Belief in a just world (*add section C items*) | |

| | |
|---|---|
| Belief in the myth of meritocracy (*add section D items*) | |
| Endorsement of color-blind ideology (*add section E items*) | |
| Denial of historical and present racial issues (*add section F items*) | |
| Denial of reality of Whiteness and White privilege (*add section G items*) | |
| Empathy bias (*add section H items*) | |
| **Total Score** (*add all items*) | |

Compare your total score to the rating scale that follows. The higher your overall score, the greater the degree to which your worldviews conflict with the realities of racism, which suggests that you need to address the sources of your denial. Domain-specific scores above 3 reflect considerable conflict between your worldviews and the realities of racism.

| Total Score | Interpretation |
|---|---|
| 0 to 10 | Low denial |
| 11 to 20 | Moderate denial |
| 20+ | Severe denial |

# REFLECTION

After completing and scoring the worldview assessment, write your responses to the following questions.

Does your score reflect a conflict between your worldviews and the realities of racism? If so, to what degree?

_____

_____

_____

_____

_____

What is your emotional reaction to your scores?

_____

_____

_____

_____

_____

What is your level of openness to interrogating and challenging worldviews that maintain racism?

_____

_____

_____

_____

Although how you make sense of the world is deeply personal, the extent to which your worldviews are incongruent with anti-racist values is not. Worldviews that deny racism and legitimize racist ideologies ultimately serve to *maintain* racism and, therefore, influence the lives of others around you. Because these worldviews can undermine your anti-racist efforts, to overcome this barrier, you must move past denial and move into acceptance, which is the focus of the next skill.

## ACCEPT: A Skill for Overcoming the Denial of Racism

The existence of racism is not up for debate within anti-racism allyship. To be an ally, you must accept racism for what it is without getting derailed by your emotional reactions to it. This type of acceptance is akin to the notion of radical acceptance in DBT, which is about accepting situations that you are unable to change or that you deem unfair. Practicing radical acceptance when it comes to racism does not mean you believe racism cannot be changed in the *future*; rather, it means you acknowledge racism's existence in the past and present.

Importantly, acceptance is not the same thing as approval. Acceptance does not mean that you agree with racism; it means that you see racism for what it is so you can enact change where possible. Acceptance opens you up to the possibilities of how to change the painful realities of racism, which is necessary to prevent the long-term suffering caused by racism. To move from denial to acceptance, you must cultivate an attitude of *willingness*—willingness to change how you think about racism, willingness to change how you think about the world, and willingness to cope with racism's harsh truths (we will talk more about willingness in chapter 6).

Once you are willing to accept racism's realities, you can practice the ACCEPT skill, which offers a step-by-step approach for overcoming the temptation to deny racism. This skill is useful in any situation where you notice yourself denying the existence of racism. It can also be used in situations when BIPOC are expressing that racism is apparent and you find yourself struggling to accept these claims. Although offered in a linear fashion, this skill does not necessarily have to be used sequentially and instead offers a number of different strategies for moving from denial to acceptance.

## "A" Is for Address Sources of Denial

Accepting the reality of racism is to address any possible sources of denial. As we discussed earlier, these sources of denial can manifest in many intentional and unintentional ways, including social dominance orientation, just-world beliefs, and the myth of meritocracy. As you read about these possible sources of denial, which seemed the most relevant to you? Similarly, after scoring your worldview assessment, which of your worldviews conflicted the most with the reality of racism? Remember, your worldviews are not isolated beliefs; they inform how you perceive your reality and that of those around you. To overcome the tendency to deny or downplay racism, you must continually question how your worldviews may inform your perception of reality.

## "C" Is for Check in with Reality

Moving from denial to acceptance also requires checking in with reality. What are you telling yourself about racism? What truths or realities may you be rejecting? At the root of denial is an aversion to accepting uncomfortable truths. When your worldviews conflict with reality, it can be tempting to respond by reasserting *your* interpretation of the situation.

For example, perhaps you write a paper questioning whether microaggressions exist. A group of scholars then critique your work and accuse it of perpetuating racial bias. You might react angrily to the implication that you and your work are racist and demand that the scholars identify where, in your work, you used a racial slur. However, you must ground your understanding in facts. While you may not have used a racial slur in your paper, remember that racism does not have to be overt for it to "count." To check in with reality, you may reflect on which worldviews are resulting in such a narrow, outdated conceptualization of racism and use your new understanding to proceed more effectively. In chapter 1, we walked you through the BASICS of considering the multifaceted and systemic forces that contribute to racism in a given context. This skill is integral to checking the facts and challenging any worldviews that may undermine your anti-racist efforts.

## "C" Is for Create Community

Creating community with other White anti-racist allies is valuable to ensure the sustainability of your commitment to anti-racism worldviews. It will also allow you to process any problematic worldviews and missteps without the emotional labor of your BIPOC peers and loved ones. Addressing the sources of denial and checking in with reality requires you to identify your missteps and then actively challenge the worldviews informing them. Although this process can be done in isolation, it is much more effective when done with others who share your anti-racist values. Therefore, connecting with other allies can bolster your success in maintaining a lifelong commitment to anti-racism.

## "E" Is for Embrace Discomfort

Embracing the discomfort that may arise when challenging your worldviews can feel like a tall order. Confronting your role in maintaining racism may incite feelings of shame, defensiveness, and self-disgust. Your first impulse might be to turn away from these emotions and thoughts. While it may feel better in the moment, this unwillingness to turn toward difficult emotions can make it harder for you to challenge your worldviews. The antidote to avoidance is acceptance. Instead of struggling against difficult emotions or judging yourself for their presence, acceptance is about making room for these emotions and thoughts while changing your relationship to them.

As part of this process, Sue (2015) advocates that White people intentionally remember as many experiences as they can where they said, thought, or did racist things, and sit with all of the negative feelings that come with these memories. This process allows White people to confront the difficult emotions, like shame, that might sit in the unconscious. Do not underestimate the gravity of this step—this is an extraordinarily difficult and long-lasting process. In fact, the chapters in section III are specifically designed to help you process the emotional discomfort of this work.

## "P" Is for Practice Self-Accountability

In order to overcome the denial of racism, it is imperative to open yourself up to opportunities for growth and self-reflection. One way to ensure that you are growing in your anti-racism allyship is to practice self-accountability. Self-accountability is the act of taking responsibility for your actions without excuses. Although it may be easier to shirk responsibility when you recognize that you endorse worldviews that are aligned with racism, self-accountability means taking ownership of your endorsement of these worldviews, reflecting on how you came to accept these worldviews as truth, and figuring out ways to change these worldviews. Self-accountability is change-oriented and solution-focused, and it encourages you to be open to growing rather than staying stuck in the same place. We believe that by practicing self-accountability, you can find better ways to move forward in your future anti-racist efforts.

## "T" Is for Tap into Your Best Self

Finally, as you confront the discomfort of moving from denial to acceptance of racism, it is important to tap into your best self. Engaging in anti-racist work is predicated on the assumption that becoming a better ally is a value or goal of yours. Therefore, throughout this book, we will encourage you to assess and tap into your values as an anti-racist ally. Reconnecting to these positive intentions is crucial in sustaining your anti-racist allyship, as it can reduce resistance and create an atmosphere of psychological safety when engaging in challenging discussions about racism. Tapping into your best self means reminding yourself of your motivations for engaging in this work. It is the difference between saying, "Wow, I made a racist comment and now everyone will think I am a horrible person" and "I made a racist misstep *and* I know I can do better." Doing so requires an explicit commitment to approaching anti-racism more flexibly, which we will explore in the next chapter.

# Why Use the ACCEPT Skill?

If you think back to the T-shirt company story from chapter 1, you can imagine why Jim Sr. and some people in management were motivated to downplay, trivialize, or outright deny the concerns brought up by workers. Addressing these concerns can be admittedly uncomfortable and require change. Yet holding attitudes and worldviews that deny racism is antithetical to being an anti-racist ally. These views obstruct anti-racist work and maintain the status quo. By using the ACCEPT skill, you can confront the roots of that denial and pull them out in a way that leads to sustained change.

## CHAPTER SUMMARY

In this chapter, you learned about a key cognitive barrier to anti-racist work: the denial of racism. We walked you through understanding where this denial might come from, including several common beliefs, values, and attitudes that conflict with anti-racist goals. To address this barrier, you explored your own worldviews and discovered how they may work to maintain a racist society. You then learned how to challenge sources of denial by applying the ACCEPT skill. Being able to move from denial to acceptance prepares you to approach the complexities of anti-racism more flexibly, which is the focus of the next chapter.

## CHAPTER 4

# Resolving Allyship "Dilemmas": From Rigidity to Flexibility

Reading through the previous chapters, you have likely started to realize that *effective* anti-racist allyship is complex. These complexities may even seem contradictory. For example, by now you know that racism did not begin with you *and at the same time,* you have a responsibility to end it. These complexities may even prompt the burning sensation of "But, but . . . you just said . . . wait . . . how can it both be not my fault and my responsibility at the same time?!" In these moments, engaging in allyship can truly feel like a tug-of-war of conflicting messages with no apparent resolution in sight. There just has to be a "right" way to do this, right? We're here to tell you there's not! This insistence on a "right" or "only" way of doing things represents another cognitive barrier to effective allyship: rigid thinking.

## What Is Rigid Thinking?

Rigid thinking is a type of all-or-nothing thinking that removes the nuance from the conversation and makes it difficult to adapt to new or changing environments. Unfortunately, this type of thinking can lead to more prejudiced attitudes and is even a hallmark of what is known as the prejudiced personality (Allport, 1954; Verkuyten et al., 2020). The prejudiced personality is marked by *dichotomization*, or the tendency to split reality into one category (e.g., good) or another (e.g., bad). When it comes to race, this might involve characterizing groups in rigid ways (e.g., "Christians are trustworthy" and "Muslims cannot be trusted").

Rigid thinking is also characterized by a need for definiteness, which is marked by an intolerance for ambiguity and a clinging to past solutions (Allport, 1954). This need for definiteness can promote oversimplified understandings of social issues that maintain racist worldviews, such as a belief in a just world. Therefore, rigidity maintains prejudice and hinders your ability to engage in anti-racism work.

# Rigid Thinking Versus Dialectical Thinking

Throughout your anti-racism journey, you are certain to encounter seemingly conflicting messages about how to best work toward your anti-racist goals. Unfortunately, rigid thinking can make it difficult to integrate new or conflicting information within the anti-racism space and to persist toward your anti-racism goals. For example, anti-racist allies have shared with us that one of the hardest dilemmas they have had to overcome is the seemingly contradictory messages inherent in anti-racism work—messages like "Step up by speaking out (loudly) against racism" and "Step back by not talking over BIPOC."

When confronted by such messages, allies tend to react in one of two ways: They either speak out against racism and insist they are being a good ally even if their approach causes harm, or they don't speak out at all for fear of getting it wrong. Both of these options reflect the underlying assumption that only one message can be right. However, neither of these options alone supports effective anti-racist allyship!

Rather than engaging in "either/or" rigid thinking, we propose using an "and" approach—or what is called dialectical thinking. Dialectics is all about balancing two seemingly opposing views, such as:

- "I am doing my best" *and* "I can do better."
- "I am disappointed in your actions" *and* "I still care about you."
- "I see where you are coming from" *and* "I do not agree with you."

This way of thinking is the basis for DBT, which is a particularly helpful form of psychotherapy for clients who have challenges reconciling seemingly irreconcilable beliefs. Although the concept of dialectics can seem new or even confusing to some, many White people unknowingly engage in a dialectical process when trying to navigate Whiteness and their relation to it, such as when they both notice race *and* deny the existence of racism (Todd & Abrams, 2011). Therefore, it is likely that you have already used dialectical thinking in some way before, and our goal is to help you transfer this dialectical thinking approach to your anti-racism efforts.

# AND: A Skill for Going from Rigidity to Flexibility

To help you apply a dialectical thinking approach to your anti-racism work, we have developed the AND skill, which you can use when you find yourself in a state of inflexibility and either/or thinking. This sequential skill can get you unstuck when confronted with an anti-racism dilemma. It is for those tug-of-war moments—helping you let go of the metaphorical rope to instead do more effective anti-racist work.

## "A" Is for Approach the Conflicting Messages

The first part of the AND skill is to approach the roadblock in your head. Ask yourself: "What are the conflicting messages? Where are these messages coming from? What are the pros and cons of taking each message to the extreme?" In this first step, you are working on sitting with the experience of openly exploring the conflicting messages and simply understanding what they mean.

## "N" Is for Notice the Kernels of Truth

The second part of the AND skill is to notice the kernels of truth in the seemingly opposing messages. At the heart of these ideas, what part is true? In this part of the skill, your goal is really to distill the parts of the seemingly conflicting messages that are the most important. These are the parts that will become elements of a more flexible and dialectical path forward.

For example, let's say you are attempting to balance these two messages: "I have to be a good ally to enact change" and "I will make mistakes as a White ally." As a White ally, it is true that you are always striving to do the best you can to dismantle racism, but the reality is that no one is perfect, so you will inevitably make mistakes along the way. These mistakes can serve as learning points that continue informing your growth and development as an ally. By highlighting the underlying truth in each of these messages, you pave the way for the next step in this skill, which is to determine a dialectical path forward.

## "D" Is for Determine a Dialectical Path Forward

In the last part of this skill, you use the kernels of truth to bring together the most valuable parts of each message and form a more balanced, dialectical understanding of the situation. This involves combining and resolving the parts of the conflicting messages that initially seemed like a dilemma. Returning to the previous example, you might reconcile the message "I have to be a good ally to enact change" and "I will make mistakes as a White ally" by developing the following balanced view: "Making and recovering from mistakes is a normal part of the anti-racism journey."

Determining a path forward might also involve adding language that tempers the extremity of the messages, such as "sometimes" or "in certain cases" (e.g., "Sometimes I make mistakes" rather than "I am a failure"). It can also involve using language that highlights the lack of universality across situations and contexts, such as "In all-White settings, speaking up might be more effective." This step is challenging and requires a willingness to sit through difficult emotions and work toward acceptance of uncertainty, while letting go of the need for definiteness.

# Using the AND Skill to Step Up and Step Back

There are innumerable dialectical dilemmas that can interfere with your ability to engage in anti-racist allyship. As we discussed earlier, one of the most common dilemmas is being asked to step up *and* step back at the same time. Here, we go through the steps of using the AND skill to resolve these conflicting messages and strengthen your determination and efficacy to push forward.

# Approach the Dilemma of "Stepping Up" and "Stepping Back"

Martin Luther King Jr. once said that, "In the end, we will remember not the words of our enemies, but the silence of our friends." The idea here is that White silence is violence, meaning that when White allies do not use their privilege to speak out against racism, they are complicit in allowing racism to continue. White silence also puts the burden of anti-racist work on Black folks, which comes with greater social costs, as BIPOC who speak up against racism are perceived as more hypersensitive (Kaiser & Miller, 2003) and are subject to more antagonism (Czopp & Monteith, 2003).

With this recognition that loud gestures from White allies *can* be effective at making BIPOC feel safe and included, many White people take initiative, grab the mic, and get into the middle of the stage—ready to be as loud as possible about racism. What can possibly go wrong?

Well, one big thing that can go wrong is "centering"—that is, making it about you. This is perhaps best exemplified by a 2019 article by Ijeoma Oluo, where she describes a situation with a White woman whose response to an anti-racism talk was to complain about how it did not seem to help her gain Black friends. When you center yourself, it makes it hard to hear the voices of BIPOC who are already doing the work. The priority, instead, becomes what *you* want or what *you* think is best. These types of actions, which make the White speaker the focal point (e.g., "Wow, how brave of you to speak up as a White ally") are not only unhelpful but also harmful because they detract attention away from dismantling racism and increase the chances that you will sing the wrong tune entirely.

In response, you may then jump on over to the other side of the dilemma and think, "Stepping back is the way to go!" You may head "backstage" and focus on listening. You commit to self-education and stay quiet so as to avoid all of the consequences of stepping up loudly. From this position, the chances of you accidentally hogging the mic are limited, and you are certainly not making it about you.

Again we ask, what can possibly go wrong? Well, without the support of White allies, BIPOC can be left exhausted as they constantly fight against racism on their own, referred to as racial battle fatigue. In addition to having to contend with the consequences of racism, BIPOC are then using up any remaining energy to fight against a system that dehumanizes them every day. Therefore, simply stepping back and hanging out backstage is not an option either.

## Notice the Kernels of Truth in "Stepping Up" and "Stepping Back"

At this point, you're noticing that stepping up has negative consequences (like taking up space) and stepping back has negative consequences as well (like *not* taking up space)! You might feel like you are being pulled toward the center of the stage and behind the curtains at the same time, which can feel overwhelming. It might seem like no matter what you do, no matter what direction you go in, you are going to mess up and cause harm.

This is a good time to step back and notice the kernels of truth in each message. For example, speaking up is critical because it helps counteract the effects of racial battle fatigue, but stepping back is also important so you don't talk over BIPOC voices. From this perspective, you can determine that both speaking up and stepping back are vital at the same time. You then start to figure out how to bring these two parts together—how to move the "song" forward without taking center stage *or* hiding backstage.

## Determine a Dialectical Way to Both "Step Up" and "Step Back"

Taking a dialectical path forward in this situation is akin to being a backup singer. Just as using background vocals can make a song stand out and help it grow in popularity (Nunes & Ordanini, 2014), you need to assume the role of a backup singer by making your voice clearly audible without making the song about you. This can look a lot of different ways in the world of anti-racism. For example, you could join in on anti-racist initiatives that are already going on in your organization or follow local and national BIPOC activists and take their lead. You can also leverage your capital and your resources, such as grant money, to support BIPOC researchers, who have been deeply engaged in this work for years, as opposed to inserting yourself into this area now that it's trendy and topical.

# Practice Using the AND Skill

Now comes your opportunity to practice using the AND skill with another common anti-racism dilemma: "Notice and be aware of race and racism" (message 1) and "Do not reduce BIPOC to their race and experiences of racism" (message 2). Use the following prompts to walk through the AND skill and determine how to best resolve this dialectical dilemma.

First, **approach the conflicting messages**. What are the benefits and drawbacks of message 1? For example, one benefit is that you may be able to call out racism when it happens rather than staying silent, and one drawback is that this may result in a tendency to speak over BIPOC and not center their interpretations of particular incidents.

_____

_____

_____

_____

_____

_____

_____

Similarly, what are the benefits and drawbacks of message 2? For example, one benefit is that you are able to see BIPOC with more breadth (e.g., identifying their resilience and rich culture), and one drawback is that you might inadvertently downplay the effects of racism by focusing too much on their strengths at the expense of minimizing their pain.

_____

_____

_____

_____

_____

_____

_____

Second, **notice the kernels of truth** of each message. What parts of the message are the most important? For example, it is necessary to be vigilant about racism *and* it is critical to view BIPOC in a multidimensional way.

_____

_____

_____

_____

_____

_____

Third, how can you **determine a dialectical path forward**? How can these two statements be combined in a way that brings together the most valuable parts of each side to form a new meaning, understanding, or solution? For example, you might say, "I notice racism and I do not define BIPOC based on racism."

_____

_____

_____

_____

_____

_____

For further practice, we encourage you to use the AND skill to practice resolving other dilemmas, such as:

- "Use your platform to draw awareness to BIPOC causes" and "Don't profit (either financially or socially) from BIPOC causes."
- "Check in on your BIPOC friends after race-related tragedies" and "Don't burden BIPOC with check-ins only after race-related tragedies."
- "Don't center your emotions" and "Notice and honor your emotions."

- "BIPOC are the authorities on their experiences of racism" and "Not all BIPOC think and feel the same about racism."
- "Listen to BIPOC directly when learning about social justice" and "Don't expect BIPOC to educate you about social justice."
- "I have made racist missteps in the past" and "I am committed to undoing racism and engaging in effective anti-racism."

## Why Use the AND Skill?

Because of the complexities of anti-racism, there can be a strong desire to have a single, simplified checklist of concrete "truths" that you must adhere to. However, rigidly approaching anti-racism and clinging to the belief that there is only one way to be an ally can create stagnation and undermine your anti-racist efforts. On the contrary, when you use dialectical thinking, you can overcome the derailing effects of all-or-nothing thinking. In this way, you are able to think flexibly and consider alternative perspectives, which allows you to move forward and navigate stuck points with ease.

## CHAPTER SUMMARY

In this chapter, we explored the seemingly contradictory messages inherent within anti-racist allyship and discussed why approaching these with a rigid mindset can make it hard to know what to do. This uncertainty can result in confusion, anger, and frustration. Yet know that being an ally means not only dismantling the systems of White supremacy that threaten BIPOC, but also learning how to navigate the tensions of anti-racist allyship across contexts and situations. In chapter 5, you will build on what you have learned thus far by checking in with your values to keep going in your fight against racism.

# Mapping Your Anti-Racist Values: From Incongruence to Congruence

As you work to overcome your misunderstanding of racism (chapter 1), aimless approaches to allyship (chapter 2), denial of racism (chapter 3), and inflexible thoughts about racism and how to end it (chapter 4), you might start to feel exhausted or overwhelmed. Succumbing to this exhaustion is how many allies find themselves only engaging in anti-racism during Black History Month or after high-profile incidents of racism. While these fleeting engagements may be well-intentioned, they do not map onto the anti-racist value of *consistent* engagement in action. In this chapter, we introduce the idea of looking inward to assess your personal values and mapping them onto anti-racist values.

## What Are Values and Why Do They Matter?

It is often stated that living a "values-driven life" is central to living a happy life. However, not only do we rarely sit down and take inventory of our personal values, but we often fail to define what values are and why they matter. Values are important personal beliefs or standards that guide how you wish to live your life. Values can be individual (i.e., those that motivate your own actions) or collective (i.e., those that represent shared beliefs and motivations). Either way, values reflect what you consider important and worthy, and they provide the basis for the development of your individual beliefs, attitudes, and decisions.

While the range of possible values that you can hold is vast, personal values generally fall into ten overarching types: universalism, benevolence, tradition, conformity, security, self-direction, stimulation, hedonism, achievement, and power. What distinguishes one type of value from another is the aspirational or motivational goal that it inspires you to pursue (Schwartz, 2012). For example, universalism motivates you to engage in actions associated with understanding, appreciating, and protecting the welfare of all people and the environment. Some examples of personal values that fall within this category include social justice, equality, environmental justice, and peace.

Other values may be characterized by more self-focused motivations or goals. For example, power motivates you to take actions that enhance your social status, prestige, and control or dominance over people and resources. Authority, wealth, and social power are examples of common personal values that fall in this category. In the following table, we summarize the ten categories of personal values developed by Schwartz (1992, 2012) and include examples of personal values within each category.

| COMMON TYPES OF PERSONAL VALUES | | |
|---|---|---|
| **Value Type** | **Defining Goal or Motivation** | **Examples of Personal Values** |
| Universalism | Understanding, appreciation, and protection for the welfare of all people and for nature | Equality, social justice, unity, wisdom, peace, environmental justice |
| Benevolence | Preservation and enhancement of the welfare of people you are in frequent personal contact with (e.g., family, friends, community members) | Altruism, honesty, forgiveness, loyalty, love, responsibility, helpfulness, generosity, friendship |
| Power | Pursuit of social status and prestige, control or dominance over people and resources | Authority, dominance, prestige, wealth, status, control |
| Achievement | Personal success through demonstrating competence according to social standards | Ambition, influence, intelligence, success, competence, perseverance |
| Tradition | Respect, commitment, and acceptance of the customs and beliefs that traditional culture or religion provide | Humility, modesty, respect for tradition, cultural authenticity, faith, duty, respect for elders, history |

| Conformity | Restraint of actions and impulses likely to upset or harm others and violate social expectations or norms | Obedience, self-discipline, compliance, decorum, respect for authority |
| --- | --- | --- |
| Security | Safety, harmony, and stability of society, of relationships, and for yourself | Stability, order, reliability, family security, social order, cleanliness, trust |
| Self-Direction | Independent thought and action through choosing, creating, and exploring | Creativity, freedom, curiosity, independence, autonomy, authenticity, courage |
| Stimulation | Variety, challenge, novelty, and excitement in life | Adventure, novelty, spontaneity, change, risk-taking |
| Hedonism | Pleasure and sensuous gratification for yourself, seeking enjoyment and self-indulgence | Pleasure, indulgence, amusement, relaxation, comfort, luxury, passion |

Given that values underlie your goals, they are powerful motivators for action. The more important a value is, the more likely you are to act in ways that increase your likelihood of attaining the goals aligned with that value. For example, the more important benevolence values (e.g., helpfulness, generosity, friendship) are to you, the more likely you are to help a neighbor in need or show up to plan a friend's birthday dinner. Likewise, achievement values (e.g., success, competence, perseverance) may inspire you to persevere in the face of setbacks toward success. Understanding your values and how you make meaning and purpose in life is a quintessential part of the human experience.

## What Are Conflicting Values and Why Do They Matter?

Values can be compatible, conflictual, or irrelevant to each other. In an ideal context, your most important values will be compatible with each other and drive motivational goals that complement each other or that serve as motivators for a single action. For example, in most contexts, the values of justice and equality are compatible and align with goals that you can obtain simultaneously (e.g., contributing to local activism efforts in your community and advocating for more equitable school funding). The goals and actions associated with these values share the defining motivation to protect the welfare of others (i.e., universalism values).

However, when your values are in conflict, they are likely to interfere with your respective goals. For example, if you prioritize humility and social recognition, it may prove difficult to reach the goals associated with these values because the actions consistent with humility (e.g., speaking little about yourself) are likely to clash with the actions required to attain social recognition (e.g., promoting your accomplishments).

Still other times, values can be irrelevant to each other. For example, the value of success is unlikely to impact situations where you want to prioritize the value of forgiveness (e.g., when you want to reconcile with a good friend after an argument). Both of these values reflect desirable goals that are unrelated or irrelevant to the attainment of the other.

Assessing whether your values are compatible, conflictual, or irrelevant is an important part of living a values-driven life. While your overall constellation of values may remain stable, how you prioritize them in your day-to-day life will vary, as it is virtually impossible to simultaneously prioritize every value across contexts. Without critically exploring how your values relate to each other, you run the risk of missing times when conflicting values are stagnating your actions or influencing your attitudes.

## What Are Anti-Racist Values and Why Do They Matter?

As we talked about earlier, values can be either personal (life principles that guide your own behaviors) or collective (shared principles that guide what is considered right and desirable in a community or society). Collective values go beyond your personal values and actions to influence the functioning of society as a whole. They shape the goals and aspirations of organizations that operate in society. The influence that collective values can have on a society cannot be overstated.

Collective values typically develop in response to historical, social, or economic threats, such as natural disasters, mass political dissent, and outbreaks of infectious diseases (Fischer & Boer, 2016; Gelfand et al., 2011). Existential threats to the shared goal of maintaining a functioning society often rally individuals to come together and engage in action guided by shared values that reduce or eliminate these threats. For example, the existential threat of climate change has shaped a growing scientific and cultural revolution informed by values such as universalism and benevolence.

As you can imagine, one of the most prominent and ever-present threats to the functioning of US society is racism. Most Americans would agree that racism, and its continued impact on the lives of BIPOC communities, is an undesirable social ill that threatens the maintenance of a fair and equitable American society. From the time when European settlers forcibly displaced and massacred Indigenous communities, to the ongoing erasure of Indigenous peoples and their rights, racism has represented an ongoing and deep threat to the survival of these communities. Indigenous communities have consistently advocated for their rights in the face of these threats, centering collective values of community, cultural authenticity, and dignity.

Similarly, the long history of state-sanctioned violence against Black Americans, from the brutality of the Transatlantic slave trade to the historical and ongoing incidents of police brutality, persists as an existential threat to Black communities. In response to this chronic and pervasive threat, social collectives of anti-racist advocates and allies have emerged throughout history. These collectives, such as the Movement for Black Lives, highlight the ongoing racism and injustice experienced by BIPOC communities and promote a shared set of values aimed to reduce or eliminate these threats. These collective anti-racist values shape the goals and aspirations of individuals and organizations that consider themselves aligned with anti-racist efforts.

But what *are* anti-racism values? Anti-racist values are the collective values that promote goals and actions that contribute to dismantling racism and creating an anti-racist, inclusive society. At an individual level, this includes striving to work against racist attitudes in yourself and others and working to eradicate racial injustice in society more generally (Blum, 1992). Anti-racist values can include multiculturalism, solidarity, respect for individuals, inclusivity, liberation, resistance, and equity. These values shape the goals and aspirations of both individuals and organizations that consider themselves aligned with anti-racist efforts.

Engaging in anti-racist action requires prioritizing values such as these, which focus on protecting the welfare of *all* people, and deprioritizing values that are incompatible with the goal of creating an anti-racist society. Examples of values that can derail your anti-racism efforts include conformity, tradition, and power (Fischer & Smith, 2006; Schwartz et al., 2010), as these values are all likely to motivate behavior that maintains the status quo. For example, when faced with the task of renaming buildings previously named after racist historical figures, many people oppose these efforts on the basis of values such as tradition, prestige, and respect for history. In this example, maintaining the status quo (by not removing the historical figures) is equivalent to passively maintaining systems of racism and oppression.

Everyone has their own system or personal hierarchy of values that is constantly evolving. It is virtually impossible to prioritize all of your personal values across all contexts. However, anti-racist action requires you to prioritize collective anti-racist values. Critically reflecting on the intersection of your personal and collective (anti-racist) values is the only way to ensure that you have a solid understanding of your compatible and conflicting goals.

# Case Study: When Conflicting Values Lead to Empty Promises

To illustrate the importance of assessing personal and collective values when engaging in anti-racist work, we introduce Vanessa, who has been a longtime advocate of anti-racism at her local adolescent mental health clinic. As the assistant director of the clinic, Vanessa is regularly tasked with making big-picture decisions (e.g., planning clinic outreach, creating website content, establishing community partnerships). Two years ago, after joining several anti-racism book clubs, Vanessa was embarrassed by her clinic's lack of progress in comparison to other mental health agencies. Multiple book club members shared that their organizations had adopted anti-racist mission statements, started "safe space" initiatives to encourage intergroup dialogue, and even applied for grants to fund more positions for BIPOC therapists and community partners.

In response, Vanessa was inspired to lead the charge on creating an anti-racism mission statement for her clinic. Vanessa wanted to show that her clinic was on the right side of the fight against inequality and racism. She formed a mission statement committee with several other members at the clinic, and after two months of brainstorming, she was satisfied with the clinic's statement and proudly added it to the clinic website:

*We believe that anti-racism is essential for providing high-quality care to all of our clients. We are committed to building a strong and supportive community where people from all backgrounds and walks of life can feel welcomed and valued. As part of this commitment, we also strive to partner with the community and to incorporate the perspectives and needs of our clients into the design and delivery of our services. We believe that having a diverse team and strong partnerships with the community are essential for providing culturally competent care to our clients, and we are dedicated to creating a workplace and health care environment that is inclusive and respectful of all individuals.*

*We also recognize that racism is a pervasive and harmful force in our society that impacts the well-being of BIPOC individuals and communities. We are committed to being anti-racist in all of our policies and practices. We are committed to actively working to identify and eliminate any barriers or biases that prevent clients from accessing our services and to challenge and change any systems or structures that perpetuate racism and inequality. We are dedicated to creating a safe and welcoming environment where clients from all backgrounds can receive the support and treatment they need and where everyone is treated with respect, compassion, and understanding.*

A year later, employees began asking Vanessa when the clinic would start adopting policies consistent with the new mission statement's focus on equity, social justice, and community building. Although Vanessa personally valued equity and social justice—and she had every intention of hiring BIPOC therapists and community liaisons—the clinic director was unsupportive of making any changes to the clinic's hiring practices. Vanessa didn't challenge the director's position, as she held the clinic director in high regard and it went against tradition to question the director. Pushing back on the decision could also influence the outcome of Vanessa's annual review.

When Vanessa expressed the news to employees, she was met with judgment and frustration—much to her surprise. A few employees even accused her of paying lip service to anti-racism values and not actually caring about these values enough to put them in action. Vanessa could not understand why these employees did not see that she had put in her best effort! She valued anti-racism and equity just as much as everyone else, but there was nothing she could do. Offended that others would dare insinuate that she did not value anti-racism, Vanessa chose to avoid any further conversation about the clinic's anti-racism efforts.

## REFLECTION

Answer the following questions to consider Vanessa's values in this scenario.

What conflicting, compatible, or irrelevant values might be salient for Vanessa in this dilemma?

_____

_____

_____

_____

_____

_____

How are Vanessa's values influencing her action and inaction?

_____

_____

_____

_____

_____

_____

In this scenario, it is clear that Vanessa holds anti-racist values (e.g., equity, social justice), but she holds several other potentially competing values as well (e.g., authority, respect for tradition, relationship security, ambition). Vanessa's unwillingness to reflect on her personal values—and the extent to which certain values were incompatible with each other—stagnated her efforts and ultimately led her to act in ways inconsistent with her anti-racist values. She could have avoided this stagnation if she had critically reflected on and clarified her values.

Taking a step back in moments like this and critically reflecting on points of conflict can seem daunting. However, with time and practice, we believe you can become more effective in overcoming these predicaments. One way to do so is to use the MIRROR skill, which we discuss next.

# Looking in the MIRROR: A Skill for Clarifying Your Values

Building on what you've learned about the importance of values, this sequential skill is designed to help you look in the "mirror" to help you identify your core values and identify overlap with anti-racism values. Remember that engaging in anti-racist action requires anti-racist values.

## "M" Is for Map Your Values

In the first step of MIRROR, the goal is to map out your personal values. To do so, think about the following questions and write down your answers in list form.

How do you wish that your closest family members would describe you? How about your friends and colleagues?

_____

_____

_____

_____

_____

What qualities do you seek in a romantic partner or friend?

_____

_____

_____

_____

_____

Think about someone you admire. How would you describe them?

_____

_____

_____

_____

_____

_____

## "I" Is for Interrogate the Meaning of Your Values

In the second step, go deeper and identify *why* you chose these values in the first step. Think about the following questions and write down your answers:

Why do you think these values matter?

_____

_____

_____

_____

_____

In what way might the world be different if everybody embodied these values?

_____

_____

_____

_____

_____

What does it mean to live out these values?

_____

_____

_____

_____

_____

What behaviors would you say are associated with these values? Try to come up with at least five to seven specific behaviors that, in your opinion, are aligned with these values.

_____

_____

_____

_____

_____

## "R" Is for Rank Your Values by Importance

Ideally, your values will inspire you to engage in actions that are simultaneously aligned. For example, when you value justice and equality, this can propel you to support community organizations that are designed to eliminate racial oppression and change racist policies. However, there can be times when your values will conflict. For example, if you value both pleasure and persistence, you may need to choose between these two values when deciding whether to embark upon a new activity that is potentially a source of both enjoyment *and* discomfort. Therefore, it is helpful to make decisions about which values are most important to you right now.

You can use the space here to rank your top five values. Please note that this is a fluid process. What used to be important to you before might not be important now, and what is important to you now might not be important in the future.

1. _____

2. _____

3. _____

4. _____

5. _____

## "R" Is for Relate Your Values to Anti-Racism-Congruent Values

This fourth step of MIRROR asks you to relate your top five personal values to the anti-racist values. To what degree are your values compatible with anti-racist values?

---

---

---

---

---

## "O" Is for Observe Whether Your Values Are Incongruent with Anti-Racism

In the fifth step of MIRROR, we ask you to reflect on the opposite questions. Which of your top five values conflict with anti-racist values? In what ways are they incongruent?

---

---

---

---

---

## "R" Is for Reassess Your Commitment

In this final step, we invite you to take an honest look at the overlap between your personal values and the values that are critical for engaging in anti-racist work. There might be a few different outcomes here, which have different implications for reassessing your commitment to anti-racism.

### Outcome 1 (Strong Alignment)

There might be both significant overlap between your personal values and anti-racism-congruent values *and* lack of overlap between your personal values and anti-racism-incongruent values. In this case, you are doing great, and the next step is to make sure your behavior aligns with your values. You can do so by working to create concrete anti-racist goals that have the potential to make measurable change in dismantling racism. If you find that you are having difficulty setting these goals or taking action, we recommend that you continue reading on to chapter 6 to confront and address any sources of ambivalence and indecision that might be getting in the way.

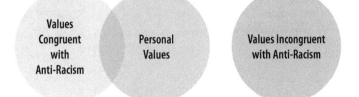

## Outcome 2 (Mild Alignment)

You might notice that there is some overlap between your personal values and anti-racism values *and* some overlap between your personal values and values incongruent with anti-racism. In this case, you could take several different routes. If you are open to readjusting your values, then you may want to think about what barriers are holding you back. If you feel ambivalent about changing your values or ambivalent about dealing with the consequences of prioritizing anti-racist values, we encourage you to proceed to chapter 6. If this whole process feels too anxiety-provoking for any reason, to the point that it is hard to continue, you may want to skip to section III to learn how to manage feelings of anxiety that arise in allyship.

## Outcome 3 (Diffuse Alignment)

You may also find that there is no overlap between your personal values and anti-racism values *and* also no overlap between your personal values and values incongruent with anti-racism. If this is the case, it may be a good time to pause and assess how this lack of overlap is maintaining racism. If you feel this lack of overlap is not a big deal, we encourage you to return to chapter 1 to further reflect on the ways racism can be maintained, even by things that seem inconsequential, and how maintaining racism leads to harmful consequences for BIPOC's wellness and safety. Also, similar to outcome 2, you may want to ask yourself if you are open to readjusting your values. If so, consider whether there are any barriers that could get in the way of fostering more overlap between your personal values and values that are congruent with anti-racism.

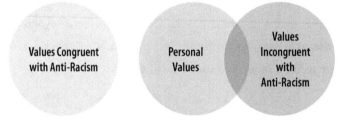

## Outcome 4 (Strong Misalignment)

Finally, you may discover that there is little or no overlap between your personal values and values congruent with anti-racism *and* significant overlap between your personal values and values incongruent with anti-racism. In this case, it may be a good time to take a step back and reevaluate your priorities. It is possible that you are not currently in a place where focusing on anti-racism makes sense for you. We encourage you to revisit chapter 1 to deepen your understanding of racism and to ignite the motivation that initially led you to buy this book.

# Why Use the MIRROR Skill?

Values are important because they give you purpose and direction, which fuel your ability to live a rich and meaningful life. However, if you are unclear about what your values are, you might engage in behavior that is inconsistent with your values, or you may fail to engage in behavior that *is* consistent with your values. Both of these scenarios can decrease your self-respect and impair your ability to engage in anti-racism work.

In addition, being unclear about your values and how they relate (or don't) to anti-racism can increase the likelihood of *performative allyship*, a type of superficial allyship that appears to promote change but doesn't actually reflect a true commitment to ending racism (Kutlaca & Radke, 2023). People and organizations who engage in performative allyship may do so because they value being liked, want to manage their image, or want to distance themselves from scrutiny or conflict. They do not value (or truly understand) what it means to promote an anti-racist agenda, which leads to surface-level actions that are taken at the expense of actions designed to create true change. As a result, BIPOC are harmed, and genuine attempts to foster equity and inclusion are suppressed. By using the MIRROR skill, you can avoid the pitfalls of performative allyship and take a hard look in the "mirror" at your own values. Figuring out the extent to which your values are congruent with anti-racism work will guide you toward the next steps.

## CHAPTER SUMMARY

In this chapter, you learned about what values are and why they matter in guiding your life. You learned that personal values can be aligned with, misaligned with, or irrelevant to anti-racism. To support your process of clarifying and mapping your personal values, we led you through the MIRROR skill, which helped you better understand how your values are congruent or incongruent with anti-racism work. We hope this skill enhances your ability to look inside and radically accept where you are right now in your anti-racism journey.

## CHAPTER 6

# Bolstering Your Anti-Racism Action: From Ambivalence to Commitment

In chapter 5, we guided you through an exploration of and a (re)commitment to your values. Routinely checking in with your values not only enhances your stamina to keep going when anti-racism work becomes challenging and overwhelming, but it also allows you to persist in value-directed anti-racism behavior when you experience a conflict between your willingness and unwillingness to do the work. This internal conflict is known as ambivalence, and it is a common cognitive barrier to anti-racism engagement. In this chapter, we discuss what ambivalence is, explore factors that contribute to ambivalence in anti-racism work, and introduce a step-by-step skill to help you identify and overcome sources of ambivalence in your life.

## Getting Stuck: Confronting Mr. Devil's Advocate

Let's imagine you attend a presentation at work about your company's culture. During the presentation, the speaker notes that your company's standards of professionalism (expectations for physical appearance, language, and so forth) have roots in Eurocentric values. For example, the company requires that employees keep their hair in a "neat" hairstyle, which they define as straight hair, and only allows the use of "standard American English," excluding dialects such as African American Vernacular English. The presenter outlines how these standards of professionalism may inadvertently promote racist agendas that disenfranchise BIPOC employees. In the post-presentation Q&A, your manager, whom we will call Mr. Devil's Advocate, says, "Isn't it better to have high standards in the workplace rather than to just let everyone dress, talk, and behave the way they want to? Are you suggesting we just abandon all sense of order in the workplace for the sake of being 'politically correct'?"

You immediately recognize the body language of your BIPOC coworkers: Their eyes widen and they begin shifting in their seats and glancing around the room. You think to yourself, "I do not want to let racist comments go unchecked *and* I do not want to be a troublemaker and embarrass my manager in public." You decide to let it go. In this hypothetical scenario, you may have felt a pull between "speak up and explain to Mr. Devil's Advocate the problematic elements of his statement" and "do not make this situation awkward and jeopardize professional relationships," which ultimately resulted in your not speaking up. Navigating this pull is crucial for anti-racist allyship.

## REFLECTION

Has there been a time when you wanted to engage in anti-racism work but something kept you from doing so? What thoughts did you have during that moment?

_____

_____

_____

_____

_____

_____

_____

_____

# What Role Does Ambivalence Play in Anti-Racist Allyship?

During your anti-racism journey, you will be confronted with new ideas and behaviors, many of which will stretch you out of your comfort zone. Because of this, you may experience ambivalence, or the psychological conflict that arises when you feel torn between alternatives or hold opposing viewpoints about a situation. For instance, one way that White allies can engage in anti-racism is by educating themselves about anti-racist topics. This may involve joining an anti-racism book club, listening to BIPOC-led podcasts, and attending a training on relevant issues. Yet self-education requires time, intention, and monetary resources. Given this, White allies may feel torn between their desire to devote time to this deep work and their desire to use their time in other ways, particularly if they feel too busy. Allies might also have a part of themselves that wants to engage in self-education and another part of themselves that wants to bypass this step because it does not feel like "enough."

Ambivalence is not the same thing as feeling neutral or indifferent; rather, ambivalence occurs when a person holds strong positive *and* negative associations at the same time. Therefore, ambivalence is intrinsically dynamic, and to overcome it, allies must be willing to confront the conflict head-on and to engage in a continuous process of resolution over time.

# Why Might You Experience Ambivalence Along Your Anti-Racism Journey?

Ambivalence is an inescapable part of your allyship journey, and it can be brought on by a number of factors. First, as we mentioned in chapter 3, certain worldviews, such as the belief in a just world, can perpetuate racism and White supremacy culture. Allies may experience ambivalence when they are overly attached to these worldviews because, although they want to do the good work of anti-racism, it may feel too threatening to accept that the world is unfair. It can feel too threatening to redefine your sense of the world and your place in it. It can also be difficult to reevaluate your worldviews when the common urge for White allies is to tenaciously cling to the belief that racism resides in others, and not in themselves (Sue, 2017).

Second, ambivalence can be connected to difficulties in thinking dialectically. At its core, ambivalence represents a conflict between willingness and unwillingness—between wanting to do something and simultaneously not wanting to—which is a conflict that requires the reconciliation of two opposing sides. When people struggle to use dialectics to resolve this internal conflict, it can actually activate more extreme either/or thinking. As a result, when confronted about their ambivalence, allies may rigidly dig their heels into their existing views instead of trying to make space for new ways of thinking.

Third, White allies can experience ambivalence if they fear that consequences will arise as a result of engaging in anti-racism allyship, such as the loss of personal or professional relationships and resources (Malott et al., 2019). For example, if a person continuously calls out every single racist remark during a family gathering, they may be excluded from family functions or made to feel as if they are the problem. Similarly, someone who constantly calls out racism in the workplace might be overlooked for promotions and seen as antagonistic, adversarial, and not a team player. In addition, ambivalence is often viewed desirably when an issue is controversial—and given that issues of race, racism, and anti-racism are still widely contested within the US, people may remain ambivalent in order to appear as if they have a fair and balanced view (Maio & Haddock, 2004).

Fourth, because ambivalence occurs when you hold strong positive *and* negative associations at the same time, it can be distressing to acknowledge and accept these emotional complexities. Ambivalence is indeed an unpleasant experience, and these unpleasant feelings are further intensified when you actually start preparing to take action as opposed simply *thinking* about taking action (van Harreveld et al., 2009, 2015). Further, even if someone is motivated and willing to take action, they may feel ambivalent about their ability to confidently manage the many emotive challenges that can occur along their anti-racism journey. As a result, White allies may simultaneously hold a deep desire to do anti-racism work while experiencing emotions that hinder their ability to act on these desires.

Fifth, ambivalence can arise when you feel stuck between the desire to change and the desire to remain the same. We believe that many White allies are genuinely interested in the idea of living in an anti-racist society in which everyone is treated equally, but they also don't want their lives to change much—changes that could include giving up the privileges and comforts they are accustomed to. For instance, what if White employees had to remain in their current positions and salaries for longer in order for BIPOC coworkers to get the promotions they deserve? Or what if funds had to be diverted from predominantly upper- and middle-class White neighborhoods to distribute funds more equitably? Findings show that White allies are less likely to support equity-based policies if they believe these policies will take resources away from them and be given BIPOC (Reichelmann & Hunt, 2022). Similarly, when it comes to reparations, many White Americans support *symbolic* gestures (e.g., an apology) but do not support *actual* directives, like direct payments to the descendants of enslaved people (Reichelmann & Hunt, 2022). Thus, White people may want to make strides toward creating a society in which people are treated equally and also not want to make the necessary sacrifices to prioritize BIPOC equity, wellness, and safety.

Finally, White allies can experience ambivalence when they have unresolved internal conflicts that impede their sense of readiness to engage in anti-racism. One such internal conflict is a lack of clarity regarding their values. For example, when individuals do not speak up against a racist remark in the workplace, it might be because they are unsure whether they truly hold anti-racist values. They may also be unclear about the values that are motivating their decision *not* to act, such as the desire to handle conflict and sensitive matters in private. Relatedly, White allies may be uncertain about which values are most important in general or in a given context. For example, when confronted with a colleague who says something racist in the workplace, an individual may value calling out racism *and* handling conflict in private. This person would need to decide which value ranks as most important in this situation and then act in accordance with that value. Ultimately, in anti-racism work, it is imperative that you frequently realign your values and priorities so the wellness and safety of BIPOC is your number one priority.

## REFLECTION

What has contributed to your ambivalence as an ally?

_____

_____

_____

_____

_____

_____

# CLEAR: A Skill for Moving Beyond Ambivalence

Now we will guide you through the CLEAR skill, which will help you confront your ambivalence and move you from indecision to action. As we walk you through this sequential skill, we will refer back to the Mr. Devil's Advocate example at the beginning of this chapter.

## "C" Is for Challenging Your Assumptions and Worldviews

The first question to ask yourself is "Is my ambivalence to call out Mr. Devil's Advocate rooted in my attachment to assumptions and worldviews that perpetuate White supremacy?" For instance, perhaps it feels too threatening to consider the possible racist elements of your company because you are attached to the belief that your company must be either "all good" or "all bad." This can also reflect an inability or unwillingness to hold the following dialectic: that your company can consist of positive elements and, at the same time, be vulnerable to reifying systems of oppression. If this first question resonates with you, it is imperative to consider how this need to hold onto the belief that your company is "all good" perpetuates oppression and White supremacy.

Additionally, perhaps you are strongly attached to your identity at this company, so any critique of the company feels like a personal criticism. Many people get their identities wrapped up in the workplace when they internalize White cultural norms that prioritize professional identities, degrees, titles, and accomplishments over lived experiences. Thus, the need to protect your company's reputation can be attached to a desire to preserve your own self-image and worth.

Although worldviews and assumptions are often deeply held, challenging them is necessary to move you past ambivalence. If you find yourself questioning how your views and beliefs may be contributing to your ambivalence, it may be a prime time to confront these worldviews. Perhaps revisit the worldview assessment introduced in chapter 3. Can you uncover the source of these views and assess their usefulness in relation to your goals for anti-racist allyship? Can you hold space for the views you have *and* acknowledge room for growth and flexibility on those views?

## "L" Is for Losing Relationships

The second step is to ask yourself whether your ambivalence is related to fears that you will lose personal or professional relationships. Although it would be ideal if you could call out racism while still maintaining relationships with people who have perpetuated harm, the reality is that when you repeatedly call out colleagues, family members, or friends and hold them accountable for what they say and do, it can lead to conflict or ruptures in relationships.

For example, are you worried that calling out Mr. Devil's Advocate will scar the relationship or cost you your job? Given real power differentials across different work environments, are you worried that conflict or relationship ruptures will potentially jeopardize your future personal or professional opportunities? Also, if you speak out in support of BIPOC and anti-racism, are you concerned that other White peers might judge you or no longer want to associate with you?

If you find yourself worried about how others might judge you or how this will negatively impact your future professional opportunities, take some time to engage in problem-solving. For example, if you lose friends in the workplace, can you seek community elsewhere where people have shared values around anti-racism? If a colleague retaliates after you call them out, can you leverage other connections and sources of support to minimize the impact of their retribution? Can you rethink the timing or approach of your anti-racist effort to minimize major consequences? We discuss additional strategies for managing relationship dynamics that emerge in anti-racism work in section IV.

## "E" Is for Enduring Emotional Distress

Next, ask yourself whether part of your ambivalence is related to a desire to avoid emotional discomfort. For example, does the thought of calling out Mr. Devil's Advocate make you feel anxious about potentially embarrassing him or making the situation awkward or uncomfortable? Do you fear displays of open conflict? Do these distressing thoughts and emotions lead you to want to avoid the situation and disengage altogether?

One way to combat avoidance is to learn distress tolerance skills that can help you manage the discomfort of approaching the situation. Such skills can include doing a quick mindfulness meditation, using guided imagery to imagine yourself successfully coping with possible tension that could result from the callout, and offering yourself cheerleading statements or affirmations, like "You can do this" or "This may be hard, and you can handle it." Ultimately, distress tolerance skills, which we discuss in chapter 8, can help you manage your emotional responses in helpful ways.

## "A" Is for Accepting Changes to the Status Quo

At this step of the skill, ask yourself whether part of your ambivalence is being fueled by a resistance to change the status quo. Resistance to changing the status quo can come from (1) a fear of losing your status and privilege within an organization or environment or (2) a failure to fully confront the degree to which the status quo harms BIPOC and reinforces White supremacy. In the example of Mr. Devil's Advocate, it would be vital to ask yourself, "Is prioritizing Eurocentric standards more important than creating an inclusive environment where other types of values are brought to the forefront?" and "Is continuing to allow colleagues to make problematic remarks worth potentially losing BIPOC members within an organization?"

When you notice resistance to changing the status quo, make sure to approach the moment with a commitment to value-consistent behavior. If one of your values is justice, it is imperative that you reconnect with this value and recommit to acting in ways that honor the value of justice for *all*.

## "R" Is for Resolving Internal Conflicts

In light of the different internal conflicts that can maintain ambivalence, the final question to ask yourself is "What internal conflicts do I need to resolve to feel ready and able to challenge my assumptions, potentially lose relationships and opportunities, endure emotional distress, and challenge the status quo—all to ensure equity and justice for all?" Within the prior discussions of C, L, E, and A are recommendations that you can use to address internal conflicts across these four domains.

Additionally, stay connected to your values as you work through internal conflicts within each domain. If you notice yourself feeling uncertain about how to move forward in a values-driven way, ask yourself, "Do I know what my values are and which values are most salient in this situation?" (For more detailed support in clarifying your values, return to chapter 5.) All in all, the ultimate question to come back to is "Am I willing to act *in spite of* these conflicts in order to persist in anti-racist action?"

# Why Use the CLEAR Skill?

When White allies are apathetic to social justice issues in professional and personal settings, it has negative consequences for BIPOC well-being, belongingness, and performance (Erskine & Bilimoria, 2019). Although ambivalence is not the same as apathy or indifference, persistent ambivalence and inaction can be perceived as a lack of interest or concern in undoing racism. Further, when you give in to ambivalence rather than acting in ways consistent with anti-racist values and behaviors, you can experience decreased self-respect and authenticity. By reminding yourself of these consequences of ambivalence and refocusing your attention on the benefits of taking action, you can recenter and engage in action that contributes to the betterment of your local and global community.

## CHAPTER SUMMARY

Ambivalence is a common part of life that can often become magnified during the process of engaging in anti racist action. When ambivalence emerges, turn toward the ambivalence and interrogate its sources using the CLEAR skill so you can move forward. All in all, we acknowledge that this is not easy work, and it would be a disservice to act as if true anti-racism allyship won't cost you anything. Yet, with the use of these skills, you will be emotionally and behaviorally prepared to handle the costs of anti-racism work, and know that, with time, the gains associated with building an anti-racist society will outweigh the losses.

# SECTION III

· · · · ·

# OVERCOMING EMOTIONAL BARRIERS TO EFFECTIVE ANTI-RACIST ALLYSHIP

## CHAPTER 7

# Understanding Your Emotions: From Unawareness to Discovery

Allyship is wrought with emotional landmines, and without the adequate skills, emotions can impede your anti-racist allyship efforts. The first step in skillfully handling your emotions is to understand what they are and how to label them. In this chapter, we introduce the importance of emotions, describe how your White racialized identity can influence your emotional experiences, discuss why managing your emotions is a vital skill for anti-racism allyship, and guide you in labeling your emotions to gain more emotional clarity along your allyship journey.

## What Are Emotions?

Emotions reflect complex experiences that are made up of different components, including your feelings, thoughts, and physical sensations. For example, the feeling of sadness may relate to the thought "I want to be left alone" and correspond with certain physical sensations in your body, like heaviness and fatigue. Conversely, the feeling of excitement may relate to thoughts like "I can't wait to share the news!" and correspond with sensations like butterflies in your stomach and a burst of energy. Emotions can also elicit certain behaviors that are consistent with how you feel. Sadness often leads to self-isolation, emotional eating, or excessive sleeping, while excitement often leads to initiating conversations with strangers, seeking out time with friends, or taking a risk on a new adventure. Emotions can also be prompted by external events, like watching a movie, or internal factors, like having an upsetting thought.

Emotions are a normal and natural part of life, and there are many different emotions you can experience. One way to categorize your emotions is as either primary or secondary emotions. Primary emotions are those that you experience in direct relation to a prompting event. That is, primary emotions are "fast-acting"— they happen right after the event that brought them on. For example, if someone cuts in front of you in line at the grocery store, you will likely feel irritated or angry. In this scenario, anger or irritation is the primary emotion because it occurred as a direct consequence of being cut in line.

Secondary emotions are the emotions you experience *in response* to a primary emotion. They are the feelings you have about your feelings. Continuing with the grocery store example, if you believe that it is wrong to feel angry, you may judge yourself for feeling this way and then feel guilty or ashamed as a result. In this case, guilt or shame would be the secondary emotion.

## Why Are Emotions Important?

One reason emotions are important is because they tell you when something in your life needs attention. They offer valuable information about your current circumstances that can sometimes be experienced as a "gut feeling" or intuition. For example, we often experience fear when our needs for safety and security are not met. We may also experience anger when our need for respect and validation is violated.

Second, emotions influence your actions and motivate you to act in situations. For example, when you step into the street and see a car quickly approaching, fear motivates you to jump back onto the curb, which protects you from getting run over. Similarly, guilt lets you know when you've wronged or hurt someone, which can motivate you to apologize, make repairs, and avoid future missteps. Without emotions, you wouldn't feel compelled to seek safety, nurture your relationships, or achieve your goals. You would essentially be a rudderless ship while navigating the complexities of life.

Third, emotions allow you to communicate your internal experience to others. For example, when you feel sad or stressed, your expression of that feeling lets others know that you need some help or comfort. Similarly, when you feel happy, you can communicate that to others and allow them to share in that joy. There are many ways in which we express our emotions—not only through our words (verbals) but also through our body language, facial expressions, tone of voice, and so forth (nonverbals). For example, frowning, having a slumped posture, and speaking in a monotone voice might communicate to someone that you are feeling sad, whereas smiling and speaking in a dynamic way with lots of arm gestures can communicate that you are feeling happy and excited.

Unlike primary emotions, secondary emotions do not provide information about your immediate needs and situation. Rather, they reflect the social, cultural, and familial messages that you received about emotions while growing up. They are essentially learned responses about how you think you "should" or "should not" feel. For example, if you were punished for expressing sadness or anger as a child, shame will likely emerge when you experience these emotions, even when they are appropriate in a given situation. Secondary emotions can also cover up more vulnerable feelings that you were taught to numb or push away. For instance, if you learned that feeling hurt or sad is a sign of weakness, then you are likely to become angry with yourself whenever you feel this way.

In addition, unlike primary emotions, secondary emotions do not pass quickly—they stick around. If you are not careful, they can even override your initial emotional experience and prevent you from getting helpful information or communicating your needs. For example, if you feel ashamed for experiencing sadness after a breakup, you may attempt to hide your sadness from close friends and family rather than reach out to them for support.

## REFLECTION

What messages did you receive about emotions while growing up?

_____

_____

_____

_____

_____

_____

# How Does Being White Affect Your Emotions?

There is a difference between the emotions you experience as a result of your own personal encounters and the emotions you have as a result of your social group membership (Goldenberg et al., 2020). For example, you can experience pride after acing a test you studied long and hard for, and if you are a sports fan, you can experience group-based pride when your team wins a game. There are also certain emotions you are more likely to experience, and to experience intensely, when your White racial identity is brought into the foreground (Mackie et al., 2016).

For example, imagine that you attend a required diversity training at work, and the presenter starts discussing White privilege and the various advantages White people receive merely for being White. Upon hearing this information, you notice yourself feeling guilty. This guilt did not arise because you committed a personal wrongdoing in the moment but, rather, because you were prompted to consider the *collective* harm caused by the systems that have prioritized your racial group over others. Or perhaps you find yourself feeling angry and resentful about what seems to be a constant focus on racism and attempts to spur racial progress for BIPOC. These emotional experiences are referred to as White guilt and White rage, respectively, because they reflect a collective, group-based emotional experience that is rooted in concerns for the *group* rather than the individual (Anderson, 2016).

Theorists of White fragility propose that when these collective feelings arise, they are often intense (DiAngelo, 2018) because they connect deeply to who you are as a person and how others perceive you. Although group-based emotions can be uncomfortable, they can also function to help the group achieve its goals, which can vary depending on the emotion and situation. For example, eliciting White guilt during a protest against racism may serve to motivate White allies to engage in action and to repair the collective harm that has been caused to BIPOC. However, stirring up White rage during an All Lives Matter political campaign may function to mobilize White people to vote against policies designed to eliminate racial inequities. Therefore, you must understand these emotions and their connection to your racial group membership, or they can otherwise lead to prejudice, which ultimately hinders your anti-racism efforts.

# Why Is Emotional Awareness Key to Effective Anti-Racist Allyship?

Consider the previous example about attending a mandatory diversity training on White privilege. What do you think would happen if you felt guilt or anger and were unaware of these emotions?

_____

_____

_____

_____

_____

If you answered that being unaware of these emotions would make everything worse, then you are correct! When you ignore your emotions or do not know how to label your feelings, you can experience a "boomerang" effect where the emotions just come back, sometimes even stronger than they were before. This ends up increasing your *emotional reactivity*, or the tendency to have frequent and intense emotional reactions that are out of proportion to the situation. For example, if you experienced White guilt during the workshop, you might overreact to the workshop material and become easily offended. You might also complain to your boss and colleagues that the presenter had an "agenda" to make White people look bad. In the case of White rage, you might lash out at the presenter or act impulsively by filing a complaint with HR where you accuse the presenter of harassment and "reverse racism." These intense emotions can take on lives of their own even long after the incident, such as finding yourself boycotting all future anti-racism trainings hosted by your company.

A lack of emotional awareness and increased emotional reactivity can harm your anti-racist efforts for various reasons. First, they prevent you from tapping into the useful information that your emotions are trying to communicate to you. For instance, White rage may cue you to the fact that your worldviews and beliefs are feeling threatened, which could encourage you to return to chapter 3 to further explore and undo any worldviews you have internalized that function to deny or minimize the reality of racism. Second, a lack of emotional awareness and increased emotional reactivity can lead to counterproductive action urges. For example, attacking the workshop presenter, becoming defensive, and boycotting future anti-racism trainings would all block the success of anti-racism efforts, whether these actions are intentional or not. (We will discuss how to counter these counterproductive action urges in chapter 10.)

Ultimately, a lack of emotional awareness and increased emotional reactivity keep you stuck and unable to move forward in your anti-racism journey. To get unstuck and be an effective ally, you need to learn how to notice and label your emotions, which is the focus of the DETECT skill.

# DETECT Your Emotions: A Skill for Noticing and Labeling Your Emotions

A vital first step in understanding your emotional state is to practice emotional labeling, which is the process of naming your emotions with greater specificity. Instead of relying on unclear, superficial descriptors like "I'm fine," "I'm okay," or "I feel bad," emotional labeling asks you to consider the full spectrum of emotions to describe how you feel in a given moment. To support you in this effort, we have developed the following step-by-step skill.

## "D" Is for Describe the Precipitating Event

As we mentioned previously, emotions can be caused by external or internal factors, which are known as *precipitating events*. When you first notice an emotion, start by trying to identify what prompted it. Consider asking yourself, "Did something happen in my environment?" or "Did I think about something that led me to feel this way?" When you gain more awareness of these precipitating events *as they occur*, especially in the context of anti-racism, you can better connect your emotions with certain triggers. This insight can help you make informed decisions on how to problem solve or cope with these kinds of situations in the future.

## "E" Is for Examine Bodily Sensations

Remember that emotions can elicit various physical sensations. Anger may cause muscle tension, headaches, increased heart rate, or a feeling of heat in the body. Anxiety may lead to nausea, shortness of breath, shakiness, or stomach pain. Sadness may elicit fatigue, an ache in your upper chest, or a sense of heaviness in your body. Therefore, checking in with your current physical sensations can provide useful clues into the emotions you are experiencing in the moment.

## "T" Is for Tune into Your Thoughts

Your emotions and thoughts influence each other, meaning that your thoughts can trigger certain emotions and vice versa. For example, if you're worrying about an upcoming date, this can cause anxiety. Similarly, feeling sad may cause you to have thoughts like "Nobody cares about me." Given this, a great way to home in on the emotion you are feeling is to tune into what is going through your mind. If you're consumed by thoughts regarding a conversation you had earlier in the day, perhaps you feel regretful about something you said or afraid that you have jeopardized a relationship with a close friend. Or if you find that your thoughts are constantly preoccupied with something that *could* happen in the future, such as being ghosted after a date, losing your job, or bombing an upcoming interview, perhaps you feel anxious.

Also notice whether you are having thoughts related to your experience as a White person. Perhaps you find yourself thinking, "They're going to think I am a bad ally" or "What if they think I'm racist?" These thoughts could indicate the presence of fear or anxiety. A thought like "I can't believe my family members supported a racist candidate" could also indicate the presence of guilt, anger, or disgust.

## "E" Is for Explore Behavioral Urges

Behaviors are what you do and how you act. They can include physical actions, like walking or running, and verbal actions, like telling someone you love them or verbally attacking them. Just like your emotions and thoughts influence each other, your emotions and behaviors influence each other too. For example, when you feel frustrated, you may vent about your frustrations to your friends and loved ones, which can either ease the frustration or intensify it. Because your emotions can influence your behaviors, one way to tune into your emotional experience is to pay attention to the behavioral urges you have in that moment. If you notice the urge to cut someone off mid-conversation, perhaps you are feeling frustrated. If you notice yourself wanting to lash out physically, perhaps you are feeling anger or rage.

Also consider whether your behavioral urges are related to your experiences as a White person. According to White fragility theory, White people commonly experience certain urges alongside certain emotional experiences (e.g., the urge to avoid in response to feeling White guilt). As a result, you may have the urge to shut down a conversation that you feel focuses too much on racism, which could be a sign that you are feeling anxious or overwhelmed. Or perhaps you find yourself having the urge to respond defensively after being called out for committing a microaggression toward a colleague. This urge may be the result of shame, guilt, offense, or panic. You may also have the urge to cry after hearing about the countless harms that have been enacted against BIPOC. This urge may be the result of sadness or despair.

## "C" Is for Consult the Feelings Wheel

Once you have identified the precipitating event and checked in with your physical sensations, thoughts, and urges, consult the feelings wheel that follows to identify the emotion that seems to best fit your experience in the moment. The center of the feelings wheel represents "core" or basic emotions, which are easier to identify or express. Once you identify the core emotion that best fits, move to the outer edges of the wheel to see if a more specific emotion better describes your current emotional state. For instance, if you start with "angry," zoom out to see if other related words, like frustrated, hostile, bitter, or violated, better fit your experience. The more specific you can be in labeling your emotion, the better you can understand what you are feeling.

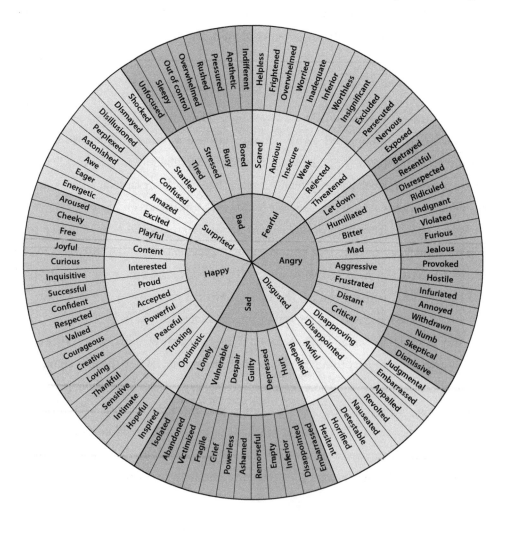

Additionally, it may be helpful to label any secondary emotions that may be present in your experience. Perhaps the precipitating event made you feel angry, and your anger has made you feel guilty as a result. Thus, the feelings wheel can be used to help you identify both primary and secondary emotions.

## "T" Is for T̲ie Your Emotional Experience to Your Racialized Identity

Once you have identified the emotion you are experiencing, ask yourself, "Am I having this emotion because of my racialized identity as a White person?" Since some of your emotional reactions may be the result of your racial group membership, ask yourself, "Is this emotion the result of a personal situation unique to me, a situation that made me aware of my White identity, or both?" Finally, consider asking yourself, "Does this emotion motivate me to protect my racial group or to prioritize the wants and needs of BIPOC?" Exploring the answers to these questions can generate new insights that could point you to more helpful solutions or ideas. If you notice that your emotions often motivate you to defend your racial group, perhaps there is a lingering worldview (e.g., social identity threat as described in chapter 3) that needs to be addressed before you can successfully move forward in your anti-racist efforts.

## Why Use the DETECT Skill?

Emotional labeling is key to cultivating emotional literacy, or the ability to identify, understand, and express your emotions. Emotions are not to be feared or avoided but, instead, understood and acknowledged. Particularly in the context of anti-racism work, it is critical to be able to acknowledge the uncomfortable and often difficult emotions that can arise when doing this work. If you are unable to accurately identify these emotions, it will be impossible to regulate them, making it difficult to keep striving toward your anti-racism goals. Knowing about your emotions can also provide critical context into any associated thoughts you are having—thoughts that could be making your emotional experience more distressing.

Emotions can be intense, but the simple act of labeling them without judgment can help you manage them better. When you are able to identify what you are feeling as you are experiencing it, you are able to create distance from your reactions and responses. This process gives you a deeper understanding of what happened and how it impacts you. You are then better able to see the possibilities for what to do next. Not only does emotional labeling allow you to feel more effective in your allyship efforts, but it also improves your overall mental well-being and allows you to feel happier and more productive.

## CHAPTER SUMMARY

In this chapter, we described how your emotions comprise your feelings, thoughts, and physical sensations. We walked you through the difference between primary emotions, which occur in direct relation to an event, and secondary emotions, which occur in response to primary emotions. We also explored how your emotions serve several functions, like communicating your needs and motivating you to take action. Importantly, being White can directly influence your emotions, particularly about racism-related issues, and result in a defensive response known as White fragility. Emotional awareness is necessary for you to tackle these emotions, which the DETECT skill was designed to help you with. As you gain more and more emotional clarity, you will have a solid foundation on which to further build your emotion regulation skills in the chapters to come.

# CHAPTER 8

# Tolerating Unpleasant Emotions: From Resistance to Willingness

As you've learned, emotions are a natural part of our everyday lives, whether they're pleasant, unpleasant, or somewhere in between. People tend to cling to pleasant emotions (e.g., happiness, excitement, joy, love) and push away emotions that are unpleasant (e.g., shame, guilt, anger, sadness). The problem with this is that when you attempt to turn away from difficult emotions, you miss out on what those emotions are trying to communicate to you. Remember that all emotions, even uncomfortable ones, provide you with valuable information about your current circumstances. Thus, it is vital to learn how to "sit with" unpleasant emotions without trying to change them or push them away. In this chapter, we review what happens in your mind and body during intense moments of distress, how your intolerance of distress is shaped by your racialized White identity, and how you can shift from distress intolerance to tolerance in the service of anti-racism allyship.

# What Happens When You Experience Distressing Emotions?

Distress, or an intense experience of unpleasant emotions, can feel overwhelming at times. This is because your limbic system, which is the "emotional control center" of your brain, responds to unpleasant emotions by activating your nervous system's fight-or-flight response. The fight-or-flight response is your body's built-in alarm system that helps you react quickly to threatening situations—priming you to either fight off the threat or run away from it. When the fight-or-flight response is activated, your adrenal glands release stress hormones (e.g., epinephrine, cortisol, adrenaline) into your bloodstream, which causes your heart to beat faster, your breathing rate to speed up, your blood pressure to increase, and the blood vessels in your arms and legs to dilate.

When you're faced with a real threat to your physical safety, like a bear you come across during your morning hike, this set of responses is necessary for survival. It prepares and motivates your body to take action so the bear doesn't eat you alive. However, the problem is that your body responds the same way to *perceived* threats to your emotional or social safety, such as someone thinking you are racist. That means that when you experience intense difficult emotions, like fear or anxiety, your body's alarm system makes it feel like all threats are created equal.

Because the fight-or-flight response mobilizes your body to take action, you can often feel a deep or urgent need to *do* something to decrease the emotional intensity of unpleasant or distressing emotions. This urgent need to do something can cause you to push away or avoid distressing emotions in your mind (internal avoidance) or take ineffective actions out in the world (external avoidance). In chapter 10, we will discuss how to counter external forms of avoidance, but in this chapter, we focus on internal avoidance by discussing the consequences of not learning how to tolerate these emotions. We also discuss how to develop a kinder, more nurturing, and more compassionate relationship with distressing emotions.

## How Does Being White Affect Your Response to Distress?

In the previous chapter, we highlighted how your emotions are influenced by your social group membership and experiences as a White person. Likewise, your experiences as a White racialized person shape your responses to emotional distress by influencing what you regard as a threat (DiAngelo, 2018; Ford et al., 2022). Because White people are not socialized to see themselves as racialized beings, they can feel threatened when they are confronted with their Whiteness. White people often live a very insular existence in which their ideas, worldviews, and behaviors are rarely challenged (DiAngelo, 2018). As a result, they often feel attacked when their privileges are brought into awareness. This then elicits a set of physiological reactions that are akin to coming across a bear in the wild, increasing the likelihood that White people will equate their perceived threats with the actual threats faced by BIPOC. However, these threats to White privilege are not *real* causes of danger. They are perceived slights that threaten the stability of social status and worldviews that Whiteness has historically provided. No matter how uncomfortable it is to read about and hear about your privilege or to be called out for a racist misstep, those things are not the same as being lynched, being brutalized and killed by police, or being deported or displaced from your home and land.

Another way Whiteness impacts emotional distress is via the right to racial comfort. As we just mentioned, White privilege often enables people to move through the world with limited challenges to their ideas, worldviews, and behaviors, meaning they are rarely out of their racial comfort zones (DiAngelo, 2018). As a result, many White people have limited practice using skills to manage the discomfort that arises when confronted with information or experiences that challenge their beliefs about race, equity, and justice. When you have experienced life in this way, you not only expect comfort but also feel entitled to it. This is especially the case given that the right to racial comfort also means there is no room for open conflict. In the context of racism and anti-racism, White racial comfort has been prioritized for years at the expense of BIPOC. Conversations about racism and anti-racism have been surveilled and minimized, in part, to not upset White individuals. White supremacy culture has created a cultural context in which BIPOC have to repeatedly experience and tolerate discomfort to appease White people.

For BIPOC, the consequences of expressing or causing discomfort can be deadly—literally and figuratively. Take, for example, the all-too-common experience in which a Black person driving or simply existing in a wealthy neighborhood is labeled as "suspicious." In this situation, the presence of a Black person may not align with the racist worldview that Black people do not belong in predominantly upper- and middle-class White neighborhoods. If this Black person is pulled over or questioned by police, it is not safe for them to express their discomfort or to challenge the racist belief system that led to their being pulled over in the first place. Instead, they must adopt a double consciousness that requires them to take on the perspective of the other person and act in ways that prioritize the comfort of others over their own. In these situations, the active decision to abandon their own comfort is an act of self-preservation.

However, for White people unencumbered by the weight of racial marginalization, that act of self-preservation is rarely, if ever, necessary. White supremacy culture is the ultimate tool of self-preservation by which White people get to remain comfortable and claim they feel threatened when they are not comfortable anymore. While the discomfort that arises during anti-racist work may have many different sources, the internal reactivity to that discomfort can feel the same. This means that learning how to soothe your emotional reactivity is not only essential for being an ally, but it is also essential in dismantling the culturally racist value that you as a White person have a right to comfort over BIPOC.

# What Is Distress Tolerance and Why Is It Helpful for Anti-Racism?

Emotions that come up in the context of anti-racist work—both pleasant and unpleasant—come and go like the waves of the ocean, and distress tolerance reflects your ability to ride those waves without clinging to your emotional experience or pushing it away. Distress tolerance also includes your ability to engage in practices that soothe your limbic system so that you can manage emotional distress without making the situation worse. It is nearly impossible to use anti-racism techniques when you are in an emotionally activated state of mind and body.

For example, after taking the worldview assessment in chapter 3, you likely recognized that you hold at least some racist worldviews. You may then have felt ashamed and engaged in negative self-talk like "Wow, I am a horrible, racist person." The idea that you are a "good person" has been threatened, activating your fight-or-flight response. When situations like this occur, you have a choice to resist the unpleasant emotions or to willingly engage with the discomfort. For many people, the initial impulse is to turn away. While this may feel better in the moment, resisting difficult emotions makes it difficult for you to reflect on your missteps and consider sources of bias that may have led to these missteps. Being closed off also prevents you from challenging your worldviews and looking for areas of growth.

Instead of struggling against difficult emotions or judging yourself for their presence, you must learn how to make room for these emotions. You must develop the capacity to turn toward these emotions and any associated thoughts. By allowing yourself to acknowledge both your emotions and your thoughts, you can reframe negative self-talk with more helpful thoughts like "I am feeling ashamed because I think others may believe I am a horrible person for the offhand comment I made. How can I move forward in a way that is consistent with my anti-racist values?" This reframe does not disengage you from the discomfort, but it does create distance between you and your emotional experience so you have space to process your emotions and recenter your anti-racist values.

Embracing the discomfort that may arise along your anti-racism journey can feel like a tall order. However, there are multiple benefits to allowing yourself to feel and tolerate uncomfortable emotions. One benefit is that when you practice distress tolerance skills, it reduces the likelihood that you will become overwhelmed by stressful situations and turn to unhealthy or harmful coping mechanisms. Such coping responses may include attempting to numb your emotional pain, minimize the impact of your actions, or deny reality altogether. You might also engage in avoidance behaviors (Bryant & Arrington, 2022), like avoiding a BIPOC colleague you unintentionally harmed or never keeping up with the news to avoid being distressed by racism-related events, despite the fact that these behaviors may lead to more serious long-term consequences (Van Dijk et al., 2013).

Another benefit of distress tolerance skills is that they give you time to figure out your needs. When you are in the midst of an intense and unpleasant emotional reaction, you are not always exactly sure what you want or need at that moment. That's because when the fight-or-flight response gets activated, the thinking part of your brain shuts down, which interferes with your ability to think clearly and make decisions. For this reason, distress tolerance skills can help you buy time until you have a better sense of the emotion you are feeling, where it came from, and what function it serves. Once you have a better understanding of your emotional experience, you can identify helpful ways to get your needs met.

A third benefit of distress tolerance is that continued use of these skills can help you recover from emotional upsets more quickly. As opposed to letting a distressing event ruin your whole day and keep you from engaging in productive anti-racist work, distress tolerance skills can help you bounce back. Even though it might not always feel like it, it can take less energy to "feel your feelings" than to fight against them.

# Learning to FEEL: A Skill for Tolerating Unpleasant Emotions

Thankfully, improving your distress tolerance skills is possible, and there are many different ways to practice doing so. One technique is to offer yourself self-encouragement statements or affirmations, like "This too shall pass" or "I can get through this." You can also self-soothe by connecting to your five senses. The distress tolerance skill we created—the FEEL skill—represents separate but interconnected strategies for tolerating unpleasant emotions. These strategies do not need to be practiced in order but, rather, represent a collection of elements that are helpful in managing unpleasant emotions effectively.

## "F" Is for Find Your Center

The first strategy within the FEEL skill is to find your center. This means finding a quiet space with no distractions and noticing what is happening in your body. In this step, you try to find the place in your body where your physical and energetic strength comes from. This could be your heart or your stomach area, wherever you feel your energy emanate. Wherever it is, you can pay attention to the sensation of that part of your body with a gentle curiosity and willingness. Sit with the sensations and just try to observe the feeling of being centered and at peace. As you become more centered, notice and try to cultivate the part of you that feels genuine commitment to making the world a just, equitable place. Connect to your inner goodness and selfless desire to bring justice to the world.

## "E" Is for Embody Nonjudgment

It can be so incredibly difficult to simply sit with a difficult emotion rather than making an evaluative statement about the emotion, yourself, or the world. However, this step in the FEEL skill is designed to help you do just that. If you notice yourself having thoughts such as "I shouldn't be this upset" or "It's so unfair that I am made to feel this way," instead try repeating to yourself, "The emotion cannot hurt me. The emotion is what it is. It is neither good nor bad." For example, you might feel sad and angry after hearing about a Black colleague's experiences with racism in your workplace. You might notice afterward that your emotions feel intense, leading you to think, "These emotions are just too uncomfortable and feeling this way is unproductive." Embodying nonjudgment would entail challenging these judgments and saying to yourself, "It hurts to feel sadness *and* sadness is not bad. It is what it is and it feels how it feels." This nonjudgment can reduce the distressing secondary emotions described in chapter 7.

## "E" Is for Embrace Difficult Emotions as a Human Experience

We have said it before, but it bears repeating: Difficult emotions are a part of life. Sometimes, having racial privilege can make you feel (even if you do not realize it) that you are entitled to being comfortable at all times. However, the reality is that difficult emotions are a part of the human experience, and difficult emotions related to anti-racist work specifically are a part of your journey as an ally. It can feel deeply uncomfortable to embrace feelings like anger or guilt, but when you try to avoid these emotions, shut them down, or rationalize them, it makes it difficult to have constructive and meaningful conversations about race and to consider your own role in racism.

Therefore, rather than rejecting painful emotions, the goal is to welcome them in and treat them with the same compassion that you would any other emotion. This means letting go of the urge to change your experience. When you notice any nagging desire to get rid of an emotion or push it away, try simply sitting with the emotion instead. You might even sit with the urge to change the emotion—nonjudgmentally observing the urge, noticing how it feels in your body, and noting what it is trying to convince you to do (e.g., to move away from the emotion). After this observation, you can set down the urge in your mind and return to nonjudgmentally sitting with and tolerating the difficult emotion.

## "L" Is for Let Your Senses Ground You

In the midst of a distressing experience, you may notice a sense of internal chaos or dissociation from your body or the world around you. To help you cope with this, we offer you a fourth FEEL strategy: letting your senses ground you. Grounding yourself using your senses can help you feel more centered and present in the current moment. If you do not have access to all five senses for any reason, that is completely okay. You don't have to engage with all of them for this step to be helpful; rather, prioritize engaging in the grounding practice in an intentional way.

If you'd like or are able to, you can start with the sense of sight. We encourage you to simply notice what you see around you, nonjudgmentally observing the colors and shapes of anything in your space. Then focus on the sense of hearing, shifting your attention to what you hear in this moment, such as the sounds outside of the room or any hums inside the room. Next, focus on the sensation of touch by noticing the feeling of the chair or ground underneath your bottom or any other sensations in your body. Then focus on the sense of smell, breathing in deeply and noticing any scents that may be wafting in the air. Finally, bring your attention to the sense of taste, either by noticing the taste in your mouth or remembering the flavor of a food that you enjoy. Letting your senses ground you in this way can help you manage the uncomfortable feelings of anti-racist work and make sure that when you respond to a situation, you are doing it from a place of peace and wisdom.

## Why Use the FEEL Skill?

Distress, discomfort, and pain are a part of the human experience and definitely a part of anti-racism allyship. Rather than having a combative or contentious relationship with these emotions, the FEEL skill allows you to develop a more caring and compassionate relationship with them. The more care and compassion you extend to your emotional experience, the more easily you will be able to navigate and recover from the intense emotional experiences that come up when doing anti-racism work. This can make your anti-racism journey truly a lifelong one that can be sustained no matter what setbacks you experience.

## CHAPTER SUMMARY

Because the brain and body get activated during times of distress, people often struggle to manage unpleasant emotions when they arise. In this chapter, we highlighted how there is no way to do anti-racism work without encountering a wide variety of stressors and distressing emotions. You cannot avoid it because the reality of racism is inherently distressing. We discussed the importance of learning distress tolerance skills, such as the FEEL skill, which can positively influence your ability to handle difficult emotions when they arise. Unpleasant emotions can be meaningful, and seeking to understand what they mean for you in the context of your anti-racism efforts can be beneficial.

## CHAPTER 9

# Checking the Facts of Your Emotions: From Fallacy to Reality

In the previous chapters, you learned how to understand and feel your emotions. In this chapter, we are going to build on your emotion-focused skill set by helping you figure out whether your emotions fit the facts in a given situation—and what to do when they do *not* fit the facts. Although all emotions provide you with information about your current experience, sometimes your *perceptions* about your current experience are not based in reality. And if you act on an emotion that is not based in reality, it can result in more distress and interfere with your ability to tackle anti-racist behaviors with calmness and intentionality.

## The Grocery Store

Imagine you are at the grocery store shopping with your 5-year-old child when you run into a Black family from your child's school. Before you know it, your child blurts out, "Look! That's the girl from school who looks like chocolate!" You feel your heart rate accelerate and you immediately begin to feel sweaty. You look at the Black parents' faces and start to notice the alarm of "They are going to think I'm racist!" ringing in your head. As the alarm rings on, you might even feel anger that your child noticed the race of their classmate and feel betrayed by their impulsive statement. To alleviate the intense panic and to ensure that the family does not think you and your child are racist, you pull your child in close and say, "That's not nice—we don't say things like that! Apologize immediately!" You then stumble over your own apology to the family and quickly walk out of the store, abandoning both your cart and the situation. When you get home, you start to reflect on why you reacted this way and where these intense emotions came from.

## Where Did Your Emotion Come From?

According to some psychological theories, our emotions are not the direct result of a particular event but, rather, the result of our *interpretation* of that event. In other words, our feelings arise from the *thoughts* we have about a given situation as opposed to the situation itself. Relatedly, White fragility theorists propose that some White people are more likely to experience intense emotional responses when they interpret a situation as conflicting with their goal to be viewed positively, such as when they believe that someone else will think they are racist (Ford et al., 2022). In the grocery store example, your feelings of intense anxiety and panic did not arise simply because your child said the girl looked like chocolate. Those feelings arose because you interpreted your child's statement as causing others to perceive you and your family as racist. It was the thought "The child's parents are going to think I'm racist!" that really got the anxiety juices flowing throughout your body.

These distorted and exaggerated interpretations that your mind automatically jumps to are known as *cognitive distortions*, or unhelpful ways of viewing the world that may be overly negative and that do not accurately reflect the facts of a situation. Psychologist and researcher Dr. Aaron Beck (1967) originally came up with six types of cognitive distortions that were relevant to depression. Since then, researchers have identified other types of cognitive distortions (e.g., Burns, 1980) and have connected these distortions to a host of emotional, interpersonal, and identity-related issues. The following is a list of different cognitive distortions.

| Cognitive Distortion | Definition |
|---|---|
| All-or-nothing thinking | A tendency to think in extremes or in a dichotomous way (the opposite of thinking dialectically) |
| Overgeneralization | Thinking that one instance of a behavior will always be applicable to the future |
| Catastrophizing | Assuming the worst will happen when an outcome is unknown |
| Personalization | Taking things personally when they are not about you or even caused by you |
| Mind reading | Assuming you know what another person Is thinking |
| Mental filtering | Only focusing on the negatives of a situation (and filtering out the positive) |
| Discounting the positive | Dismissing or minimizing your positive qualities by telling yourself they "don't count" |
| "Should" statements | Making blanket statements about how things "should" be without radically accepting how things are |
| Emotional reasoning | Assuming that how you feel is an indicator of reality ("I feel it, so it must be true") |
| Labeling | Reducing yourself or others to a label (e g , a "loser") based on one instance or experience |

When you repeatedly engage in these unhelpful thinking patterns, it can fuel depression, anxiety, and lots of unhelpful behaviors. The less accurate your thinking is, the more likely you are to perceive yourself, others, and the world in a negative way that makes you feel hopeless or anxious.

## POP QUIZ

Now it's time for a pop quiz to see if you can apply these cognitive distortions to various anti-racist thoughts. Take a moment to draw a line between each cognitive distortion and the anti-racism thought it corresponds to. You can find the correct answers at the end of the chapter.

| Cognitive Distortion | Anti-Racism Thought |
|---|---|
| 1. All-or-nothing thinking | A. "I should naturally know how to be a good ally." |
| 2. Overgeneralization | B. "I made a mistake during the anti-racism meeting last week, so I am a terrible ally." |
| 3. Catastrophizing | C. "If I can't get it right every time, I might as well not even try out anti-racism efforts." |
| 4. Personalization | D. "I must be the reason my BIPOC colleague called out racism in our company." |
| 5. Mind reading | E. "I spoke up about racism once and nothing happened, so my future efforts are pointless." |
| 6. Mental filtering | F. "I feel anxious about how I acted in an interracial interaction, which means it must have gone poorly." |
| 7. Discounting the positive | G. "I'm sure my BIPOC friend wouldn't want me to speak up on her behalf, so I'll stay silent." |
| 8. "Should" statements | H. "I keep thinking about those who didn't support my anti-racist effort even though I did get through to some people." |
| 9. Emotional reasoning | I. "I committed a racial microaggression and now I am going to be canceled." |
| 10. Labeling | J. "I used several skills from my new skills-based anti-racism workbook, but it's not a big deal." |

# How Can Cognitive Distortions Interfere with Anti-Racist Work?

As you can see, not only can unchecked cognitive distortions lead to a host of mental health consequences, but they can also hinder your anti-racist work! The more you engage in cognitive distortions without challenging them, the more likely you are to respond to your emotions in ways that make it hard to persist in your allyship efforts. Let's go back to the hypothetical grocery store incident. In this situation, the thought "The child's parents are going to think I'm racist!" reflected the cognitive distortion of mind reading. Despite the fact that there was no evidence indicating the little girl's parents thought you were a racist, just having that thought ramped up the intensity of the situation. This then put you in a state of panic, which made it hard to respond in a way that was helpful. The Black parents may have felt even worse about the interaction as a result of the harsh statement you made to your child. What could have been a celebratory learning moment with your child turned into a chaotic and anxiety-ridden mess.

## REFLECTION

What cognitive distortions show up most often in your allyship journey?

_____

_____

_____

_____

_____

_____

# Checking the FACTS: A Solution to Cognitive Distortions

As we discussed earlier, emotions arise in response to your *interpretation* of an event rather than the event itself. So if cognitive distortions happen because you are incorrectly interpreting a situation, the solution has to be to correctly interpret the situation, or what's called "checking the facts" in the language of DBT.

In the following paragraphs, we outline the steps needed to check the FACTS in a given situation. To illustrate how each step works, we'll use a hypothetical scenario. Imagine that you just finished leading a diversity meeting in your company where you were completing a racism assessment (e.g., the BASICS skill from chapter 1). A Black colleague approaches you afterward thanking you for your effort. The colleague then adds, "I noticed you used the term *slaves* in your presentation, but the correct term is actually *enslaved persons*. The term *slaves* takes away their inherent humanness whereas *enslaved persons* emphasizes what was being done to them." Just when you were starting to feel good about your anti-racism efforts, you feel crushed about making this mistake.

## "F" Is for Figure Out the Emotion

The first step you are going to take in any intensely emotional situation is to identify the emotion you're experiencing. Different cognitive distortions are associated with all sorts of different emotions, so accurately identifying the emotion is critical. You can use the DETECT skill from chapter 7 to help you with this goal, if the emotion is not immediately clear to you.

In the scenario with the Black colleague, you take a moment and realize that your body suddenly feels exhausted, as though the energy has been zapped out of you. You spend a few moments reflecting on your experience and eventually conclude that you are feeling hopeless.

## "A" Is for Acknowledge the Stories You Are Telling Yourself

After you identify what emotion you're experiencing, the next step is to acknowledge the thoughts you are having about the scenario that prompted this emotion. You might ask yourself questions like "What do I believe just happened?" and "What do I think are the implications, in terms of how I am perceived, of what just happened?" The key part here is to nonjudgmentally and truthfully interrogate how you are interpreting the situation. Even if you can immediately tell that the thought doesn't make sense, that's okay. This step is just about acknowledging the stories you're telling yourself.

Continuing with the hypothetical scenario, you might notice that the hopelessness started because you interpreted the colleague's correction as a personal attack that you are not cut out to lead anti-racism workshops. You ask yourself, "What is really causing me to feel this depleted? What do I believe this colleague's correction says about me?" After taking some time to sit with and tolerate the distress (as you learned in chapter 8), perhaps you realize that you are telling yourself the story that "No matter what I do, I will never be good enough as an anti-racist ally." Playing this story over and over in your mind makes you feel like there is just no hope.

# "C" Is for Check for Cognitive Distortions or Racist Worldviews

Now is the time for you to become a human lie detector test! At this point in the FACTS skill, ask yourself if the stories you are telling yourself are true. There are many ways to figure this out. You might check to see if these stories are rooted in any racist worldviews (go to chapter 3 for a refresher). You might also ask yourself if there is any evidence to support the stories you are telling yourself as well as if there is any evidence against them. This might involve reflecting back on your past experiences or looking up research articles or other credible sources.

If you realize the stories you're telling yourself are cognitive distortions, it means that your emotions do not fit the facts. In this scenario, you would head to the "T" part of this skill, which is the next step. But if you realize the stories are *not* cognitive distortions, then it means your emotions do fit the facts. For example, say that you feel guilty after using racist humor with your friend, and the thought you have is "I hurt my Arab American friend's feelings by making a casual joke about terrorism." Based on the fact that your friend was visibly hurt and required distance from you, the story you're telling yourself is accurate, and the corresponding emotion of guilt fits the facts. If your emotions do fit the facts, then you can skip the "T" step and head on down to the "S" step of this skill.

In the continuing example of a colleague critiquing your use of the word *slaves*, you feel hopeless and realize that this emotion occurred because you thought, "No matter what I do, I will never be good enough as an anti-racist ally." You might ask yourself, "What is the evidence that supports this thought?" Is it true that you will *never* be good enough as an anti-racist ally? Or are you turning this one incident into a never-ending pattern of defeat? This line of questioning leads you to realize that you are engaging in the cognitive distortion of overgeneralizing. Even though you have made some mistakes in the past, allies are not evaluated based on how well they get it right every single time but, instead, on how they recover from and learn from these mistakes.

You also take a moment to ask yourself if there is any evidence against this thought. In doing so, you notice that you are completely disregarding the excellent work you've done as an anti-racist ally in the past and also ignoring the complimentary feedback that you received from this same colleague, who praised your willingness to do this work. You realize that you are discounting the positive (Yes, it is possible to have multiple cognitive distortions simultaneously!) After this process, you realize that the feeling of hopelessness that washed over you came on as a result of cognitive distortions.

# "T" Is for Tackle the Distortions or Racist Worldviews

If you're at this step, it means that the stories you have told yourself are rooted in cognitive distortions or racist worldviews. At this stage, you are using all of the information you have gathered from the previous step to tackle the distorted thought. Think of yourself as a pop-up message that shows up on social media when someone shares misinformation or the Snopes website that fact-checks questionable information. Your goal is to correct the distorted thought by replacing it with a new, fact-based thought. Essentially, this step involves rewriting the script.

For example, in the hypothetical scenario with a Black colleague, you realize by this point that your hopelessness does not fit the facts and that it's time to challenge the distortion. Instead of thinking that you are a hopeless case, you remind yourself that it is normal to make missteps as an ally and that your ability to recover from these missteps is what matters. You also remind yourself that no one is born knowing the correct terms. We *all* learn as we go, particularly given that scholars regularly interrogate language to develop newer, more accurate and equitable terms. Even if you knew the most accurate terms at one point, it doesn't mean you will *always* know them because they constantly evolve, so it's your responsibility as an ally to be flexible and keep up. You might even realize that "good enough" is an arbitrary standard and that all effort is valuable and can be built upon.

Based on this information, you decide to replace the hopelessness-inducing thought of "No matter what I do, I will never be good enough as an anti-racist ally" with the more accurate thought of "It hurt to hear that I used an outdated term, and at the same time, this is a normal part of the anti-racist ally process." You may even notice gratitude toward the colleague who pointed this out to you.

If you discovered in the "C" step that you were telling yourself a story rooted in racist worldviews, it is time to tackle this as well. For example, imagine that after hearing your Black colleague's feedback, instead of having the thought that you are doomed to fail as an anti-racist ally, you thought, "But I'm a good ally! I've been doing the work. If it were *really* wrong to use the word *slaves*, I would have known by now!" In this case, you would be subscribing to the reality-denying worldview of Whiteness ("If *I* do not think it is racist, it must not be"). Before moving on to the next step in FACTS, you would use the other skills you've learned—particularly ACCEPT, DETECT, FEEL, and AND—to challenge this racist worldview, identify and sit with your feelings, and reframe your thoughts to better support your anti-racist values and efforts.

## "S" Is for Select an Appropriate Path Forward

The FACTS skill concludes by using what you have learned to take the most effective step forward. Depending on the situation, the appropriate path forward may involve changing any unhelpful behaviors you are engaging in, rectifying any harm you have caused, or using distress tolerance skills to manage any overwhelming emotions you've determined are rooted in fact. In some cases, the appropriate path forward may not require any further action on your part, especially if the act of challenging your thoughts led to a coinciding improvement in your associated beliefs, emotions, and behaviors. If your emotion does not change (or if you are upset after realizing that your emotion *does* fit the facts), then it may be time to engage in distress tolerance skills as discussed in chapter 8.

For example, after tackling the distortion about the colleague correcting your use of the term *slave*, you notice that your hopelessness dissipates and you feel much more at ease. You immediately go to your office, update the language on your presentation slides, and commit to using the new term you learned in the future.

# Revisiting the Grocery Store Example

Just to drive this skill home, let's go ahead and apply the FACTS skill to the grocery store example from earlier in the chapter and determine an alternative path that you could have used to move forward.

1.  **Figure out the emotion:** You are sweating, shaky, and feeling breathless, which helps you determine that the emotion you're feeling is anxiety.

2.  **Acknowledge the stories you are telling yourself:** You ask yourself how you are interpreting the situation and acknowledge the following stories you're telling yourself: "I feel uncomfortable, which means my child must have done something wrong," "My child is bad for seeing race and noticing the kid's skin color," and "This Black couple definitely thinks we're all racist now."

3.  **Check for cognitive distortions or racist worldviews:** After reviewing the list of cognitive distortions, you realize that you are engaging in emotional reasoning (you assume that your feelings of discomfort are evidence of your child's wrongdoing), labeling (you label your child as

"bad" for noticing the little girl's skin color), and mind reading (you assume that the Black couple thinks you are racist).

4. **Tackle the distortions or racist worldviews:** After taking some time to mindfully think through the facts, you recognize that your child was not being intentionally hurtful and that they were merely excited to see a friend from school. You also consider that the Black parents may have perceived it as an innocent comment for a 5-year-old to make. You then replace your faulty thoughts with more realistic and helpful thoughts like: "It is normal for children to notice race and doing so is not evidence of a wrongdoing," "My child is acting in a developmentally appropriate, typical way by noticing race," "There is no way to know for sure how the parents feel about my child's comment."

5. **Select an appropriate path forward:** As a result of this fact-checking, you realize that rather than admonish your child, you could instead ask them to refer to the peer by her name (rather than her skin tone) and note that she does, in fact, have beautiful brown skin. You take a breath and act effectively in the moment by turning to your child and saying, "Why don't we refer to your peer by her name? Yes, [*name*] has beautiful brown skin!" This response teaches your child a more appropriate way to refer to their BIPOC peers and also allows more space for connection and growth.

## Why Use the FACTS Skill?

The FACTS skill can help you identify whether your emotions are based in reality, which is key to managing your feelings and acting effectively in any given situation. If you have an emotion that *doesn't* fit the facts and take action based on this emotion, this will likely cause you internal conflict and create conflict in your interactions with others. If you've ever had someone take any action against you after a misunderstanding, then you know how dire the consequences can be if you don't check the facts. If you have an emotion that *does* fit the facts, then the FACTS skill can still help you figure out how to take appropriate action. For example, if you feel anger after learning about an injustice, you can validate this emotion to yourself, knowing that it is rooted in reality, and use this anger as a motivator to take a stand against racism as a White ally.

## CHAPTER SUMMARY

In this chapter, we discussed how emotions are often the direct result of your *interpretation* of an incident, rather than the incident itself. When these interpretations are exaggerated, faulty, or distorted in some way, they can lead you to experience painful emotions that interfere with your ability to serve as an ally. These interpretations can fall under a number of different categories that are called cognitive distortions. To challenge these distortions, you learned the FACTS skill, which can help you figure out whether your emotions fit the facts in a given situation and determine what to do when your emotions do *not* fit the facts. Because thoughts arise quickly in relation to your emotions, it can be easy to feel like your thoughts are objective truths even when they're not, which then intensifies your emotions. It is only when you take the time to pause, observe those thoughts, and check how consistent they are with reality that you are able to best manage your emotions.

## ANSWERS TO POP QUIZ ON PAGE 116

| | | |
|---|---|---|
| 1. C | 5. G | 9. F |
| 2. E | 6. H | 10. B |
| 3. I | 7. J | |
| 4. D | 8. A | |

## CHAPTER 10

# Overcoming Unhelpful Behavioral Urges: From Avoidance to Engagement

Throughout this section, we have reviewed the skills needed to label your emotions, recognize and tolerate distressing emotions, and determine whether your emotions fit the facts of a situation. However, it can be difficult to use these skills if you are engaging in patterns of behavior that help you avoid and disengage from unpleasant emotions, experiences, or thoughts. In chapter 8, we introduced the concept of *internal* avoidance, which occurs when you turn away from unpleasant emotions rather than allow yourself to feel and tolerate them. In this chapter, we help you to learn how to recognize and move past *external* avoidance, which occurs when you engage in unhelpful behavioral strategies that undermine your anti-racism efforts. We also introduce a skill to help you move from avoidance to engagement.

## The Book Club Ally

Annie, a White ally, is a proud member of her local Accountable Anti-Racist Allies (AAA) book club. At the most recent book club meeting, Annie suggested a book by Dr. Do-Good based on the many rave reviews she had heard about the book. However, to Annie's surprise, her suggestion was met with significant pushback. A book club member shared that Dr. Do-Good had a long history of making derogatory remarks about Asian American women and felt offended by Annie's suggestion that the club support this problematic author. Annie felt utterly embarrassed and guilty that she did not fully vet the author before making her recommendation. After noticing the disapproving faces of her fellow AAA members, particularly the BIPOC members, Annie feared she would be viewed as racist, so she became defensive and stated, "How was I supposed to know that this author had a history of making these comments? Weren't the book's rave reviews a sign that the club should at least consider the book?" When other members attempted to highlight the issues with Annie's response, Annie became visibly upset and stormed out of the book club meeting. She also called another White member after the meeting to discuss how she felt "ganged up" on by some of the BIPOC members who were "being too sensitive."

## REFLECTION

If you were Annie, what emotions would have come up for you in this scenario? How do you typically approach these emotions?

_____

_____

_____

_____

_____

_____

_____

# What Is Behavioral Avoidance?

As discussed in chapter 8, we tend to welcome pleasant emotions more readily than unpleasant emotions. When an emotion is overwhelming, we often feel a deep or urgent need to *do* something to decrease the emotion's intensity. And, often, this involves using behavioral avoidance strategies that give us an escape or distraction from the unpleasant emotional experience. When we use behavioral avoidance, we experience an unwillingness to sit with unpleasant or unwanted internal experiences (e.g., thoughts, emotions, sensations, memories, urges) and do things to escape or avoid those experiences even if doing so is pointless or interferes with our values in life (Hayes et al., 1996).

Behavioral avoidance is not all bad—when used flexibly and intentionally, it can be appropriate at times. For example, when you feel angry during a conversation, you may have the urge to lash out and say something that you might regret. Choosing to temporarily walk away from the conversation may allow you to escape those feelings of anger and prevent the argument from escalating. While you are intentionally avoiding that internal experience of anger, you are doing so flexibly with the intent of revisiting the conversation.

However, when you engage in behavioral avoidance inflexibly, habitually, or without evaluating how helpful it actually is in a particular situation, it can be counterproductive (Hayes-Skelton & Eustis, 2020). For instance, you might need to set a boundary with a friend who is taking advantage of you but avoid doing so because you don't want to experience the anxiety this will cause you. Or you might repeatedly downplay your needs to avoid feeling any discomfort when your friend neglects those needs. In both scenarios, behavioral avoidance only serves to undermine your goals and values. If you don't set limits and you allow your friend to continue walking all over you, you might eventually explode and start an argument the next time they cross a boundary. Or worse, it could lead you to slowly abandon the friendship altogether. Either way, behavioral avoidance wreaks havoc on your friendship and compromises your values of honesty, harmony, and respect.

As you can see, while behavioral avoidance might allow you to avoid unpleasant emotions in the short term, repeatedly engaging in these behaviors ultimately leads to numerous consequences over the long term, which becomes especially concerning in the context of anti-racism allyship.

# How Do Common Behavioral Avoidance Strategies Hinder Anti-Racist Efforts?

Since behavioral avoidance can take on many forms, there are no absolutes in terms of how someone may act in order to avoid an unpleasant emotion. However, there are some common action urges that accompany certain emotions. Sadness, for example, is often accompanied by the urge to socially withdraw, fear is often accompanied by the urge to run away, anger is often accompanied by the urge to lash out, and happiness is often accompanied by the urge to approach and engage with others.

When it comes to unpleasant emotions, another common urge that people have is to deny their emotional experience and convince themselves and others that everything is okay. For example, someone who is in a toxic relationship might deny the hurt their partner's abusive behavior is causing because this would result in too much pain and grief. Or someone struggling with substance use might deny the disappointment and shame they feel when they drink every night because doing so would be too uncomfortable of a truth to bear.

Similarly, in the context of anti-racism, people can experience a range of unpleasant emotions and accompanying action urges that allow them to avoid or deny their emotional experience. In fact, research shows that White people often use avoidance-based approaches to manage difficult emotions around race (Howell et al., 2013), many of which involve disengaging from the situation or their emotions. These avoidance strategies can have severe impacts on BIPOC, as they can lead to punitive measures against BIPOC and result in anti-racist initiatives shutting down.

For example, learning about Black history can contribute to the well-being of Black youth (Chapman-Hilliard & Adams-Bass, 2016), and Black children also report having a preference for education that aligns with their cultural background (Sampson & Garrison-Wade, 2011). However, many White teachers experience emotional discomfort about topics related to Black communities and therefore avoid discussing race in the classroom (Levine-Rasky, 2000). This avoidance maintains Whiteness (Picower, 2009) and has a direct negative impact on BIPOC.

To illustrate further, let's consider the case vignette at the start of the chapter. Annie appears to strongly value anti-racism, as evidenced by her commitment to the AAA club. However, the threat of being seen as "problematic" for her misstep led her to experience several unpleasant emotions. She felt fear and anxiety about being perceived as racist or being "canceled" by BIPOC book club members, and she felt guilt because she made a mistake that was harmful to others in the book club. However, in an effort to avoid these unpleasant emotions, Annie acted on several ineffective behavioral urges. First, she became defensive by minimizing the impact of her recommendation and doubling down on her belief that reading the book would be beneficial despite the author's racist history ("Weren't the book's rave reviews a sign that the club should at least consider the book?"). Second, when Annie was confronted with constructive criticism that brought up feelings of guilt, she abruptly left the book club meeting. By leaving, she was able to avoid continued comments that may have increased feelings of guilt, but she also denied herself the opportunity for accountability. Third, in an attempt to deflect blame away from her, she called another White group member to center the conversation around accusatory statements ("They're ganging up on me") and put-downs ("They're too sensitive").

Collectively, these actions served to reduce the intensity of Annie's unpleasant feelings—she no longer had to feel fear or guilt now that *she* was the victim. Centering herself as the victim likely wasn't a conscious effort to manipulate her fellow group members, but it was Annie's way of trying to escape her distress and shame. While Annie may have felt the intensity of her emotions decrease after engaging in these avoidance strategies, she ultimately undermined her efforts to grow as an ally, diminished the efforts of the book club to be a safe learning community for all members, and ruptured the trust the other allies had in her. Because she used behavioral avoidance strategies in an inflexible and habitual way, Annie did not act in accordance with her values, which resulted in more distress for Annie and those around her.

In situations where you are called out for a racial misstep, you might find yourself acting like Annie by becoming defensive, throwing your hands up in defeat, or disengaging from anti-racism efforts altogether. You might even center *your* emotions, thoughts, and intentions in order to reassure yourself that you are in the right. It is common to want to deny or minimize responsibility for your actions when you want to avoid feeling guilt or regret. Unfortunately, as we saw in the case of Annie, these strategies result in outcomes that are inconsistent with anti-racism values and that harm BIPOC.

The following list illustrates several common behavioral avoidance strategies that White people may use in an attempt to avoid feeling unpleasant emotions when they're confronted with issues of race and racism.

| Emotion | Behavioral Avoidance Urges |
|---|---|
| Guilt | Minimizing racism, equating your individual experiences of unfairness with systemic racism (or other forms of oppression), denying responsibility for the impact of your actions, redirecting conversations away from race or racism |
| Anxiety, worry, or fear | Opting out of anti-racism spaces, seeking comfort from others, refusing to take accountability, denying racism, scapegoating those who cause discomfort |
| Anger | Defending yourself, insisting that others are wrong, becoming defensive when topics of race or racism arise, denying racism, fixating on a person's "tone" or way of calling you out, demanding or expecting apologies from people who call out your missteps |
| Sadness | Refusing to engage with sensitive or painful material, not listening to BIPOC's experiences |
| Hopelessness or powerlessness | Tuning out in conversations about racism, minimizing racism, disengaging from information and discussions about racism |

## REFLECTION

What behavioral avoidance strategies do you commonly engage in? What emotions are you typically trying to avoid?

_____

_____

_____

_____

_____

_____

# Learning to OPPOSE Behavioral Avoidance: Engaging in Effective Anti-Racism Action

When you give in to behavioral avoidance urges, you are allowing ineffective behaviors to direct the show. But it does not have to be this way. Here, we outline the steps needed to OPPOSE behavioral avoidance. This skill is informed by the "opposite action" skill in DBT, in which you simply do the *opposite* of what your urge is telling you to do. By engaging in actions that are the opposite of your urge to avoid, you can reclaim control and choose a course of action that is consistent with your values as a White ally.

## "O" Is for U̲nderve the Urge to Engage in Behavioral Avoidance

Overcoming behavioral avoidance in anti-racism work requires first bringing a mindful awareness to the urge to avoid. This means you notice the urge *as it arises* and pay attention to it, on purpose and without judgment. There is no need to judge yourself for having the urge to avoid an unpleasant emotion—that is a natural human reaction. However, just because you have the urge to avoid does not mean you have to act on the urge. By mindfully observing the urge, you are able to gain some distance from it and reconnect to the present moment and what is most important to you.

## "P" Is for P̲inpoint the Emotion
## You Are Trying to Avoid

Once you notice the urge to avoid, ask yourself, "What emotion am I trying to avoid or disengage from?" To help with this step, we encourage you to use the DETECT skill from chapter 7, which is designed to help you understand, identify, and label the emotion you are feeling as you are experiencing it. In fact, having this basic emotional literacy is crucial for being able to implement the OPPOSE skill. By pinpointing your emotion (e.g., guilt) and connecting it to your corresponding avoidance urge (e.g., the urge to shift blame to others), you can gain greater emotional clarity and expand your emotion regulation skills.

## "P" Is for P̲ause to Consider the Consequences
## of Your Behavioral Avoidance

As you have learned, behavioral avoidance can be helpful at certain times. When used flexibly and intentionally, it can be appropriate in preventing a situation from becoming worse. For instance, imagine you make a racial misstep and feel extremely hurt, embarrassed, and sad about the impact of your actions on others. Consistent with these feelings, you notice tears welling up in your eyes. Although crying would allow you to feel your feelings, crying has been found to take on heightened meaning in interracial contexts (Accapadi, 2007). In particular, when a White ally cries in interracial contexts, their tears can be used to reprioritize White people and their experiences over the experiences of BIPOC, which in turn reinforces White supremacy. Therefore, in this circumstance, making the *intentional* choice to disengage from your emotions and to avoid crying until you are alone would be an example of effective action. But if you respond to your emotions by denying accountability for your misstep or reiterating how harm was not your intent (despite your actions' negative impact), these actions invalidate the experiences of those you have harmed, which could center you, the ally, over the goal of undoing racism. Therefore, it is necessary to reflect on the consequences of your urge to avoid and determine whether it impedes being an effective anti-racist ally.

## "O" Is for <u>O</u>rganize a List of Effective Actions

If you have identified that engaging in behavioral avoidance is unhelpful and antithetical to your anti-racism values and goals, you can then generate a list of all the possible *opposite* actions you could take that would be consistent with your values. For instance, if you have the urge to redirect conversations away from race and racism, what would be all the ways you could act in an opposite manner? If you get stuck on what those opposite actions might be, consult this chart, which provides an overview on common effective behavioral responses.

| Emotion | Effective Behavioral Responses |
|---|---|
| Guilt | Recognizing and acknowledging racism and its consequences, admitting when you are wrong or mess up, engaging in reparative actions, persisting in difficult anti-racism conversations, accepting responsibility |
| Anxiety, worry, or fear | Fully engaging in anti-racism spaces and conversations, embracing discomfort or negative feelings, taking accountability with emotional bravery, tolerating uncertainty, releasing the need for perfectionism or expectations that you will be the "perfect" ally |
| Anger | Actively listening to BIPOC, taking a step back, leaning in calmly, safely finding an outlet for your anger, reflecting on the source of your anger |
| Sadness | Tolerating distress, exposing yourself to the material that you think will make you sad, listening to BIPOC's experiences |
| Hopelessness or powerlessness | Reminding yourself of why you are doing this work, acknowledging the emotional drain and exhaustion that can happen, remembering that change is slow |

## "S" Is for Select the Most Effective Action

Once you have generated your list of possible opposite actions, select the most effective action. It may help to consider which action is most feasible or doable in a given context. For example, if you make a racist statement during a one-time speaking engagement but are not called out on it until after the fact, it may be too late to make a public apology to the audience in the moment. However, it may be feasible to send a written apology to the host and ask that they email it to all registered attendees. Therefore, picking the most effective opposite action will depend on the various contextual elements of the situation.

## "E" Is for Enact a Specific Plan to Implement the Effective Action

It is not enough to generate a list of possible actions and to select the most effective action if you do not actually engage in the action. Therefore, you must *do* the action that is opposite to your urge if you want to overcome behavioral avoidance. Toward this end, you will need to create a plan for how you will carry out this opposite action. For example, if you decide to send a written apology to the host of your speaking engagement, your plan may involve dedicating time later that evening to draft an apology letter that acknowledges the harm you caused, asking your spouse to review the letter, making any necessary adjustments, and then sending it. (You will learn more about how to make reparations with the REPAIR skill in chapter 11.)

Remember, your plan may need to entail doing the opposite action over and over. Behavioral avoidance urges can be strong and intense, and reducing the intensity of such urges may require doing the opposite action repeatedly until you notice your avoidance urge dissipate. But don't despair—if you use the opposite action *all the way*, it will work with time and practice.

# Revisiting the Book Club Ally Example

To see how the OPPOSE skill can work in practice, let's reconsider the case vignette with Annie. When the other book club member pointed out Annie's misstep, she could have taken the time to nonjudgmentally reflect on the emotions and corresponding action urges she was experiencing in that moment. This process could have helped her to get some distance from her intense emotional discomfort and allowed her to consider the consequences of giving in to behavioral avoidance in this context. In doing so,

Annie would have realized that minimizing the impact of her book recommendation and insisting on its value were inconsistent with her values as an anti-racist advocate.

Using the list of effective actions as a guide, she could then have selected several behavioral responses that were the opposite of her urge to avoid. For example, Annie could have acknowledged her misstep and apologized for suggesting a book written by a problematic author. She also could have verbally validated her peers' concerns and thanked them for sharing this information with her. In addition, rather than leaving the meeting early, she could have stayed to show her willingness to persist in difficult conversations and to meaningfully take in helpful feedback from anti-racist peers. Finally, instead of calling another group member to center Annie's feelings, Annie could have used distress tolerance skills, like the FEEL skill from chapter 8, to soothe herself in the face of her intense emotional overwhelm. Strategies like these would have allowed Annie to demonstrate *real* support for anti-racism and BIPOC.

## Why Use the OPPOSE Skill?

We all experience the urge to avoid unpleasant emotions. Unfortunately, when avoidance is your first-line response and you don't consider the consequences of your behaviors, it can lead you to make choices you later regret. Remember that strong emotions can override the logical part of your brain, so if you don't stop to mindfully reflect on your emotions and identify the unhelpful avoidance urges that accompany these emotions, you may act in ways that are not aligned with your values. Therefore, the primary benefit of using the OPPOSE skill is to not let your avoidance take the wheel. Although behavioral avoidance may provide relief in the short term, it can negatively impact your life choices over time and stagnate your anti-racism efforts.

# CHAPTER SUMMARY

In this chapter, we discussed the role of behavioral avoidance in managing unpleasant emotions. Even though avoidance is a natural response to unpleasant emotions, giving in to the urge to avoid can disrupt your work as a White ally, especially given that many urges are antithetical to anti-racist action. Avoidance is tempting because it can feel good! The more you avoid, the less discomfort you feel, making you want to avoid even more. However, avoidance behaviors like minimizing racism, becoming defensive in response to racial missteps, and disengaging from discussions about racism all invalidate the experiences of BIPOC and keep you from being an effective ally. To overcome the urge to avoid and engage in more effective actions, you learned the OPPOSE skill, which helps you do the opposite of what your behavioral avoidance urge tells you to. Doing this takes courage, but the more you practice it, the easier it will become. With this tool in hand, as well as those from the preceding chapters, you are now ready to start navigating the complexities of interpersonal barriers to anti-racist allyship.

# SECTION IV

· · · · ·

# OVERCOMING INTERPERSONAL BARRIERS TO EFFECTIVE ANTI-RACIST ALLYSHIP

## CHAPTER 11

# Recovering from Racist Missteps: From Rupture to Repair

People often say that mistakes are proof you're trying, and in the world of anti-racist allyship, this is definitely true. Anti-racist work is hard and complex, and you have so many barriers to overcome on the route to becoming an effective ally. Despite your best efforts, this complexity means missteps *will* happen. When it comes to racist missteps, it's necessary to remember that *how* you respond to the misstep is more important than the misstep itself. In this chapter, we outline what a misstep is and guide you through the process of repairing harm after a misstep has occurred.

## Theo the Therapist

Let's imagine that Theo, a mental health therapist, is working in a hospital, and the day starts off with the usual morning rounds with the treatment team. He starts to share with the group that he recently spoke with a client on the phone whom he wants to take on as a new client. Someone on the team looks at the potential client's file and says, "Actually, her file says she prefers a Black therapist who will understand her experiences as a Black person." Theo immediately replies, "She's Black? That's weird because she didn't sound Black to me!" After the weight of his comment hangs in the air for a moment, Theo adds, "Oh, come on, you *know* I didn't mean it like that. She just . . . sounded White!" Noticing that his BIPOC colleagues do not immediately assuage his distress, he says, "Y'all are so sensitive! Fine, I won't take the client on. Can we just move on now?" He then disengages from the rest of the meeting and does not bring up the incident again.

# What Is a Racist Misstep?

As you've probably guessed, Theo's action was an example of a racist misstep, and it most likely caused a rupture in his relationship with his colleagues. His comment, which assumed that Black people sound a particular way, is just one type of misstep out of a plethora of different kinds. In the following table, we outline several different types of racist missteps that you, as a well-meaning White ally, might engage in.

| Racist Misstep Type | Definition | Example |
|---|---|---|
| Implicit bias | Mostly automatic, largely unconscious negative assumptions made about BIPOC | A White medical doctor assumes that a Black patient is exaggerating their pain and declines to prescribe them needed pain medications. |
| Racial micro-aggressions | Intentional or unintentional slights or remarks that are denigrating, dehumanizing, or invalidating to BIPOC | A White employee states that their new Latinx coworker speaks English well. |
| Centering oneself | Directing attention away from anti-racist work toward yourself, including your personal preferences and feelings | In a town hall meeting to provide support for BIPOC after a recent racist incident in the news, a White woman spends a significant amount of time talking about how hurt she was by the incident and how bad she feels about what happened. |
| Nonverbal behaviors | Engaging in nonverbal actions that communicate mistrust, disgust, or disdain toward BIPOC | After a visibly Muslim couple sits next to a White man at the airport, he immediately gets up and walks to the other side of the waiting area. |

| Derailing anti-racist efforts | Interrupting, resisting, and halting racial progress through both intentional (e.g., holding up policy changes) and unintentional (e.g., becoming unresponsive when you are responsible for a particular action) behaviors | On an anti-racism committee, a White member repeatedly expresses pessimism that anti-racist changes can be made, offering only critiques of the changes without proactively trying to offer solutions. |
|---|---|---|
| Cultural appropriation | Using an element of a BIPOC's culture (e.g., language, dress) in a way that is unwelcomed by many people in the group and reflects a lack of knowledge about historical context | A White woman applies a bindi (a traditional, circular mark worn by some Hindu, Jain, Sikh, and Buddhist women) to wear at a music festival. |
| Erasure and inadequate attribution to BIPOC | Taking the ideas and work of BIPOC without properly acknowledging the original source | After an Indigenous social media content creator makes a video illustrating the contributions of Indigenous peoples to science, a White content creator replicates the video frame by frame and does not give the original creator credit. |

# Why Does Repair Matter?

As we mentioned earlier, how you recover from a racist misstep is of the utmost importance. To highlight this, imagine you are at a subway station when someone bumps into you, leading you to fall over. If that person ignored what they did and kept power walking past you, you'd probably be fuming. But if they stopped immediately to help you up and offered a genuine apology, you might still be mad, but you probably wouldn't be *fuming*. This is because engaging in an act of repair communicates to the harmed person that you take responsibility for what happened and that you are committed to not doing it again.

# What Is an Effective Anti-Racist Repair?

Repair can look a number of different ways. For example, reparative action could include a particular gesture or action, or an apology. For our purposes, we define it as any effort taken to mend or reconcile a relationship after a rupture has occurred. Not all repair attempts are equal; there are many ways repair attempts can go wrong, ranging from simply not doing anything at all to inadvertently making the situation worse. When thinking about anti-racist repair, there are several considerations that are relevant to each stage in the process, including understanding why the misstep occurred, clarifying your motives for repair, embodying cultural humility, regulating your emotions, understanding the context in which the misstep occurred, managing your expectations for the repair's outcome, and committing to behavior change. In the following paragraphs, we discuss each of these considerations in more detail.

## Understand the "Why"

Before engaging in reparative action, it is critical to understand why the misstep was a misstep in the first place. Imagine that at a parent-teacher conference, a teacher meets the father of three Black students and asks, "Wait, are you the father of *all* three kids?" At that moment, the teacher might think she is asking an innocent question and might even say, "I was just curious—I didn't want to assume." Despite her innocent or curious intentions, this question reflects a misstep because it invokes the "baby mama" stereotype, which characterizes Black women as having children by multiple partners.

It is also important to understand what caused the misstep. In the parent-teacher conference example, the teacher's question—and the fact that she likely does not ask this same question of White fathers—could have been caused by her internalization of stereotypes about Black women in particular and Black heterosexual families in general. Without understanding that her comment was a direct result of her internalization of these harmful stereotypes, she would not have information about what she needs to work on. Therefore, taking the time to process and reflect on the "why" behind the misstep is critical.

## Clarify Your Motives

It is also necessary for you to get clear on your motives for repair and to make sure that you are engaging in reparative action for the right reasons (e.g., genuine remorse, alignment with anti-racist values). When you apologize because it's forced or because you want others to perceive you more positively, it often backfires because disingenuousness is palpable. One study found that apologies rooted in a fear of consequences are associated with *less* forgiveness compared to apologies motivated by more genuine motives, like self-blame (Mu & Bobocel, 2019). Another study found that voluntary atonement is also perceived as more worthy of forgiveness compared to imposed atonement (Watanabe & Laurent, 2021). Thus, the more you understand why a misstep was a misstep, and the more you genuinely experience and demonstrate regret, the more likely you are to engage in reparative action that is intrinsically motivated.

## Embody a Spirit of Cultural Humility

When engaging in reparative action, you need to approach the interaction in the spirit of cultural humility. Cultural humility refers to an ongoing commitment to self-reflection and learning about groups that are different from you. Patallo (2019) suggests that cultural humility encompasses collaborative partnerships, mutual respect, and an attitude of genuine curiosity toward your own and others' cultural identities. This means that even if you have the most racially diverse friend group, have BIPOC family members, or have won prestigious awards for your anti-racism work, you never reach the status of an "expert ally" who is invincible against missteps. Your good intentions and your accolades do not mean that you won't mess up sometimes, nor do they absolve you of the need to take responsibility for your missteps. Accepting that missteps can happen is critical!

## Use Emotion Regulation Skills

If being an ally is a key aspect of your overall sense of self, a misstep can feel shocking and deeply inconsistent with how you see yourself. As a result, you'll likely need to be prepared to practice the emotion regulation skills from the last few chapters to engage in effective reparative action. You might need to tolerate a lot of painful emotions, including shame, regret, and disappointment, to meaningfully take responsibility for the harm you have caused. Otherwise, you may be tempted to over-apologize even when the person harmed said the misstep was minor. Over-apologizing in an attempt to minimize or soothe your own guilt makes the situation about you and unfairly puts pressure on the BIPOC person to minimize their reaction to the harm and center yours.

In addition, when you don't use emotion regulation skills, you might try to avoid or minimize your unpleasant emotions by issuing a quick apology just to get the situation "over with." However, such an apology can come across as disingenuous. In fact, some research demonstrates that apologies that come later (rather than sooner) are actually perceived more favorably because the person who was wronged may feel more heard and understood (Frantz & Bennigson, 2005). It could be that taking longer to apologize communicates that you are taking the situation seriously and carefully considering the best way to respond. Therefore, to minimize the likelihood of offering a rushed apology, it could be helpful to offer an immediate response that is brief and note that you need more time to process and figure out the best way to handle the situation.

## Consider the Context

In addition to your approach to the repair, you also have to acknowledge that the context of the racist misstep matters and that there is no one-size-fits-all approach to the actual repair process. Later in this chapter, we offer guidelines that will help you decide what the most effective action can be, but it is up to you to really think through several details. For example, if the racist misstep was public (e.g., committing a microaggression in a group meeting), then perhaps the repair should also be public (e.g., in a subsequent meeting of that group). If, in the repair process, the person who was harmed asks for a specific type of reparation (e.g., a change in a particularly biased procedure at work), then your repair should include a plan to address those specific requests.

## Watch Your Expectations

The work is not over yet! You will still need to regulate painful emotions after you engage in a reparative action, especially if you have certain expectations for the outcome of the repair. For example, even without realizing it, you might expect the other person to spare your feelings of guilt by making you feel better about what happened or by minimizing how much your behavior actually harmed them. You might also expect them to forgive or comfort you once they realize just how bad you feel about what you did. Despite these urges to seek forgiveness or comfort, it's important to just sit with the uncertainty and regret you might be experiencing. Even if you give the most eloquent apology, BIPOC do not owe you forgiveness.

## Grow from a Racist Misstep

The most critical action you can take post-repair is to change your behavior. An apology and a gesture will mean absolutely nothing if there is no commitment or resolve to ensure that the misstep does not happen again. It's therefore extremely vital for you to take responsibility to create a game plan for how you are going to change your behavior in the future. This could involve reading a book or attending workshops related to the misstep. If your misstep involved a microaggression, perhaps you can read books or watch videos about racial microaggressions. If your misstep involved an instance of implicit bias, perhaps you can set up systems to automatically detect implicit bias in the decisions you're making. Either way, you have to remember that the process of repair should include both short-term and long-term plans. At the end of the day, it's *your* responsibility to figure out what to do to ensure the misstep does not happen again, though you can, of course, request feedback from others.

# The REPAIR Process: Managing the Aftermath of a Racist Misstep

After the emotional flurry of engaging in a racist misstep, it is necessary to take a moment to think through the most effective way to respond. Similar to a wound, the way you approach the healing process matters. Whereas effective wound care (e.g., keeping the area clean) can lead to healed skin, improper wound care can lead to even worse consequences on top of the wound (e.g., introducing bacteria, leading to infection). As we noted earlier, there is not a single repair process that works the same across *all* situations. Instead, we offer you the REPAIR skill, which will guide you through the critical components necessary for you to craft an effective repair.

## "R" Is for Recognize What Caused the Misstep

The first part of the REPAIR skill is to recognize what caused the misstep. Doing so requires working backward from the misstep to figure out all the things that led up to that moment. Let's take the "centering oneself" example from the racist misstep table included earlier in the chapter, in which there was a town hall meeting for BIPOC following a racist incident in the news. At the town hall meeting, a White woman we'll call Chatty Cathy spent a significant amount of time talking about how hurt she was by the incident and how bad she felt about what happened. Although Cathy's feelings were understandable and valid, her inability to tolerate distress made it so that *her* pain was spotlighted and that BIPOC attendees were unable to talk about their feelings and reactions. Upon reflection, Chatty Cathy realized that her misstep—centering herself and taking up too much space—occurred because she lacks distress tolerance skills and doesn't know what it means for White folks to center themselves in BIPOC-designated spaces. The more she understands the cause of the offending behavior, the less likely she is to repeat it in the future.

## "E" Is for Evaluate Your Emotional Reactions

There's a reason we introduced you to the emotion regulation skills *before* the interpersonal skills in this book—it's because your ability to identify and manage your emotions are foundational skills for overcoming the interpersonal barriers that emerge in anti-racist work. You have to be aware of the emotions you experience after a racist misstep so that you can proceed effectively. This process of evaluating your emotional reactions is what the second step of the REPAIR skill is about.

To illustrate how this can look, let's take the cultural appropriation example from the previous racist misstep table. Here, a White woman—let's call her Festival Frances—wore a bindi to a music festival. After sharing a picture of herself wearing the bindi on social media, she is gently called out in the comments section by her fans for cultural appropriation. Her fans note that she likely had good intentions and that they still respect her as a person. Festival Frances feels shame, but since she doesn't use the DETECT skill from chapter 7, she doesn't recognize this is what she is feeling. In an attempt to justify her behavior, she immediately starts posting examples of other White people who have worn bindis (and maybe even finds a single blog post where a Hindu person says this behavior is okay). However, if Frances had taken a moment to pause, she would have recognized that she was feeling shame and allowed herself to tolerate this emotion using the FEEL skill from chapter 8. In turn, she might have been more likely to convey her shame in a way that allowed for a repair to be effective.

Similarly, it's possible that Festival Frances might feel angry because she was "attacked," in her eyes, by her social media fans. She then might lash out, accusing "woke" culture for viciously attacking her, despite the reality that the callouts were quite gentle. Rather than doing this, Frances could take a moment to notice her anger and determine that it does not fit the facts (using the FACTS skill from chapter 9). This could help her to reduce her anger and consequently not say something that will make the situation worse.

## "P" Is for Pay Attention to Your Motives

As we mentioned earlier, the motives behind your repair matter, which is why we recommend really looking inward and asking yourself, "What is driving my desire to repair?" If you notice that you are engaging in a repair process because you feel obligated to or because you are worried about negative consequences (e.g., "I don't want to get canceled"), then it might be time for a pause.

For example, imagine that you are preparing to meet with your Middle Eastern coworker to apologize after you told her that she looked "so exotic" as a compliment, and others in the office pointed out that it was problematic. You notice yourself having thoughts such as "Ugh, if I don't apologize, I am going to get canceled by the whole office. Why do I have to do this? I know she knows I had good intentions." These thoughts indicate that your motive for apologizing is driven by a fear of being negatively judged by your coworkers. You might ask yourself what is driving the resistance to a genuine apology and use the tools we've offered so far (including the ACCEPT skill from chapter 3 to tackle problematic worldviews or the CLEAR skill from chapter 6 to push through ambivalence) to overcome this resistance. If, on the other hand, you notice that your desire to repair is coming from a place of genuine remorse and a desire to do better, you can let that motive guide the remainder of your repair process.

## "A" Is for <u>A</u>pologize in a Way That Takes Responsibility

Although verbal apologies may not be feasible in every scenario in which a misstep occurs (e.g., committing a microaggression to a passing stranger), there are times when the repair process should involve verbal apologies. But just because we may have learned about the importance of saying sorry in childhood doesn't mean we naturally know how to do this effectively. In fact, apologies can go awry, especially in anti-racist work.

To illustrate how the repair process can go wrong, let's consider another example from the previous racist misstep table: erasure and inadequate attribution to BIPOC. After an Indigenous content creator makes a video illustrating the contributions of Indigenous peoples to science, a White content creator we'll call TikTok Taylor replicates the video frame by frame and does not give the original creator credit. Let's imagine that TikTok Taylor responds to being called out in one of the following ways:

1. She makes a video with the message, "Everyone takes everyone's ideas on TikTok. Sorry you're mad, but that's just how this works."
2. She privately messages the original creator and says, "Sorry for the mix-up. I took the video down."
3. She responds to her followers' callout comments by saying things like "Why does everyone have to make everything about race? I guess I'll take it down if everyone is going to harass me."

What do all of these responses have in common? In each of these attempts, TikTok Taylor is not stating what she did wrong or taking responsibility for her actions. Having a clear statement of what the misstep was and *why* it was a misstep communicates to the harmed party that you take responsibility for the misstep. Imagine, instead, that Taylor made a video in response to her misstep and said things like "I am sorry that I stole an Indigenous creator's work and passed it off as my own, which showed that I did not respect their artistry or ideas" and "This kind of behavior is problematic because it erases Indigenous peoples' work and contributions in a society that has violently done so for hundreds of years." You can see how in this case, Taylor is clearly stating what she did without sugarcoating it or minimizing its impact. Thus, she is apologizing in a way that takes responsibility for her actions.

## "I" Is for Invite Feedback, Not Forgiveness

In the context of racist missteps, asking for forgiveness can add a lot of undue pressure on the BIPOC person who was harmed to quickly process their reactions to the misstep. Furthermore, asking for forgiveness can often be a way to assuage your own guilt so that you can "move on" and not think about the incident.

Instead of asking for forgiveness, we suggest that you ask for feedback in a way that is consistent with cultural humility. There are two things you may want to get feedback about after a misstep, assuming someone has taken the time to let you know that your behavior was harmful. First, you can ask for feedback about whether you understand the issue correctly. Consider the racial microaggression example from the racist misstep table, in which a White employee tells her Latinx coworker that he speaks English very well. When she is called out for this problematic comment, she interprets this to mean that she is not allowed to give Latinx people compliments. By getting feedback on the issue, she can come to realize that it is okay to give others compliments, just not compliments that assume Latinx people do not speak English well.

Second, you can tentatively, and in a non-demanding way, ask for feedback about future steps. This could mean asking if the harmed person wants you to resolve the situation in a particular way. However, this does not let you off the hook from doing your own homework. In fact, we recommend that you first identify ways you can repair the harm and then communicate that you are open to specific requests. For instance, in the implicit bias example in our racist misstep table, a White medical doctor we will call Invalidating Ian assumes that a Black patient, Michael, is exaggerating his pain and therefore declines to prescribe Michael needed pain medications. To help repair the misstep and get feedback about future steps, Invalidating Ian may talk to Michael directly and ask, "In addition to writing you that prescription and reading up on how to tackle racial empathy gaps in medicine, is there anything I can do to make this right?" The patient might have nothing to offer, which is perfectly okay, or he might make a request, such as asking to be introduced to another doctor with whom he might be more comfortable. Either way, asking for feedback about whether the harmed person wants a particular repair centers them and their needs, which is an indication that you are taking their concerns seriously.

## "R" Is for Resolve to Change Your Behavior

As the old adage goes, the best apology is changed behavior. Why might this be true? Changing your behavior communicates two things: (1) that you understand why the racist misstep behavior was problematic and (2) that you are so concerned about not harming BIPOC that you actually want to exert effort to do things differently. Let us examine one more example from the racist misstep table: derailing anti-racist efforts. Derailing Donald sits on an anti-racism committee, where he repeatedly expresses pessimism that changes can be made and only offers critiques of proposed changes without proactively trying to offer solutions. After months of this behavior, several committee members grow increasingly frustrated and invite him to no longer be on the committee. He protests this suggestion, reaffirms his commitment to the mission, and asks what he can do differently. The members suggest to Donald that he can do several things differently: do more listening than talking; before speaking, ask himself if the comment he's about to make is helpful; and actively work on problem-solving. He agrees to all these things.

However, in the next meeting, he starts off by saying, "I don't mean to be negative, but I looked at our department's budget, and there's absolutely no way we can offer fee waivers to BIPOC applicants. And by the way, can we talk about how complicated the application process is?" Once again, the committee's anti-racism efforts are derailed, and those who spoke with him about his behavior deem his attempt at repair a complete failure. Imagine, however, that at the next meeting, when Donald is asked for an update, he says, "Although there wasn't initially room in the budget for fee waivers, I found several internal funding mechanisms to support this anti-racist effort and would be happy to take the lead on an application." In this scenario, it is clear that he has taken the time to process the feedback and he has a plan for implementing changed behavior in a way that is consistent with anti-racist work. You can imagine how if you were a member of this committee, you might feel hopeful and excited to continue working with him. Who knows? You might even change his name in your head from "Derailing Donald" to "Determined Don."

# Why Use the REPAIR Skill?

Without knowing how to adequately respond to a misstep, you run the risk of committing another misstep, undermining your relationships with BIPOC, and self-sabotaging your own anti-racism efforts. Using the REPAIR skill is one way to ensure you stay aligned with your anti-racist values and preserve your relationships with BIPOC and other allies. Using this skill—which encompasses multiple elements of reparative action—is also in line with research showing that reparative action that includes more elements is perceived as more effective than reparative action with fewer elements (Lewicki et al., 2016). When you engage in reparative action, you want to make sure you are maximizing its effectiveness to truly undo the harm that has been caused.

## CHAPTER SUMMARY

Although it would be nice to never commit a racist misstep, missteps are inevitable when you're truly engaging in anti-racist allyship. In this chapter, we highlighted common types of racist missteps, explained how they occur, and described how ineffectively responding to these missteps can often dig you into a deeper hole. We also talked about how you can craft meaningful reparative actions that include recognizing what led to the misstep in the first place, appropriately managing any difficult emotions you feel as a result of the misstep, attending to your motives for repair, apologizing and taking responsibility, inviting feedback about how you can do better, and resolving to make the necessary changes to prevent the misstep from happening again. Once you are able to take accountability for your missteps via the REPAIR skill, you are better equipped to turn your attention to others, especially when it comes to calling out other people who make missteps, which is the focus of the next chapter.

## CHAPTER 12

# Calling Out Racism: From Passiveness to Assertiveness

Allies receive numerous messages about how to best show up in anti-racism work. One message is that you should speak out loudly against racism, which can be done by calling out racism in your workplace or in interactions with family and friends. However, if you've ever sat across from a colleague, friend, or family member who has said something problematic, you know that calling out racism can be a struggle. You may lack the skills to do this effectively or worry about hurting someone's feelings in the process. The purpose of this chapter is to provide both reflection guides and skills to strengthen the connection between your anti-racism allyship goals and actions. Toward this end, we describe what calling out racism entails, outline its benefits, discuss the barriers that make this difficult, and introduce a skill that can bolster your confidence in calling out racism.

## What Do We Mean by "Calling Out Racism"?

At its core, calling out racism is about identifying and challenging instances of racist behavior, language, or attitudes you witness, whether those instances are intentional or unintentional. Calling out racism can include pointing out racist comments made by a colleague or highlighting how a family member's joke reflects prejudiced or racist stereotypes about BIPOC communities. It can involve educating others about the impact of their words or actions, or simply expressing discomfort or disapproval when witnessing racist behavior. Although some people propose a distinction between what it means to "call in" (e.g., have a private, deeper discussion) and "call out" (e.g., engage in a public confrontation), we use the term *call out* in a flexible way that allows you to choose a delivery context that makes sense for any given situation. The language you use to describe your actions is less important than the actions themselves. In other words, whether you describe what you do as "calling out" or "calling in" is up to you. The critical part is that you challenge instances of racism effectively.

For some White people, calling out racism is only done as an act of "virtue signaling"—that is, publicly expressing opinions or sentiments intended to make *yourself* look good. We want to be clear that virtue signaling is not only ineffective but also misguided. Calling out racism isn't about separating yourself from "problematic White people" or situating yourself as "better than." Rather, it's about challenging racism at the individual level in ways that are likely to promote meaningful change. So when we talk about calling out racism, we mean intentionally calling attention to racism and making requests for change.

## REFLECTION

What comes to mind when you think about calling out racism?

_____

_____

_____

_____

_____

_____

_____

_____

# Bella the Bystander: A Case Vignette

Bella, a White ally, belongs to a group chat with several work colleagues from different racial backgrounds. One morning, she opened the group chat and saw that her White colleague Ryan made a racist comment about a Latinx customer he had interacted with: "I tried to stay calm, but the spicy Latina in her just came out!" Bella felt her eyes widen and her mouth fall open in disbelief as she read the message. She would have never expected her colleague to make such a comment, much less in a work group chat. She hesitated for a moment, wondering if she should say something, but noticed that no one else in the chat responded to the comment. As the conversation continued without any acknowledgment of the racist comment, Bella felt increasingly anxious and uncomfortable. She knew Ryan's comment was wrong and hurtful, but she didn't want to risk making things awkward or damaging her relationships with her colleagues. She also worried that if she spoke up, Ryan might retaliate, making Bella the target of harassment. She wondered what her BIPOC colleagues might be thinking or feeling, and why they too weren't speaking up. Ultimately, Bella decided to remain silent and check in with her BIPOC colleagues privately.

Over the next few days, Bella couldn't shake the thought that she had let herself and others down by not speaking out against the racist text message. When that same colleague continued to make similar jokes in person, she felt a rising sense of helplessness. She felt like she was fumbling another opportunity to challenge harmful behavior and promote greater understanding and empathy among her colleagues. But how could she call him out without "making a scene" or making him feel like she was attacking him? What if she came across as too pushy or judgmental? What if her BIPOC colleagues thought she was acting like a White savior? They didn't say anything either, so maybe it wasn't a big deal? Bella once again decided against speaking up and instead considered starting a separate group chat with her "non-problematic" White colleagues and BIPOC colleagues.

## REFLECTION

Have you had a similar experience as Bella? Why might it be helpful for her to push through her concerns and say something to call out the comment?

_____

_____

_____

_____

_____

_____

_____

_____

# Why Is It Important to Call Out Racism?

Situations like that of Bella the Bystander are far too common, and they get in the way of undoing racism. To challenge oppressive structures and create change, you need to do the opposite of Bella and call out racism when it occurs. By explicitly naming the racism that is present in a particular situation, you can help raise awareness of how certain thoughts, words, and actions perpetuate racism. In fact, researchers have found that when White people are educated about how racism is perpetuated, it actually increases awareness of White privilege and decreases racial color-blind ideologies—ideologies that keep racism going (Hochman & Suyemoto, 2020). Therefore, calling out racism helps increase our collective awareness of racism, privilege, and the negative consequences of adhering to a color-blind worldview.

Further, calling out racism begins to dismantle patterns of White silence and leads to increased collective anti-racist actions. Research has found that when people are taught to confront prejudice, not only do they learn how to speak out against discrimination, inequity, and racism, but the people in their social networks subsequently become more willing to do so too (Paluck, 2011). These findings make sense because when you hear others express strong anti-racist views, it increases your own willingness to condemn racism (Blanchard et. al, 1994). Therefore, calling out racism has the potential to change social norms in your networks, communities, and systems, and decrease the likelihood of racist interpersonal incidents continuing to occur.

Finally, calling out racism can support the personal and professional well-being of BIPOC. As we have stated many times in this book, racism is a pervasive social and structural ill that harms the mental and physical health of BIPOC, limits their opportunities, and makes it hard to have a society that is based on trust and collaboration. When people exhibit perceived apathy to social justice issues, both in professional and personal settings, it can have negative consequences for BIPOCs' well-being and sense of belonging. Conversely, when people act as allies and call out racism, it can reduce prejudice, promote positive interracial relations, and improve the well-being of both allies and marginalized groups. Therefore, the benefits of calling out racism are far reaching and have profound effects on the personal and professional lives of BIPOC.

## Why Is It Important for *White Allies* to Call Out Racism?

Although speaking up against a racist incident is important for everyone, it is especially important for White allies to bear the burden of this task for several reasons. First, speaking out against racism has much higher costs for BIPOC compared to White people. For example, when BIPOC employees speak out, they are more likely to be perceived as less likable and less competent, and they are often subject to harsher social punishment (Kaiser & Miller, 2003). This can lead to poorer mental health, decreased job satisfaction, and loss of job opportunities (Rosette et al., 2008). BIPOC are literally risking their interpersonal relationships as well as their job security and livelihood when they call out racism. BIPOC folks are aware of these very real consequences, which often results in disparate work experiences for them relative to their White peers. It is for this reason that Bella's BIPOC colleagues may have chosen not to speak up about Ryan's "spicy Latina" comment, rather than, as Bella assumed, because they were not bothered by the comment. While White allies who speak out about racism may also be perceived as less likable, the costs are not the same.

Second, calling out racism as a White person not only dismantles patterns of complacency and inaction but also leverages White privilege to protect BIPOC from the disproportionate costs of speaking out. By leveraging this privilege, White allies can take on some of the undue burden that BIPOC often carry in efforts to dismantle racism. This is true in professional and personal settings. When White allies speak out about racism, they not only reduce the costs to BIPOC, but they also increase the benefits for both themselves and BIPOC. For instance, research shows that when White allies speak out, BIPOC are more likely to experience a sense of belonging in their social and work environments. Relatedly, White people who engage in anti-racist work consistently report a stronger sense of purpose and connection to social justice (Nelson et al., 2011).

# What Gets in the Way of Calling Out Racism?

There are a variety of barriers that can get in the way of your ability to call out racism. One of these barriers is the inability to recognize racism (or racist missteps) when they occur. Many White people have not been exposed to or educated about racism and its effects, and they may not recognize it when they encounter it. Further, White people benefit from the privileges that come with being a part of the dominant cultural group in many societies, which can make it harder for them to recognize or understand the experiences of BIPOC. This is a large part of why we began this book with a discussion of what racism is and introduced you to a skill to recognize it (the BASICS skill from chapter 1). It's important for allies to have a sound, working definition of racism in order to become more masterful in recognizing racism when it occurs in the moment.

Another barrier to calling out racism is ambivalence, which may lead you to simultaneously want to call out and *not* call out racism. In fact, when White allies are faced with the potential consequences of calling out racism, they often struggle with indecision to act. Much like Bella's experience, this indecision, or ambivalence, leads to stagnation. Bella's fear of damaging relationships and being perceived negatively were clearly driving her ambivalence, which ultimately undermined her ability to act in alignment with her values to call out racism. In an ideal world, Bella would have benefited from using the CLEAR skill from chapter 6 to move from indecision to action. She also would have used the OPPOSE skill from chapter 10 to work through any unpleasant emotions she experienced at the thought of speaking up. Instead, she remained silent and did nothing to challenge and dismantle racist behaviors and workplace norms. Since ambivalence gets in the way of your ability to actively call out racism, you need to ask yourself what may be driving your ambivalence in these situations.

Even after working through ambivalence, many allies, like Bella, struggle with yet another barrier to calling out racism: not knowing how to do it. We acknowledge that there are many ways that calling out racism can go awry—not all forms of calling out are created equal. Calling out racism can be ineffective if it's done in a way that's too passive and what's being called out is lost. Or perhaps it is done in a way that is too ambiguous such that a clear request for change is missing. It can also be ineffective when people call out racism in a way that focuses on the other person's character rather than the racist action, which can lead to defensiveness and hostility from the person being called out. The task of navigating these potential pitfalls can seem insurmountable. While there are a multitude of ways your callout can go wrong, there are also a number of ways to improve your ability to call out racism and avoid these pitfalls. For this barrier, we specifically designed the CALL OUT skill.

# CALL OUT: A Skill for Effectively Confronting Racism

The CALL OUT skill is a stepwise process for effectively and assertively calling out a racist incident in the moment and making a request for change in a way that increases the likelihood of a positive outcome. This skill is also designed to help you effectively communicate with the other person and navigate any conflict that arises. In terms of the acronym, CALL teaches you *what* to say, whereas OUT teaches you *how* to say it.

## "C" Is for Clarify What Happened

The first step in calling out racism is to clarify what happened by explaining the factual details of what was said or done. Sticking to the facts of the situation means that you are not expressing your feelings, opinions, or perspectives or asking for anything at this time. Rather, you are simply setting up the conversation by using facts. This gets everyone on the same page about what occurred, which is vital for all subsequent steps. When there is not a shared understanding of the facts of the situation, it undermines communication and makes it more difficult to navigate conflict. Therefore, describing the incident and focusing on the *specific* language or behaviors that were racist allows everyone in the conversation to develop an accurate understanding of the issue being addressed.

## "A" Is for Acknowledge Possible Intentions

It is possible that you will encounter resistance or defensiveness after you clarify the specific language or behaviors that were racist. This is because when people are called out, they assume that they are being perceived as acting in bad faith or intentionally being racist. As a result, people often instinctively redirect the conversation to their *good* intentions, sometimes in an effort to absolve themselves of any blame or fault. When people redirect the conversation in this manner, you want to minimize their defensiveness or resistance to engaging in constructive dialogue.

One way to do so is to acknowledge the person's possible intentions. In some cases, people do intend to be racist or cause harm, but for many people, racist missteps happen despite their good intentions. Here, it is important to clarify that what someone *intends* to do and the actual *impact* of what they do are not the same. For example, while you may intend it as a compliment to tell a BIPOC person how articulate they are, the impact of this message is that it communicates your implicit shock or surprise that a BIPOC person can speak intelligently. This underscores your negative assumptions about BIPOCs' ability to speak well.

The point is, even if someone has good intentions, their words or actions can still cause harm and perpetuate racist attitudes and beliefs. When you acknowledge that someone may have had good intentions *and* still said something racist, it can create a more open conversation and prevent the conversation from being derailed or diverted to a focus on intent versus impact. Ultimately, remember that calling out racism is about addressing harmful behavior and attitudes, not about attacking the individual as a person or trying to make them feel bad.

## "L" Is for Lay Out the Reasons It's Racist

Once you have objectively described what happened and stated the importance of impact versus intention, you need to provide concrete feedback on why the behavior was racist. In some cases, individuals may be unaware of the historical and cultural implications of certain words or phrases and may not immediately understand how something they said or did could cause harm. For example, a person may compliment an Asian American woman by stating, "You speak English so well" and not realize this is a microaggression that presumes that all Asian Americans must be from countries in which English is not their first language.

In other cases, individuals may act or speak in ways that reinforce harmful stereotypes because these stereotypes have been normalized within the context of a White supremacist society—a society in which miseducation and exposure to racist propaganda are commonplace. For example, a person may blame issues within Black communities on "absent fathers," making statements like "The real problem with the Black community is that the fathers are never around. Kids need father figures to be raised right!" Statements such as these are often the result of inaccurate information or propaganda; in fact, data actually show that 59.5 percent of Black fathers live with their children (Jones & Mosher, 2013). As an ally, it is important that you use your privileged position to take advantage of opportunities to correct any misunderstandings that perpetuate racism. When you describe *why* something is racist, it identifies the underlying biases and prejudices that may be contributing to the behavior or language, and it helps to educate others on why certain words or actions are harmful.

## "L" Is for List Possible Solutions

Once you've described the event and stated why it was problematic, it is imperative to be clear about what your request for change is and to present possible solutions. The key is to be as clear, specific, and behaviorally oriented as possible. By including a clear request for change, you are both providing a solution to the conflict and asking the person to take responsibility for their actions and to commit to making a change. Possible solutions can involve apologizing for the harm caused, educating themselves on the impact of their behavior or language, or taking steps to actively work toward becoming more aware of their biases and prejudices. Intentionally directing the conversation toward your request for change helps shift the focus from blame or shame toward constructive action and accountability.

## "O" Is for Observe Your Internal Reactions

Confronting someone about their racism is not without personal cost; even when done effectively, it can be emotionally taxing. When you confront someone about their racist behavior or language, it can elicit a range of personal emotions, including anger, frustration, fear, and sadness. Therefore, when following the CALL steps, pay attention to your own internal reactions. If you don't acknowledge and make room for these emotions, it can undermine the effectiveness of the conversation and your own well-being. For one, this is because if you are not aware of your own internal reactions, you may unintentionally react in ways that escalate the situation or shut down the conversation. For example, if you don't notice that you are feeling irritated, you might act on this emotion by saying something unhelpful like "Ugh, there's just no point in trying to educate you."

Second, when you fail to observe your internal experience, you may become overwhelmed by your own emotions and shut down. For example, if you don't take the time to process that you are feeling frustrated, you might immediately act on the urge to exit the situation without actually calling out the racist behavior. Both of these scenarios ultimately result in missed opportunities to educate and advocate for change. Therefore, taking a moment to pause and recognize your emotions and urges allows you to approach the conversation with more intentionality and thoughtfulness.

## "U" Is for Use Humility

One of the risks of calling out racism is that it can easily become a power struggle, where the focus is on proving who is right or wrong. This can lead to defensiveness, anger, and ultimately, a breakdown in communication. Practicing humility can help to shift the focus from blame or shame toward learning and growth. As a White ally, it is unlikely that you have never misstepped or caused harm. It is often helpful to connect with that shared experience between yourself and the target of your intervention and to approach from a place of humility.

For example, if you are calling out someone for using language that is appropriative of Indigenous cultures (e.g., referring to something as a "spirit animal"), you can take some time to reflect on when you learned about this topic and recall that you were not born with this knowledge—you had to obtain it somehow. Reminding yourself of this can soften your emotions in the moment and allow you to empathize.

Using humility also means considering how *you* would want to be called out for saying something problematic or racist. Calling out is not designed to be antagonistic but, instead, direct and respectful. To be clear, this does not mean that you should treat someone who is enacting harm with unconditional kindness. Ultimately, it is about being intentional about aligning with the part of the individual who may be open to change as you presumably have been in the past.

## "T" Is for Tolerate Resistance

As an ally, your role is to push back on White supremacist norms in whatever ways you are able. This means pushing back on every oppressive action, norm, policy, and behavior that is within your power to challenge. Unfortunately, the reality is that you will not change every heart you attempt to correct. To effectively call out racism, you must know that resistance will come and learn how to tolerate it by remaining clear, firm, and persistent, even in the face of this resistance.

It is important to note that remaining clear, firm, and persistent does not mean that you need to engage in drawn-out arguments or unproductive conversations. Remember, you are calling out a behavior or action and making a request for change. You are not interested in receiving additional context or engaging in philosophical arguments about what is or isn't racist. Here, you want to use one of the principles of DBT by thinking of yourself as a "broken record." When a record gets stuck, it keeps repeating the same thing over and over. Similarly, when a person wants to argue and go back and forth with you, you want to be a broken record by redirecting the conversation away from these attempts at deflection and repeating your main request for change. For example, you can repeatedly insist, "In the future, please use appropriate language to refer to immigrants."

If you notice that after repeating your main request for change, a person is unwilling to adhere to this request, it is vital to know when to disengage from the conversation. This doesn't mean that you should disengage at the first sign of tension, discomfort, or conflict, but that you can yield and walk away if the person displays a pattern of indifference, apathy, or extreme rigidity about their original point or comment. Not everyone will honor your offer for feedback or request for change, and the degree to which you push back may be guided by the context of your relationship. For example, if the person is someone who reports to you and that you work with often, it may be worthwhile to engage further.

## Using the CALL OUT Skill: From Bella the Bystander to Bella the Brave

Calling out racism in practice can feel overwhelming, just as it did for Bella the Bystander. She was consumed by the fear of saying something wrong or possibly damaging her relationships with her colleagues. However, by using the CALL OUT skill, she had some structure to guide this difficult conversation. After deliberation, she determined that because of the nature of her relationship with the offending colleague, she would feel more comfortable reaching out to him privately and decided to do so via text. To psychologically prepare for this, she engaged in a brief deep breathing exercise before diving in.

She then sent her colleague a text message to get the conversation started. Here's their exchange, with annotations explaining the CALL OUT process.

*8:27 AM*

> Hey Ryan, just wanted to check in about something really quick. The other day in the group chat, you talked about having a hard interaction with a Latinx customer and because the customer was upset, you referred to her emotional experience as the "spicy Latina coming out of her." I know you were just trying to be funny and didn't mean it to be intentionally hurtful—I get that.

Here, Bella starts off with the first step in CALL OUT, which is to clarify what happened in objective terms.

She acknowledges that his intention was to be funny, not harmful.

> But saying this kind of stuff invalidates Latinas' experiences and makes it seem like their emotional experiences are nonsensical or inappropriate.

She lays out the reasons why this is problematic by explaining that he is relying on a harmful stereotype about Latinas' emotionality, one that is often used to invalidate their experiences.

*8:28 AM*

At this point, Bella notices that she is becoming frustrated that Ryan doesn't seem to be taking this seriously. She takes a moment to breathe and process her feelings before she responds.

> I didn't mean it in a bad way at all. I feel like being spicy is actually a good thing, lol! 😂 I wish my pasty White self was a little bit more spicy! 🌶️🌶️🌶️

*8:35 AM*

> Like I said, I know you didn't mean it to be harmful, but even if you didn't mean it that way, it is still harmful. I know that I sometimes make jokes in the heat of the moment 🔥 (no pun intended) and it's cringey to realize what I said was actually not funny at all. Anyway, please take a second to read this brief article I'll send a link to—it's written by a Puerto Rican clinical psychologist and talks about why saying these kinds of things can really negatively impact Latinas.

Here, Bella shares her own experience with making missteps. She expresses humility and empathy for Ryan, which may help him to overcome his defensiveness.

*8:36 AM*

> It still just doesn't feel that serious. 😕 IDK what you even want me to do.

*8:38 AM*

> Glad you asked, lol! I think you really need to do something to repair. I actually have this book called *Beyond Fragility* that has a whole chapter that teaches you a skill called REPAIR. It will walk you through everything you need to address this. Do you want to borrow it?

Bella is listing possible solutions that Ryan can use to address this misstep. She believes that he needs to issue an effective apology, so she is providing him with a resource that can help him do that.

*8:40 AM*

> I guess . . .

*8:41 AM*

> How about I leave it in your office tomorrow morning and then we can meet during lunch to discuss your REPAIR plan? I'm happy to give feedback.

Even though Ryan continues to express resistance, Bella is persistent and direct. She is straightforward without being rude, and throughout this whole experience of CALL OUT, she is attending to her emotions and managing them in service of being as effective as possible.

Bella and Ryan enact their plan the following day. After reading the REPAIR chapter, Ryan issues an apology in the group chat and describes his plans to learn more about anti-Latinx racism to ensure he won't make the same misstep again.

## Why Use the CALL OUT Skill?

Complacency and inaction in the face of racism are antithetical to your goals as an ally to create a world that is more inclusive, empathetic, and equitable for everyone. As a White person who has benefited from systemic racism and White privilege, you have a responsibility to use your privilege to help to undo racism by calling it out when you see it occur. Although you may struggle with *how* to do this and lack confidence in your ability to do this well, the CALL OUT skill provides you with a script for how you can leverage your privilege to intentionally challenge instances of racism across various settings, including at work, at school, and in your personal relationships. Using the CALL OUT skill to approach conversations about racism can help promote more constructive dialogue, which can ultimately improve your ability to communicate about racism, help you build stronger relationships with other White people and BIPOC, and lead to greater impact in changing the culture of racism.

## CHAPTER SUMMARY

When you remain silent in the face of racism, you allow it to continue. Therefore, this chapter clarified what it means to call out racism and why doing so is beneficial. We also introduced the CALL OUT skill so you can challenge racism in interpersonal contexts intentionally, clearly, and with an increased sense of self-efficacy. This skill gives you a structured way to approach an anti-racist action that requires quite a bit of courage. Our hope is that this skill takes the guesswork out of the critical ingredients of calling out racism. Using this skill is also a key aspect of letting BIPOC know you bear witness to the racism they experience. By bearing witness to racism and doing something about it, you are fundamentally validating and supporting BIPOC, which we elaborate on more in the next chapter.

## CHAPTER 13

# Communicating Care: From Centering Yourself to Validating Others

Being an effective White ally requires showing up for BIPOC in many ways. One way to do so is to provide compassionate verbal support when BIPOC share their experiences with racism. Responding with compassion means allowing BIPOC's experiences to take center stage and not giving in to the urge to dismiss racism, give advice, or make it about you. In this chapter, we introduce the concept of validation as a way to communicate compassionate verbal support. We also review common stumbling blocks to providing validation, including how your socialization as a White person could contribute to *invalidating* responses to BIPOC, even if you don't mean for that to happen. We finish with a step-by-step skill to help you embody the necessary elements of effective validation when supporting BIPOC.

## What Is Validation?

The key to compassionate verbal support is learning how to validate others. Validation is a key concept in DBT, and it is an essential ingredient for every relationship, including your relationships with BIPOC. At its core, validation is showing another person that you understand where they are coming from. It is also about building empathy and showing that you are listening to what someone else is saying or feeling.

Validation has several benefits for your relationships with BIPOC. For one, validation shows BIPOC that you see and hear them, which ultimately communicates care. For example, if your friend tells you about being followed in a boutique clothing store, saying something like "Wow, how infuriating! It must have been so hard to be targeted in that way" shows your friend that you care enough to step into their emotional world to understand what that experience was like for them.

Second, validation removes the pressure to prove who is right or wrong in a given situation. It is not up to you to prove whether the store manager *really* followed your friend, nor is it up to you to question whether your friend correctly interpreted the manager's intentions or actions. In other words, validation is about taking the perspective of BIPOC and not debating the accuracy of what transpired.

Third, validating someone can help soothe that person's distress. Saying to your friend, "It makes sense that you'd be really upset about this" rather than "You should let it go" reduces the chances that your friend will become defensive or feel re-traumatized by your invalidating response.

## How Do White People Invalidate BIPOC?

As we have reviewed in several chapters of this book, BIPOC individuals experience painful acts of racism on a regular basis. These racist acts can manifest as limited systemic support in the workplace or microaggressions from peers and colleagues. BIPOC also deal with repeated media coverage of the mistreatment of their community members as we have seen with the endless videos documenting police brutality toward Black people, hate crimes toward Asian Americans, and savage detainment of Latinx immigrants. Unfortunately, when BIPOC people encounter racism and share these experiences with White people in their lives, they may be met with a host of unhelpful and invalidating responses.

Here is a chart informed by mindfulness educators and social workers Trinh Mai and Jean Whitlock (2022) that overviews the common ways White people invalidate BIPOC's experiences of racism. We also provide some examples of what validating responses can look like.

| Common Reaction | Examples of Invalidating Responses | Example of a Validating Response |
|---|---|---|
| Invalidating and minimizing the impact | • "Everyone is disrespected sometimes."<br>• "Don't let this ruin your day."<br>• "You're strong. I know you'll get through this."<br>• "Just don't think about it anymore." | "I'm sure it's really painful to be disrespected like this." |
| Not believing that it's racism; asking a lot of questions | • "Just playing devil's advocate, do you *really* think it was about race?"<br>• "How did you approach them?"<br>• "Did you say something that could have been misinterpreted?" | "What you experienced was not okay." |
| Highlighting the perpetrator's innocent intentions | • "I don't think they had bad intentions."<br>• "Remember, they're going through a lot. They aren't at their best."<br>• "He cares about his staff; I'm sure he is not intentionally ignoring you."<br>• "They just participated in the anti-racism meeting last week, so I know they mean well." | "Regardless of why he said it, it's still a racist comment that is hurtful." |
| Rushing to problem-solving | • "You can always contact HR if you feel like you are being discriminated against."<br>• "What do you want me to do about it?"<br>• "Why don't you sue?" | "This is a lot to process. What can I do to support you in taking the time you need to figure out how you want to proceed?" |
| Defending the status quo | • "Those beliefs were common back in their day."<br>• "Sometimes those attitudes are generational."<br>• "People are just like that sometimes."<br>• "Well, we have to respect tradition." | "It's a shame how often some folks are stuck in the past, and there is just no excuse for it." |
| Needing reassurance from the fear of being seen as racist | • "You know I'm on your side and I'm not a racist, right?" | "Thank you for sharing your experience. You should not have to experience things like this." |
| Tone policing | • "You really need to calm down."<br>• "People aren't going to listen to you if you don't chill out."<br>• "You catch more flies with honey than with vinegar."<br>• "The language you're using is polarizing."<br>• "When you're ready to talk about this in a rational way, let me know." | "Your emotions are valid and it's more than okay to be angry about this." |
| White centering | • "The same exact thing just happened to me."<br>• "I've been marginalized too because of my [insert other identity, such as your gender identity, sexual orientation, etc.]."<br>• "I experience hair discrimination too. Someone in my family told me my curly hair looked 'messy.'" | "I can't even imagine what it's like to experience what you went through." |

## POP QUIZ

It's time for a pop quiz! Read the following scenario, then consider the possible responses that are listed beneath it. Below each response, write whether or not that response is validating and why. If it is not validating, also offer suggestions for improvement. Once you're done, compare your answers with the correct answers provided at the end of this chapter.

Imagine you are a physician and one of your Black colleagues comes into the breakroom upset that a patient's family has requested a different physician over her. She begins to cry and says that she thinks the change was requested because she is Black.

1. "It's hard for me to help when you get emotional."

_____

_____

_____

_____

_____

2. "You can always sue if you feel like you are being discriminated against in the workplace."

_____

_____

_____

_____

_____

3. "Wow, that must have been so disheartening."

_____

_____

_____

_____

_____

4. "What can you do? Some people are just stuck in their ways."

_____

_____

_____

_____

_____

5. "I had a similar experience. Let me tell you about it . . ."

_____

_____

_____

_____

_____

6. "You should never have to experience being targeted because of who you are. It sucks that we live in a society that doesn't value Black women."

_____

_____

_____

_____

_____

7. "Thank you for sharing this with me."

_____

_____

_____

_____

_____

8. "You're strong. I know you'll get through this."

_____

_____

_____

_____

_____

# Why Do White People Struggle to Validate BIPOC?

There are many reasons why invaliding responses can emerge, one of which is unresolved or unaddressed problematic worldviews. As we mentioned in chapter 3, worldviews are a set of core beliefs, values, and attitudes about society, including ideas about racism. One worldview that can influence invalidating responses is Whiteness. When White people adopt and internalize aspects of Whiteness—the worldview that rests on the assumption that White people and their ideas, views, and beliefs are superior to others—they can end up invalidating BIPOC due to their conscious or unconscious acceptance of the belief that their ideas about racism are superior to the ideas of BIPOC who have actually lived with racism. This may result in responses like "Was it really about race?" or "*I* don't think they were being racist," which implicitly communicate that White people are the authority on what, or who, is and is not racist.

Whiteness also places White people at the center of society, which creates a dynamic where White people, and their interests, perceptions, and emotions, are catered to. This leads to "White centering," in which White people and their cultural values and norms are situated at the normal center of the world (Saad, 2020). This centering can manifest in a number of ways, and one common way it shows itself during interracial interactions is when White people co-opt the focus of a conversation away from BIPOC toward themselves. For example, if a BIPOC person tells a story where they felt targeted due to their race, a White person may share an experience about a time *they* felt targeted. They may also take up space talking about how sad, distraught, or angry *they* feel about the BIPOC person's encounter. Although these statements may aim to foster connection (e.g., "See, I get it, too"), the *impact* of such statements is to resituate White people at the center and to relegate BIPOC to the margins of their own experiences of racism—thus, continuing to perpetuate dynamics in which it's never just about BIPOC and their experiences.

As we also noted in chapter 3, Whiteness gives way to another worldview, which is the idea that the world is fair and that people get what they deserve. This worldview, coupled with unchecked implicit biases about BIPOC, can manifest as invalidating responses. For example, if someone holds the belief that the world is fair *and* they consciously or unconsciously believe that Black Americans are criminal, suspicious, and untrustworthy, they may make invalidating statements that imply that BIPOC are to blame for the racism they encounter. Upon hearing that a BIPOC person was pulled over by the police, a White person may ask, "Were you driving over the speed limit?" or "Was your taillight out?" which implies "What did *you* do?" In order to provide a validating response, like "That must have been scary," White people need to release the belief that the world is a fair place as well as work to overcome their implicit biases.

Invalidating responses can also occur via tone policing, which is the act of disregarding or criticizing a person's point of view because it is communicated in an emotional manner. This can involve comments like "Your language is divisive" or "When you're ready to talk about this in a rational way, let me know." Tone policing can also occur when people condemn protests and comment more on *how* protestors behave than the actual issue that led to the protest in the first place (e.g., police brutality, unfair housing practices). In this powerful quote from anti-racist activist Layla Saad (2020), she shares:

> *Imagine, if you will, experiencing an act of violence and then being asked to talk about what you experienced without expressing any strong emotions. This is clearly inhumane. To be human is to feel. To talk about pain without expressing pain is to expect a human to recall information like a robot. When you insist that BIPOC talk about their painful experiences with racism without expressing any pain, rage, or grief, you are asking them to dehumanize themselves.* (p. 51)

When you home in on the way a BIPOC person shares their experiences with racism rather than the experience itself, you invalidate BIPOC's ability to simply *be*—be angry, emotional, sad, or enraged. This invalidation may be rooted in the centuries-long practice of dehumanizing BIPOC—the process of denying or depriving BIPOC of the qualities that make them human and worthy of empathy. Also, when you focus on the way a person has expressed a point of view rather than the main point itself, you prioritize your right to comfort; in fact, tone policing mainly functions to shut down conversations *you* find uncomfortable, which is why we have the FEEL skill on tolerating this kind of distress in chapter 8. This discomfort can arise when you are uncomfortable with open conflict or when you misattribute a person's anger about oppression to a malicious attack on you or your existence. Tone policing may also be rooted in the (false) belief that conversations are only productive when they are conducted in a calm or neutral manner and that talking about emotions is a waste of time or a hindrance to fruitful human interaction.

Other times, invalidation happens through no response at all. BIPOC constantly deal with being on the receiving end of White people's silence during times of racial injustice. As we discussed in chapter 6, this silence can be driven by ambivalence. You may want to provide validating responses *and* also fear the emotional discomfort that this might bring, signifying a conflict between two opposing desires. In other words, you feel torn between a desire to show up interpersonally and another desire to protect yourself from the possibility of saying the wrong thing.

This ambivalence can also fuel behavioral avoidance. As we discussed in chapter 10, White people may disengage altogether to avoid feeling the anxiety or overwhelm of "getting it wrong." This repeated disengagement also means that White people get less practice in showing up for BIPOC, which increases the likelihood that they won't respond at all. Unfortunately, when you do not offer validating support to BIPOC due to your ambivalence, behavioral avoidance, or lack of practice, you end up centering your own barriers over the needs of BIPOC. In other words, you engage in White centering (Oluo, 2019; Saad, 2020), which ultimately reinforces a societal culture in which White people's needs and desires prevail over BIPOC's.

# Offering SUPPORT: How to Provide Compassionate Verbal Responses to BIPOC

Racism can be traumatic and emotionally draining for BIPOC, and there are specific things you can say and do as a White ally to compassionately support them during these difficult times. Yet, this way of showing up must not be tainted with White saviorism, or the belief that you, as a superior being, must step in to help or to rescue a BIPOC person or community. Rather, engaging in the step-by-step SUPPORT skill is about using interpersonal skills to build trust with BIPOC and to prevent retraumatizing them after a racist encounter.

## "S" Is for Show Genuine Concern

Offering support must start with paying attention. When a person is sharing with you their experiences of racism, treat that person and what they are telling you as meaningful. We all express concern in different ways and have unique ways of communicating; therefore, we encourage you to show concern in whatever way is most comfortable for you. You can show them you are listening by accurately reflecting back and summarizing what you heard them say or by giving them nonverbal cues, such as nodding or leaning in closer. Also, avoid expressions that communicate a lack of concern, like rolling your eyes, making a judgmental facial expression, or doing unrelated tasks on your phone. It may even be appropriate to mirror the person's body language and show rage, shock, or disappointment. Yet, be careful not to overdo it when mirroring a person's body language—remember, the focus should be on them and not you.

## "U" Is for Understand the Context

You do not need to be a racism expert to validate BIPOC. However, you do need to have a foundational understanding of the multiple systems that unjustly shape the lives of BIPOC relative to White people. Knowing this context allows you to acknowledge and accept that the BIPOC person was not targeted randomly but, rather, as a result of their race (Bryant-Davis & Ocampo, 2006). Having this insight will allow you to deeply observe the person's voice tone, body language, and behavior and to then express how their reaction makes sense given the historical and contemporary facts of the situation.

For example, if a Mexican American colleague tells you about having their citizenship questioned by a new hiring manager, you could respond with something like "I'm so sorry you had to deal with that kind of ignorance. You must be really tired of people ignorantly assuming that Mexican people don't have a right to be here in this country." To enact this step, you may need to go back to the BASICS skill from chapter 1. Using this skill can help you understand and recognize racism within a given situation and to consider the multiple elements that enable racism to exist in a particular context. You can also learn more about the ways that racism continues to affect our society by seeking out resources, including documentaries such as *13th*, *Amend: The Fight for America*, or *The 1619 Project*.

## "P" Is for Process Your Own Internal Reactions

It is possible that as you listen to someone share their experience, you may have an emotional response. This is okay and natural—you are human. The important thing to remember, though, is that this encounter is not about you and your emotional response. It is also not about your worldviews, your difficulty understanding racism, or even about your opinion about whether or not the event was racist.

We hope that the skills offered in other parts of this book can help you manage your internal reactions, whether they are related to not fully understanding racism (chapter 1), the urge to deny racism (chapter 3), ambivalence (chapter 6), difficulty naming your emotions (chapter 7), difficulty tolerating your emotions (chapter 8), or behavioral avoidance (chapter 10). Taking time to manage these reactions on the front end will allow you to show up for BIPOC, including being able to express care and empathy in a way that does not lead to you becoming overwhelmed and out of control.

## "P" Is for Prioritize the Experiences of BIPOC Over Your Own Experience

Validation must be provided in a way that centers the people most impacted (i.e., BIPOC) rather than you. This is not the time to assert that you are one of the "good ones" or to express how guilty or embarrassed you feel about the racism perpetuated by other White people. Nor is this the time to make comparisons between BIPOC's experiences and your experiences, even if you acknowledge that the experiences are different. For example, if your Black colleague discloses feeling unappreciated as a Black person in the organization, it is never appropriate for you to share how you, too, feel unappreciated as a woman or queer person in the organization. Keep the focus on the other person and their experience with racism.

## "O" Is for Offer Appreciation

There are many valid reasons why BIPOC do not feel safe around White people— safe to be their authentic selves and to speak truth to their wants, needs, perspectives, and experiences. This lack of safety comes from their countless experiences of being harmed, physically and emotionally, when around White people. Therefore, BIPOC may actually fear disclosing their experiences with racist incidents to White peers. So when a BIPOC person takes the risk to share their feelings with you (someone who is not a BIPOC with shared experiences), it is a valuable and courageous action. Make sure to acknowledge this risk and to express your gratitude. You can do so by simply thanking them for sharing their experience with you. You can even acknowledge the courage it took to share this experience with you despite the fact that White people have not been typically safe spaces with whom to share information about racism. Another way to show your appreciation is to communicate to them that you will continue to be a safe space in the future and that you are willing to make space for them whenever they need to share or process their experiences again.

## "R" Is for Resist the Urge to Give Advice or Challenge Them

It is natural to want to give someone advice when they express pain and suffering. However, when someone chooses to tell you about a particular experience with racism, it is not an invitation for you to give advice. Although you may just want to be helpful, rushing to give advice can also be the result of your own anxiety. It may be an attempt to bypass feeling powerless and to try to "fix" the problem as if racism could be fixed by a single solution or action.

The other problem with giving advice is that it can give off an air of superiority, as if you know what's right or best instead of the person who lived through the experience firsthand. It can also communicate that BIPOC do not have the ability to figure out what's right for them or to solve their own problems, which is especially problematic given long-standing biases that BIPOC are in need of White saviors. It is possible that any advice could feel like a critique of the other person's intelligence or problem-solving skills as well. Therefore, when in doubt, refrain from giving advice.

If you absolutely feel like you have valuable information or solutions to offer, *at most* ask the person if they are in a place to receive that type of information. You could ask something like "What do you need most from me at this moment—for me to give you advice or for me to listen?" You could also say something like "I have some ideas that might be helpful. Would you be interested in hearing them?" Offering questions like these gives the person space to opt in or out of hearing such solutions, ultimately prioritizing their needs over yours during the interaction.

In addition to advice giving, it is also problematic when you challenge or question a BIPOC's experience with racism. Doing so can be a form of gaslighting, in which you cause someone to question their own reality, which can magnify their already distressing emotions. Challenging or questioning someone's experience also disregards all of the cognitive effort they have likely put into considering if they have correctly interpreted the situation. In other words, although BIPOC are often accused of "playing the race card," the reality is that many BIPOC spend huge amounts of time thinking over what's happened to them and asking themselves if it was about race. So if a BIPOC person says that what they experienced was racist, trust that they know what happened to them. Even if a BIPOC person mentions that they aren't sure whether or not something was racist, perhaps validate the discomfort of not knowing rather than trying to push them in a particular direction.

Ultimately, remember to operate from a place of care and curiosity when listening to BIPOC share their experiences of racism. Don't forget that people want to be heard, understood, and supported—and those things should supersede being told what to do or what to think.

## "T" Is for Tune into the Person's Needs

A primary aim of the SUPPORT skill is to provide BIPOC with the emotional support they may need as they process their experiences with racism. However, there is a great deal of variability in how people respond to experiences of racism, and everyone has different needs. What's helpful for one person may not be helpful for another. You may have one friend who wants to talk through their feelings multiple times—for them, talking it through can be cathartic. But you may have another friend who likes to process things internally. They might need space before being ready to talk about it, and even when they do decide to open it up, it may be brief.

There may also be variability in what steps your friend may want to take. For example, after an incident where a microaggressive comment was made in a public team meeting, your friend might be comfortable with you speaking up for them. (To do this effectively, see the CALL OUT skill in the previous chapter.) However, if the same statement was said in a private meeting, they might not want you to say anything, as doing so could identify them and lead to negative repercussions (e.g., losing their job, workplace retaliation).

Thus, do not assume you know what's "best" in terms of next steps for BIPOC when they share their experience. Instead, ask about their preferences and needs. You might say, "What is the best way I can support you right now?" If the person is particularly distressed and struggling to generate solutions, you could offer different options tentatively (e.g., "I could do X . . .") in the spirit of taking on the cognitive burden to problem solve. Finally, given the injurious impact of racism, it may be helpful to ask the person if they need additional space to process the traumatic incident. Sometimes, tuning into BIPOC's needs means helping them make space for self-care.

# Why Use the SUPPORT Skill?

Racist incidents negatively impact the physical, emotional, cognitive, and social well-being of BIPOC. When these experiences are then met with invalidation—whether through disbelief, victim blaming, or denial—this can be further traumatizing and distressing for BIPOC. The purpose of the SUPPORT skill is to help you move past well-meaning intentions that can re-traumatize or re-harm BIPOC to providing verbal support that can have lasting positive effects. Although doing something you're ambivalent about, anxious about, or lack practice in is hard, it is not harder than living through pervasive racism. If BIPOC can resiliently exist in a world that devalues them and their presence, you can engage in new skills to show up for them in a caring and nurturing way.

## CHAPTER SUMMARY

Validating others with compassionate verbal support can be difficult at first if you were never taught this skill. Yet, in this chapter, you learned that, at its core, validation is simply about understanding where the other person is coming from and letting them know they can safely share their experiences with you. The SUPPORT skill guided you through the process of effective validation that can allow BIPOC to feel heard and understood. Our hope is that BIPOC will be met with more affirmation, understanding, and validation after sharing their discriminatory experiences with you, ultimately leading to long-lasting benefits to their mental health and well-being.

# ANSWERS TO POP QUIZ ON PAGE 168

1. This is an **invalidating response** because it reflects tone policing, or an attempt to force the person to communicate in a particular way before taking their concerns seriously.

2. This is an **invalidating response** because it rushes to problem solve. It also dismisses the pervasiveness of racism; if BIPOC sued every time they encountered racism, they'd be perpetually involved in legal suits. Also, although someone can sue, doing so may have disproportionate negative consequences for BIPOC relative to Whites.

3. This is a **validating response** because it is tapping into what you imagine the BIPOC's experience was and normalizing the feelings of hurt and pain.

4. This is an **invalidating response** because it both shifts the conversation away from the BIPOC's experience and communicates the message that nothing can be done.

5. This is an **invalidating response** because it shifts the conversation away from the person's experience to your experience. Even if your intention is just to say that it's a relatable experience, this response communicates that your experience is more important than the other person's encounter with racism.

6. This is a **validating response** because it shows genuine concern about Black women's lived experiences and shows that you have a deep understanding of racism.

7. This is a **validating response** because it communicates genuine concern and invites the BIPOC to feel safe bringing up these issues with you again. Particularly if the person was nervous to share their experience, expressing this gratitude can ease that nervousness.

8. Although this statement may come across as complimentary and encouraging, it is an **invalidating response** because it does not show genuine concern or that you understand the larger context of racism.

## CHAPTER 14

# Knowing When to Ask BIPOC for Help: From Exploitation to Collaboration

Throughout this book, we have emphasized the importance of dismantling a White-centric worldview so that all voices, perspectives, and values are celebrated and affirmed. Yet, as you work to unlearn the values and perspectives of White supremacy and make space to adopt anti-racist values and perspectives, you may recognize a desire to seek support or help from BIPOC. This desire can often lead to a more insidious interpersonal barrier: placing undue emotional and intellectual burden on your BIPOC friends, family, and colleagues to assist you in your anti-racism efforts.

Although we want you to join in the fight for racial justice, we also want you to respect the autonomy and humanity of BIPOC in deciding when to offer White allies direction. Collective action is critical, but failing to assess the potential impacts and burdens of requesting BIPOC assistance with your anti-racism goals can undermine your efforts. In this chapter, you will identify and resolve dilemmas related to centering BIPOC's voices and expertise while not overburdening them.

# What Is Equitable Collaboration and Why Does It Matter for Anti-Racism?

Often, when we think of collaboration, we think of teamwork in professional settings. However, collaboration can be crucial for advancing anti-racist efforts across many contexts, including (but not limited to) your professional setting, your neighborhood community, and your friends. At its core, collaboration means working together with others who share a common vision or goal and leveraging collective strengths and resources to achieve greater impact. For example, perhaps you don't know where to start in your quest to develop a deeper understanding of the historical and ongoing issues of racism in your community. You might collaborate with friends or colleagues to identify resources, such as BIPOC-written books or BIPOC content creators. Taking this approach allows you to achieve your anti-racist goals as well as to learn, share resources and perspectives, and maximize your anti-racist efforts.

Because you request help from and collaborate with others in your everyday life, seeking collaboration in your anti-racism work may seem pretty straightforward. However, collaboration in this context requires a more intentional approach—an approach that prioritizes *equitable* collaboration. Equitable collaboration is not just about working together; it is about working together in ways that uphold the values and principles of anti-racism and equity. For one, equitable collaboration requires trust and accountability. Historically, BIPOC have struggled to find White collaborators who would fight alongside them in the struggle for racial equality. When individuals are willing to engage in this fight, it can be somewhat inconsistent, which makes the accountability piece important.

Second, equitable collaboration requires clear communication and respect. Otherwise, it is easy for misunderstandings to occur. Clear communication is about transparently stating your request and its purpose, the expected time commitment, any compensation or benefits associated with the tasks, and the expected outcomes of the labor. For example, rather than just asking a BIPOC colleague to brainstorm ideas about ways to increase diversity in your department, first explain the larger context of the request. Then let the person know if there is any compensation (or other tangible benefits) associated with this request and how long the brainstorming process should take. Whether or not the person decides to help may very well depend on various aspects of the context (e.g., is the brainstorming for a nonprofit or for your upcoming book?). In terms of respect, this can entail taking the time to listen to BIPOC, especially if they have questions, feedback, or concerns about the request. For example, if your colleague agrees to brainstorm and critiques your current hiring practices, you want to make an effort to understand their viewpoint without becoming defensive or minimizing their perspective.

Third, equitable collaboration requires acknowledging and addressing the power dynamics and privileges that may exist among collaborators. Because of the racial hierarchy that has existed within the US, many White people feel entitled to unpaid assistance from BIPOC and do not truly see BIPOC as autonomous human beings who have the right to decide if and when to offer White allies support. Similarly, many BIPOC may feel as if they cannot truly say no to White people without incurring negative consequences. Too often, well-intentioned attempts to "do the right thing" and collaborate to "amplify BIPOC voices" disregard or do not acknowledge these realities—realities that absolutely influence how effective the collaboration is.

Fourth, equitable collaboration requires acknowledging and addressing the imbalance that may also exist among collaborators. Research shows that BIPOC engaged in DEI work contribute more emotional labor, experience higher levels of stress, and risk more negative consequences for advocacy than their White counterparts (Doan & Kennedy, 2022). The increased emotional burden of this work can contribute to increased isolation, frustration, and burnout (Hamed et al., 2022). Equitable collaboration requires a recognition of these imbalances and a commitment to addressing them.

# Overzealous Olivia and Overburdened Owen

The founders of CyberSerenity, a mental health tech start-up company, believed that having a diverse workforce was central to their mission to bring innovative ideas and perspectives to the digital health field and to increase health care equity. However, over time, the company's leadership began to notice some areas where they were falling short. They realized that their current recruitment and hiring processes relied heavily on recruiting from large tech conferences where most attendees were White. Therefore, White applicants were able to establish relationships with recruiters more easily than BIPOC applicants could. Some employees also had expressed concerns about company climate given the lack of BIPOC representation across different levels of management.

The company's leadership was particularly concerned that some employees justifiably felt that the company events and initiatives didn't reflect their anti-racist values.

The leadership team knew that they needed to address these issues to live up to their stated mission. They decided to form a task force to identify areas for improvement and develop actionable plans in response to employee feedback on workplace climate. The task force was made up of CyberSerenity employees from different departments and levels within the company, and their goal was to focus specifically on improving their recruitment and hiring processes and to plan a series of anti-racism workshops. In their first meeting, Olivia noticed no BIPOC employees were part of the task force. In an effort to ensure the company centered BIPOC voices in their planning, Olivia suggested they ask one of their Indigenous employees, Owen, for his input. Owen was a relatively new hire, but Olivia knew from conversations that he was really passionate about diversity in tech and had spearheaded efforts at his previous workplace related to these topics.

When Olivia excitedly approached Owen the next day, she was shocked to hear that he was apprehensive about joining the task force. Owen shared that he was already overwhelmed with managing his regular job responsibilities and the new project he was being trained to take the lead on. He was concerned that the time and anxiety of taking on such a significant role on the task force would be too much to manage on top of everything else. Olivia expressed to Owen how disappointed she was to learn that he didn't want to contribute to CyberSerenity's anti-racism efforts, particularly because his extensive expertise in this domain contributed to their decision to hire him. She assured Owen that the task force only met once a week and that as a lead project manager, she could arrange for him to be taken off the new project if that would be helpful. After Olivia's repeated attempts to reassure him, Owen asked for time to think about it. However, for the next week Olivia noticed that Owen seemed to be avoiding her.

## REFLECTION

Answer the following questions to evaluate Olivia's approach.

What (if anything) would you have done differently than Olivia?

_____

_____

_____

_____

_____

In what ways did Olivia consider components of equity in her request for collaboration?

_____

_____

_____

_____

_____

In what ways did Olivia fail to consider components of equitable collaboration?

_____

_____

_____

_____

_____

Olivia clearly has good intentions in asking Owen to join the DEI task force. She recognizes that an all-White group is limited in its perspectives, and she approached Owen because he is passionate about diversity in tech and has previous leadership experience in this area, not simply because of his race.

However, Olivia has not given Owen much reason to trust in the task force's commitment to equitable collaboration and holding themselves accountable. For example, although Olivia mentioned that the group meets weekly, she did not indicate how much time the members are expected to put in outside of these meetings or their estimated timeline for meeting their objectives; she is asking Owen to commit to an indefinite amount of time. Olivia also failed to respect Owen's preferences and goals. Her offer to take Owen off his other project was meant to be reassuring, but perhaps Owen is excited about leading that project and would prefer to continue that work.

Further, Olivia's repeated attempts to persuade Owen are putting undue pressure on him, highlighting her lack of awareness of the power imbalance between them. Owen may now feel caught between two risks: (1) that joining the task force will detract from his own goals and performance, and (2) that not joining will also be met with negative consequences—especially since Olivia revealed that Owen's DEI experience contributed to the decision to hire him, suggesting that she may evaluate him negatively if he declines to join the group.

You can see how failing to consider the components of equitable collaboration can be counterproductive to your anti-racist goals. In this case, Olivia's well-intentioned efforts to center BIPOC voices led to eroding, not building, trust and collaboration. She would benefit from exploring the barriers that are preventing her from fostering equitable collaboration, which we will discuss next.

## What Are the Barriers to Equitable Collaboration in Anti-Racist Work?

Equitable collaboration in anti-racist work involves bringing together individuals and groups to address systemic racism and promote social justice. However, numerous barriers can undermine efforts to engage in equitable collaboration, including insufficient accountability, lack of resources, power imbalances, and inadequate institutional support (Bezrukova et al., 2016). Overcoming these challenges requires ongoing evaluation and accountability to ensure that power is being shared equitably and that any barriers to equitable collaboration are adequately addressed. It is important to do this work *before* requesting assistance from BIPOC. While barriers to equitable collaboration can depend on the context of the work (e.g., professional versus interpersonal), the following are some common barriers that we propose you routinely assess to ensure your request is equitable and not exploitative.

| Common Barriers to Equitable Collaboration | |
|---|---|
| Tokenism | Including a small number of individuals from underrepresented groups to create an appearance of diversity, without actually addressing underlying issues of inequity, or relying on a small number of individuals from underrepresented groups to educate others |
| Power imbalances | Individuals from majority groups have disproportionate influence over decision-making, while marginalized voices are sidelined |
| Lack of resources | Inadequate resources, such as funding or personnel, that hinder the implementation and effectiveness of efforts |
| Inadequate expertise | Insufficient training, education, or experience in anti-racism efforts that leads to a lack of understanding and awareness among collaborators |
| Disproportionate emotional labor | Inadequate support for the emotional labor required to engage in collaborative efforts, or a lack of acknowledgment of the disproportionate psychological toll for BIPOC |
| Fragmentation of efforts | Lack of coordination or consultation with ongoing efforts that results in redundant efforts and unnecessary labor for BIPOC |
| Insufficient accountability measures | Lack of clear measures in place to monitor progress and hold individuals responsible for missteps and accountable to goals |
| Inadequate commitment | Lack of genuine commitment from organizational leadership that hinders the success of anti-racist and DEI initiatives |

Critically reflecting on these barriers to equitable collaboration is a crucial step in anti-racist work. When you request the help of BIPOC colleagues on initiatives but have unaddressed barriers, it increases the likelihood that your request will place undue burden on your colleagues. Going back to the previous example, while Olivia's intentions were clearly to make a request for meaningful collaboration, there were many barriers that prevented her request from truly being equitable. By singling out Owen as the only Indigenous employee to represent all BIPOC perspectives on the task force, Olivia unknowingly put the burden of representation on him. This may have made Owen feel tokenized and unfairly responsible for educating his colleagues on all matters related to race, diversity, and inclusion. Olivia's request also inadvertently placed an additional burden on Owen, who was already overwhelmed with his existing job responsibilities.

Further, Olivia's insistence on Owen joining the task force, despite his initial apprehension, reflected a lack of respect for his personal boundaries and capacity. Equitable collaboration requires respecting individual limits, fostering mutual trust and open communication, addressing power imbalances, and engaging in shared decision-making. Although it was likely Olivia's intention to prioritize these components, by not critically reflecting on her approach and assessing potential barriers to equitable collaboration, she undermined her efficacy and alienated a colleague.

# The DEI CALCULATOR: A Skill for Prioritizing Equitable Collaboration

Determining whether your request for collaboration is equitable or exploitative can seem overwhelming. There are many components to consider when determining whether you should ask a BIPOC colleague, friend, or family member to collaborate on DEI or anti-racist work. Depending on the context of the request, different barriers and components of equitable collaboration may be within or outside of your control. However, it is still important to consider them when assessing the appropriateness of your request for collaboration. To guide you in making sure your request is equitable instead of exploitative, we offer the DEI CALCULATOR skill. This skill walks you through the core components of equitable collaboration and provides structure for determining whether your request adequately promotes and embodies these components.

## "D" Is for Demonstrated Collaboration

It is imperative to demonstrate collaboration so the person you are asking to collaborate with knows that you are working *alongside* them. Let's imagine that this year in your workplace, you want to celebrate Black History Month by having a dedicated event. You plan to ask your Black coworker to put on a Black History Month event and encourage them to find others to help them. Would this approach demonstrate collaboration? No! Instead of just asking them to figure it out on their own, you can rethink your request and ask your Black coworker to work *with you* to put on the event. You can be specific about your intention to collaborate and explain that you would be able to dedicate three hours a week for two months to work with them in planning the event. This revised request is much more collaborative, and your coworker is less likely to feel alone and overburdened.

## "E" Is for Equity

To avoid coercion and exploitation, make sure there is an equitable power balance where you make it clear to the other person that there are no consequences for saying no to your request. Imagine that you are working on your company's anti-racism mission statement and ask your BIPOC employee for assistance reviewing the draft you come up with. When asking the employee, you reiterate that this is optional and that there will be no consequences if they prefer not to review your work for any reason. You tell them that you know it can be hard for them to say no but also encourage them to decline your request if they would prefer not to take it on for any reason.

You can see how in this scenario, the BIPOC employee would not feel coerced to take on this task, particularly if they have a trusting relationship with you and actually feel comfortable saying no. Compare this to if you were to simply tell the employee, "This anti-racism statement is important to me, and I would appreciate it if you reviewed it at your earliest convenience. Would that be okay?" without explicitly recognizing the power imbalance and inviting your colleague to say no for any reason. In this case, they may not feel comfortable declining for fear of direct or indirect consequences.

## "I" Is for Interest

Many people mistakenly think that just because someone is a person of color, they are automatically interested and knowledgeable about DEI or anti-racism issues. This is not the case! While it is true that most BIPOC have probably experienced racism, it doesn't mean that they are interested in taking on anti-racism endeavors. Assuming otherwise is highly problematic and can lead to stereotyping and tokenization, which in turn, can lead to a lot of incorrect assumptions about BIPOC.

It would make much more sense to ask a BIPOC to collaborate on an anti-racist endeavor if they have previously spoken about their passion for such issues and have actively participated in past initiatives. Their stated interest and documented history of active participation is a relatively good sign that you are not relying solely on their identity when determining whether they would be appropriate to ask for collaboration. In contrast, asking a BIPOC person to collaborate on anti-racism work when they have not stated an interest in this work or have no history of participating in related initiatives means your request is likely rooted in an overgeneralization about BIPOC.

## "C" Is for Capability

The fourth consideration is about capability. Similar to the interest component of the DEI CALCULATOR, you cannot assume that all BIPOC have the expertise or skill set needed to do anti-racist work. Like any other endeavor, anti-racist work requires specific skills, knowledge, and experiences that not all BIPOC have (or want to have). Imagine that you ask your Pakistani American friend, who is an artist, to contribute to an anti-racist art show solely because they are Pakistani American and completely disregard their lack of experience or expertise in anti-racism. This would be an example of a scenario where the person clearly does *not* have the capability for the task. However, if you approach a different Pakistani American friend who has a proven track record of leading and participating in art-based anti-racist initiatives, that would be an appropriate choice, since they would be a knowledgeable and experienced partner for the anti-racist art show you want to put on.

## "A" Is for Appropriate

Imagine that you work at a college counseling center and you ask an Asian American therapist colleague to work with you to develop an outreach program to increase the number of Asian American students you serve. Whether this is an equitable collaboration request depends entirely on whether the task is appropriate given the colleague's role. It is not an appropriate role simply because of their identity! If this employee's job description specifically indicates that they will support and lead anti-racism-related outreach initiatives within the organization, then the request would be appropriate. If, however, this employee was hired to take the lead on a completely different aspect of the counseling center (e.g., compliance with state regulations), then this request would be inappropriate.

## "L" Is for Limited

The scope of a particular request can make a big difference in the decision to ask for collaboration. Be very clear about the scope of the task and make sure that it is as limited (versus recurring) as possible. The time required to engage in these efforts disproportionately impacts BIPOC, and when you leave the timing of the request vague, it places BIPOC at a disadvantage in determining whether or not they have the time or capacity to collaborate. For example, inviting a Black colleague to participate in a one-time panel discussion about representation in your field would be a more appropriate request than asking them to lead a monthly workshop series with no clear end date. Emphasizing the limited nature of your request can be extremely important.

## "C" Is for Compensation

We noted earlier that BIPOC are often disproportionately overburdened with DEI-related labor. Often, adjustments are not made to their workload, nor are they given additional compensation for such labor. This has a negative effect on BIPOC, both because this pattern can deplete their cognitive and emotional resources and because it can keep them from doing their actual job for which they are being evaluated.

Imagine that you are the chair of the French Language department at a research-focused university. You ask your Moroccan American employee, an assistant professor, to take on the new role of DEI director of the department. You explain how this position requires that they spearhead DEI initiatives, conduct assessments and evaluations of initiatives, and serve as an internal consultant for other faculty and students. If this request were to come with a course release (meaning that the faculty member is exempt from teaching an otherwise required course) or additional salary, it may be appropriate. If, however, you offer no additional compensation besides a "we would appreciate your service," then the request is likely to cause a significant burden to the professor. While other colleagues are completing work that actually plays a role in their tenure and promotion (e.g., conducting research and publishing their findings), the Moroccan American professor's scholarship could stagnate as a result of this role. Thus, it is up to you to think creatively and work hard to find ways to compensate BIPOC for their labor.

## "U" Is for Useful

When you are asking for collaboration on an anti-racism endeavor, it is critical to make sure that the effort is actually useful for the BIPOC person you're asking. There should be at least *some* clear benefit to them doing this work. While you may benefit from their collaboration, you should not assume that the benefit is mutual or equitable.

For example, imagine that you know your colleague is becoming more interested in DEI-related work and wants to eventually take on a related leadership position related to DEI endeavors. However, at the moment, their job title and responsibilities do not have such a component. If you were to invite this colleague to join a high-profile DEI task force, in which there are numerous opportunities for relevant professional development and job-related networking, and the chance to positively influence organizational change, then this endeavor is likely to be useful to them. However, if you ask them to participate in a small, powerless committee and offer them no benefits, it is unlikely to be useful for them to participate in this activity.

## "L" Is for Long-Term Goals

Given how laborious anti-racist work can be, make sure that the endeavor you are asking a BIPOC to collaborate on is a meaningful one that is part of a larger, long-term anti-racism goal. For example, imagine that you work in a racially diverse school and you approach a coworker about participating in a "Diverse Alumni" project, where BIPOC alumni are invited to come to the school and talk about their career and how they got to where they are. You explain how this project is part of a larger, long-term goal to shift the culture of the school to be more inclusive and a place where students from all racial groups can feel a sense of belonging. You share that you had focus groups with students and that they specifically requested events like this because they would find it meaningful. Now, compare this to if you were to ask the BIPOC teacher to come to your classroom and talk about their favorite food from their "culture." You can see how in the second example, the request would be a somewhat random one-off activity with low possibility for impact, and therefore not likely to be worth the teacher's time.

## "A" Is for Authority

Although BIPOC are often sought after to engage in various DEI and anti-racism task forces, such invitations often do not give them any power to actually implement meaningful change. Imagine that you ask an employee to develop an anti-racist strategic plan for your company. You ask them to do research on proven strategies that can maximize effectiveness, and you require that they develop at least 10 specific anti-racism goals with step-by-step strategies for achieving those goals. If you make this request without any assurance that efforts will be made to implement the plan, the employee will not have the authority to actually *do* something that would make a difference.

Imagine, instead, that this request is accompanied by an assurance that the board of directors will support giving the employee the authority, time, and resources to implement their proposed plan. In this scenario, the employee will have actual power or authority to contribute to change, which will make the effort much more meaningful and worth their time.

## "T" Is for Timing

Many requests for collaboration come with a sense of urgency. Whether the efforts start in response to a major incident (e.g., a police shooting) or are part of an ongoing larger initiative, people often center the timing of their requests without considering how it affects the potential collaborator. Perhaps you request assistance writing a statement of support from a coworker immediately following a high-profile incident or during an extremely busy period at work. The urgency of this request leaves your coworker little time to thoughtfully consider their involvement.

Or you may approach a colleague during a period of relative calm, providing them ample time to consider your request, but you fail to consider that they are up for a big promotion and are already overextended. While giving them time to make the decision is important, it is also necessary to consider whether the timing of your request undermines equitable collaboration by placing undue burden on them. Ideally, you want to make sure that the timing of your request is appropriate and isn't creating barriers to equitable collaboration.

## "O" Is for Other Resources

When seeking collaboration, it is common for people to forget to assess whether there are other ongoing efforts or resources that can be of support before they make requests of others. When you forget these existing resources, you run the risk of creating redundant efforts, which unnecessarily burdens potential collaborators.

For example, perhaps you know that your Black neighbor, who is active in many activist organizations, has made comments about housing disparities. Inspired to start a neighborhood task force, you consider asking them to help you gather housing discrimination statistics in your city. Without first checking whether there are existing resources available (e.g., a local housing disparity report), you risk overburdening your neighbor and duplicating efforts. You might also discover that your neighbor has already gathered these statistics and is using them in meaningful ways in your neighborhood. In this case, it would make much more sense to step up to assist your neighbor with their existing efforts.

## "R" Is for Relationship

Finally, consider the context of the relationship you have with the person you are seeking collaboration with. Relationships with friends and colleagues are dynamic, so ask yourself if the request you are making is appropriate for this relationship. Perhaps you barely know this coworker or have had limited interactions with them, yet you ask them to take on a significant DEI responsibility or share personal experiences to help you increase your understanding of the workplace climate. This would likely not be appropriate. However, if you were to ask a colleague whom you know well and with whom you have a positive, collaborative relationship, your request for their involvement in a DEI initiative would likely be more in line with the nature of your existing relationship.

## Crunching the Numbers with the DEI CALCULATOR

We've walked you through the components of the DEI CALCULATOR and explained why they are critical for equitable collaboration. Now comes the part where you integrate your understanding of these core components and assess the appropriateness of your request for collaboration. Remember that for BIPOC, collaboration on anti-racism and DEI efforts does not come without cost (e.g., disproportionate emotional labor, higher likelihood of negative consequences and perceptions). Using the DEI CALCULATOR will help you determine if you can afford (literally and figuratively) to make your request.

As we noted earlier, each letter of the DEI CALCULATOR refers to a specific component of equitable collaboration. To help you determine whether your request is adequately addressing each core component, the following table has questions you can ask yourself at each step of the skill. Each question has a corresponding dollar amount (ranging from $0.50 to $2.00) that reflects the weighted value of each component of the DEI CALCULATOR. These are known as "equity bucks."

Go through the table and ask yourself the questions listed for each component of the DEI CALCULATOR. If the criteria have been met, add those equity bucks to the last column of the table.

| DEI CALCULATOR Component | Question | Value | Your Equity Bucks |
|---|---|---|---|
| Demonstrated collaboration | As part of your request, will you communicate that this initiative will be collaborative and that you will provide support as needed? | $0.50 | |
| Equity | Is there an equitable power balance where you make it clear to the person that there will be no consequences if they decline your request? | $2.00 | |
| Interest | Has this person expressed interest in this kind of DEI or anti-racism work? | $1.00 | |

| Capability | Does this person have relevant DEI or anti-racism experience (i.e., you're not just asking because they are a BIPOC)? | $1.00 | |
| Appropriate | Is it the person's literal job (i.e., it's in their job or role description)? | $1.50 | |
| Limited | Is this a limited task, rather than a recurring one? | $0.50 | |
| Compensation | Is the person going to be fairly compensated (e.g., pay increase, adjustment in their usual workload to create time)? | $2.00 | |
| Useful | Is there some clear benefit to them for doing this work (e.g., networking opportunities, resume building)? | $1.50 | |
| Long-term goals | Is the endeavor meaningful and part of a long-term anti-racism goal? | $1.50 | |
| Authority | Will their position in this initiative give them the power or authority to contribute to change? | $1.00 | |
| Timing | Is this a good time to ask (e.g., not after a major incident has happened)? Does the person have enough time to consider your request? | $0.50 | |
| Other resources | Have you checked for other related efforts and resources to avoid redundant work and to not overburden this specific person? | $1.00 | |
| Relationship | Is your request appropriate for this relationship (i.e., is it a reasonably close, positive, reciprocal relationship)? | $1.00 | |
| | **Total Equity Bucks:** | | |

Go ahead and crunch the numbers, adding up all of the values in the last column to determine your total equity bucks. How much money you have determines the next steps forward. Ideally, you'll have enough equity bucks to proceed confidently and make a request for equitable collaboration. In other scenarios, you may need to go back and assess what changes are needed to make your request equitable. Either way, the skill is intended to guide you through this decision-making process.

##  Less Than $5: Don't Ask!

If your equity bucks add up to less than $5, you are in the red zone, which means you absolutely should *not* make this request for collaboration. A value of less than $5 means that the initiative you are asking a BIPOC person to collaborate on is likely not part of an equitable process and therefore falls into the many pitfalls described earlier. There is a high potential to cause harm due to the inequities inherent in your request. However, all is not lost! There are still ways you can work hard and likely move your total equity bucks to the next tier. Simply review your responses and take note which questions had a score of $0. What can be done to change them? You may want to focus on the higher-value items that will give you the biggest bang for your buck, so to speak. If you are not able to move the total equity bucks to the next tier, it means you'll have to either change your request or find other White folks who might be able to contribute.

## ▽ $5 to $10: Proceed with Caution

If you find yourself with a total value between $5 and $10, you are in the yellow zone, which means that you need to think very carefully and troubleshoot before making a request for collaboration. Similar to the red zone, you need to ask yourself if there are ways to move your total to the next tier. Again, take note of which questions had a score of $0 and pay the most attention to the high-ticket items. After you engage in this troubleshooting, you need to make a decision about whether it feels fair to make the request. If you choose to proceed with the request, we encourage you to ask tentatively. You may even acknowledge the ways in which the request is flawed (e.g., "I applied for a grant to support this consultation and asked for other sources of funding, but I was not able to secure any funds. I know it is problematic that I cannot compensate you for this labor and, at the same time, I hope that I will be able to make up for that in other ways"). Additionally, if the person agrees, make sure to keep the equitable collaboration strategies in mind so as to avoid exploitation and harm. If the person does not agree, continue to problem solve so that you can get closer and closer to the green zone.

## ⯁ More Than $10: Ask with Some Confidence

If you find yourself with more than $10, congratulations! You are in the green zone. Being in the green zone means that you have made a reasonable effort to think through and address issues of power and privilege in the context of collaboration on an anti-racist endeavor. It means you have thoughtfully considered and taken meaningful steps to ensure equity and to minimize harm to your BIPOC collaborator. We encourage you to make your request confidently while also knowing that it will always be important for you to take no for an answer. (Yes, even if you have all $15.) To maximize the effectiveness of your request, we encourage you to provide as much information as possible when making the request and to clearly lay out all of the expectations and benefits of collaborating with you. As you proceed with the possible collaboration, it's important to use all of your *Beyond Fragility* skills to make sure it's as smooth and impactful of a collaboration as possible.

## Why Use the DEI CALCULATOR?

When requests for collaboration fail to incorporate trust, accountability, communication, and respect, as well as to consider power and burden imbalances, you risk causing ruptures to your relationships with BIPOC and overburdening BIPOC who are already contending with the stressors of existing in a racist society. Ensuring that collaborative work is equitable means balancing your needs for support while also promoting values of equity and justice. This can mean ensuring that resources, opportunities, and benefits arising from the collaboration are equitably distributed among all members. It can also involve ensuring diverse voices and perspectives are represented at every stage of the collaboration with a focus on power sharing, while avoiding burdening individuals with the responsibility of representing an entire group.

Acknowledging and respecting individual limits, workloads, and abilities, and not pressuring others to take on tasks beyond their capacity, are central to ensuring that a collaborative effort is equitable. However, it is impossible to ensure this without taking inventory of how context, power, and privilege may impact both the collaboration process and outcomes. Failing to consider these components of equitable collaboration increases the likelihood that your request will lead to undue burden on those you are soliciting help from. Ultimately, approaching collaboration *without* an equity lens will undoubtedly jeopardize your anti-racist efforts.

## CHAPTER SUMMARY

Throughout your lifelong journey of being an anti-racist ally, you will, without a doubt, encounter both challenges and opportunities that require collaborating with BIPOC. This is not a bad thing at all. In fact, collaboration can help foster a helpful culture of learning, mutual support, and accountability, which can strengthen your commitment to addressing racism and its root causes. On top of that, collaboration can also amplify the voices and power of marginalized communities who are most affected by racism and other forms of oppression.

Despite the importance of doing collaborative work with BIPOC, figuring out when to ask for help is quite challenging. Thus, we offered you the DEI CALCULATOR as a way to take the guesswork out of these nuanced decisions. By considering issues of power and equity in your requests for collaboration on anti-racism initiatives, you can make sure that your efforts are responsive to BIPOC needs, which can help maintain your interpersonal relationships in a way that can encourage you to continue the work of anti-racism.

# SECTION V

. . . . .

# APPLYING ANTI-RACIST SKILLS TO THE REAL WORLD

## CHAPTER 15

# Setting Anti-Racist Goals: From Performative Allyship to Powerful Engagement

Let us take a moment to celebrate the fact that you have made it to the last section of *Beyond Fragility*! By now, you have learned what racism is, what it means to be an anti-racist ally, and how to overcome many cognitive, emotional, and interpersonal barriers that get in the way of doing this work. In this section, we focus on applying these skills in the real world, starting with tackling one of the most important parts of your anti-racist journey: setting anti-racist goals. In this chapter, we dive further into how to make sure that your anti-racist work is effective and meaningful rather than superficial and performative. We start by explaining *why* setting anti-racist goals matters in the first place and then explain *how* to evaluate your anti-racist goals to maximize their effectiveness and overcome stuck points related to implementing these goals.

# Why Does Anti-Racist Goal Setting Matter?

Setting goals is fundamental to anti-racist work. Decades of research has shown that goal setting is critical for success, with there being at least four reasons why this is the case (Locke & Latham, 2002). First, goals direct your attention to a specific area. Rather than having a vague interest in anti-racism that doesn't lead to action, goal setting allows you to intentionally delegate your focus to a particular anti-racism endeavor. Second, setting goals can light a fire under you! As soon as you set an anti-racist goal, you will notice yourself building the energy and momentum needed to reach that goal. Third, when you have a particular target in mind, it becomes easier to persist through and overcome any hurdles that might pop up along the way. It can be hard to find the motivation to persevere if you only have a vague notion of what you're working toward. Fourth, goal setting can serve as a gateway to more relevant knowledge and strategies. This means that the more anti-racist goals you set out to accomplish, the more likely you are to learn unanticipated lessons and hone your anti-racist skills.

Although there are various ways to set goals, not all goals are created equal. In other words, simply having a goal is not enough—you also need to follow a particular process in setting your goals to ensure you are successful in accomplishing them. We believe this is also the case in the context of anti-racism. One way to do so is to make sure that your goals adhere to the SMART acronym by being specific, measurable, achievable, relevant, and time-bound:

- **Specific:** What needs to be accomplished and by whom? What steps need to be taken to achieve the goal?
- **Measurable:** How will progress be measured and quantified?
- **Achievable:** Can the goal be reasonably accomplished?
- **Relevant:** How does achieving the goal connect to your big-picture or long-term objectives?
- **Time-bound:** What is the timeline for accomplishing the goal? What date should the goal be completed by?

The SMART framework will help you transform vague and overly general goals into goals that are concrete and actionable. In the remainder of this chapter, we provide a skill based on the SMART framework that will help you ensure your goal is maximally effective in producing meaningful change toward ending racism.

# Ready, Set, ACTION: A Skill for Evaluating Your Anti-Racism Goals

Although we've briefly highlighted why goal setting is key, it is also important to know how to engage in goal setting along your anti-racism journey. Drawing on the SMART goal framework, we guide you through the ACTION skill, which is a step-by-step guide to determine whether or not your anti-racist goal is effective. Using this skill is a way for you to conduct a mini assessment of your goal, and we also offer ways to tweak your goal to maximize its effectiveness.

## "A" Is for Anti-Racist

The first question to ask yourself when evaluating your goal is "Does my goal *explicitly* seek to dismantle racism?" This would be a good time to check in with the BASICS skill from chapter 1 to consider whether your goal seeks to undo racism at one (or more) of the levels (individual, cultural, systemic) we identified. Instead of simply having the goal to "increase diversity," which doesn't explicitly change existing racist policies within an institution, you can make your goal more relevant to anti-racist allyship by changing it to be something like "Identify and tackle the racism-related barriers that result in BIPOC underrepresentation in my organization." In this comparison, you can see how the goal of "increasing diversity" is not *explicitly* seeking to dismantle racism.

In fact, simply targeting "diversity" without an explicit focus on dismantling racism could lead you to set a goal that has nothing to do with BIPOC. For example, a company seeking to increase its number of "diversity hires" could end up still prioritizing White people from marginalized groups (e.g., White women, White sexual minorities) over BIPOC—thus reifying White privilege and doing nothing to end racism. Not only is this inefficient, but it also undermines your ability to end exclusionary policies that affect BIPOC or to dismantle systemic racism within a particular context. Thus, this step is about really trying to make sure that your goal explicitly targets racism.

## "C" Is for Concrete

Second, ask yourself, "Is my goal specific and action-oriented versus vague and aspirational?" Imagine that an anti-racism committee is aware of the poor racial climate at their organization, as they have heard frequent complaints about how many people in the organization have committed racial microaggressions or have openly expressed problematic worldviews. As a result, the committee members decide to create the goal to "improve racial climate." Although this goal sounds nice in theory, what does it actually mean in practice? In other words, what is the committee actually going to do?

To address the vagueness of their goal, the committee might revise it as "Decrease the frequency of racial microaggressions that are contributing to a poor racial climate." You can see how in the second version of the goal, it is a lot easier to problem solve and find a specific strategy to tackle the issue. With their concrete goal to reduce BIPOC's experiences of racial microaggressions, the committee might generate a first step, such as "Implement a racial microaggression training program in the organization." Therefore, concreteness matters because it gives you direction and leads to specific, concrete action steps. Do keep in mind that it's okay for a goal to start off as vague, but it's necessary to eventually concretize the goal in a way that is conducive for taking action.

## "T" Is for Thoughtful

The third question to ask yourself is "Is my goal thoughtful in prioritizing BIPOC over my own self-interest?" It is imperative that your goal is not performative or focused on the *appearance* of being anti-racist while potentially causing harm (even unintentionally) to BIPOC. If you don't ensure that your goal prioritizes BIPOC's wellness, it is possible that your goal could inadvertently cause harm or re-traumatize BIPOC.

For example, instead of creating a goal like "Encourage BIPOC colleagues to spearhead the new anti-racism committee," it is more thoughtful to have a goal like "Provide stipend support for BIPOC who contribute their time and labor to anti-racist work." As we stated in chapter 14, it can be problematic to ask BIPOC to take the lead on anti-racism efforts that are not compensated, given that this work is largely underappreciated, time consuming, and emotionally taxing. As another example, instead of simply changing your social media profile picture to *signal* that you care about racism, it would be more thoughtful to actually get involved in activist organizations that work to dismantle racism. Thus, this step is about making sure you are clear about what's driving your goal and who ultimately stands to benefit from your goal—you or BIPOC.

## "I" Is for Impactful

The fourth question to ask yourself is "Will achieving this anti-racism goal lead to measurable change?" Anti-racist goals that are impactful can lead to tangible and sustainable changes in policies, systems, and practices that perpetuate racism. When goals do not offer any type of quantifiable change, they fall short of actually addressing the root causes of racism and only address racism in a superficial way.

For example, Lenny, a language arts teacher, might have the goal to "not use racial slurs." Although this goal is definitely consistent with anti-racism, at the same time, what impact does this really have in fostering change? It probably does not make much of an impact because it is a very basic *in*action (i.e., having the goal of not doing something) rather than actually *doing* something that can create change. Perhaps Lenny might dig deep and ask himself what he originally intended by this goal. What does he *actually* hope to achieve?

In doing so, Lenny might realize that he actually wants to address the many ways White supremacy has impacted language. For example, Lenny might learn about the concept of linguistic racism, which occurs when someone experiences discrimination based on the language or dialect they use (Baker-Bell, 2020). To enact change, it may be much more impactful for him to actively work toward dismantling racism when it comes to what are considered "acceptable" dialects in the United States. His new goal might be to "Increase awareness of linguistic racism and encourage strategies to overcome it." This might mean watching and sharing videos about different dialects (e.g., African American Vernacular English) and committing to calling out racism every time he hears inaccurate assumptions being made about language. Over time, this can lead to *measurable* change as Lenny educates his White students, colleagues, friends, and family, counteracting their belief that there is one "correct" way to speak (which is determined by White people), making them less likely to mock others' dialects, and helping achieve linguistic liberation for all BIPOC (Baker-Bell, 2020). Thus, make sure that your goal packs a punch when it comes to creating meaningful change toward anti-racism.

## "O" Is for Obtainable

Fifth, ask yourself, "Is this goal obtainable?" Although we highly encourage you to think big, it's not helpful if the goal is unrealistic. Setting goals that are not achievable can be counterproductive for many reasons. For one, unrealistic goals set you up to fail, which can then reduce your self-efficacy and lead you to give up. Second, all the time you spend on an unrealistic goal is time that could have been spent doing something that is actually obtainable and likely to be implemented.

For our purposes, obtainable goals are ones that involve actions that you can control. In contrast, unobtainable goals are those in which the changes are out of your control, the goals require perfect outcomes, or the goals require skills and resources unavailable to you at the current time. For example, setting the goal to "Eliminate systemic racism in the tech industry within a year" is admirable, yet highly unrealistic. The time frame is tight, and it's unlikely that you, as a single person, even have access to an entire industry. An alternative goal might be to "Conduct the BASICS skill within my tech company and use these insights to inform recommendations to change policies that maintain racism." While having the large-scale commitment to dismantle racism in the tech industry is significant, it's critical to build toward it by setting achievable goals that are aligned with that commitment. When you make sure that your goal is impactful yet doable given the time, resources, and skills you have, it will make it a lot easier for you to maintain momentum and not fizzle out from exhaustion.

## "N" Is for Necessary

The final question to ask yourself is "Is this goal something that's necessary for progress toward a long-term commitment to change?" If it's not, then the goal is more likely to be performative, short-lived, and disconnected from your overall goals as an anti-racist ally. But given how large of a problem racism is, each goal you set needs to be a part of a larger, intentional plan. This ensures that your goal is not just about making you feel better about yourself or doing something because it's trendy.

For example, let's say that you are on an anti-racism committee that is currently focusing on educating community members about racism. If you have the goal to "Create graphics about systemic racism," it may be unclear why such a step is necessary. Instead, you can tweak your goal to say, "Address knowledge gaps about systemic racism by creating graphics about this issue as a first step toward educating community members." You can see how making it clear that this goal is necessary for a long-term change contextualizes the goal as just one pixel in a bigger picture. In this last criterion of ACTION, you are really working on connecting a small anti-racist goal to a larger commitment, which can make it more likely that you'll continue to move toward that commitment rather than stop after the specific goal is done.

# Applying the ACTION Skill

Now let's use the ACTION skill to evaluate the effectiveness of anti-racism goals. In the following section, we present two different sample goals and go through the process of assessing whether each goal meets the criteria for each step of the ACTION skill. If it does, then no change is needed! But if it doesn't, we'll provide you with suggestions to tweak the goal so it meets the necessary criteria.

## Example 1: Educating Yourself About Anti-Racism

Let's say that you are spending time with your Filipino friend, Mark, who you haven't seen in a while. You are telling Mark about a recent hate crime that happened in your town and you make a comment about how even though you feel terrible about what happened, you don't "buy" the argument that the victim's race had anything to do with it (despite local anti-racism activists pointing out evidence showing the incident was a hate crime). This leads to you talking about how you are generally just really sick of racism—you're tired of hearing about it, you're tired of people being racist, and you just "want the world to move on already." At the end of the conversation, your friend looks uncomfortable and says, "You've got some work to do." You ask for clarification and he tells you that you've expressed racist views and that you needed to educate yourself more. After some initial defensiveness, you decide to take on this goal of educating yourself more. Let's run this goal through ACTION to see how it does!

**Original Goal:** "Educate myself more."

| ACTION Criterion | Response | Tweaked Goal |
|---|---|---|
| Anti-racist? | No, this goal is not really anti-racist. It is just about educating yourself more, without any connection to anti-racism. One way to tweak this goal is to include specific outcomes related to anti-racist action. | Educate myself more about anti-racism and apply new insights to my anti-racist work. |
| Concrete? | No, the goal is not concrete. What kind of anti-racism education are you going to do? Here you want to get really specific about your goal. Perhaps you add a time frame and you also specify the book you're going to read! | Read the book *Beyond Fragility* within the next two months and apply new insights to my anti-racist work. |
| Thoughtful? | Yes, this is a relatively thoughtful goal because it is not placing your self-interest over BIPOC. In fact, this goal is supportive because it involves reading a book written by BIPOC scholars about anti-racism and is in line with your BIPOC friend's recommendation. | Read the book *Beyond Fragility* within the next two months and apply new insights to my anti-racist work. |
| Impactful? | Somewhat. Maybe it's impactful, but specifying the desired outcome of reading the book would be even more impactful. You can modify the goal to state a specific measurable impact that you'd like it to have. | Read the book *Beyond Fragility* within the next two months and apply new insights to the pursuit of three new anti-racism goals. |
| Obtainable? | Maybe! You might not be able to read the book in two months if you have other constraints on your time (e.g., an upcoming trip, exams, a big project at work). However, for this example, let's say you do have the time to read the book. In this case, your goal is obtainable. | Read the book *Beyond Fragility* within the next two months and apply new insights to the pursuit of three new anti-racism goals. |
| Necessary? | Yes! BIPOC have repeatedly stated the need for White allies to do inner work (e.g., learn emotional and interpersonal skills) to be able to engage in effective, sustained change. Reading this book is necessary to support your long-term goal of being an anti-racist ally. To make this connection clear, you can tweak your goal once more. | As part of an overarching goal of engaging in lifelong and effective anti-racist work, read the book *Beyond Fragility* within the next two months and apply new insights to the pursuit of three new anti-racism goals. |

# REFLECTION

In the example, the goal morphed from "Educate myself more" to "As part of an overarching goal of engaging in lifelong and effective anti-racist work, read the book *Beyond Fragility* within the next two months and apply new insights to the pursuit of three new anti-racism goals." What do you think are the benefits of this transformation? How would the revamped goal lead to more effective anti-racist allyship?

_____

_____

_____

_____

_____

## Example 2: Revamp Performance Reviews to Be More Diversity Focused

Imagine that Ned directs a nonprofit organization that offers after-school programming for youth in disinvested communities. After several racism-related concerns are brought up by BIPOC employees and volunteers, Ned decides to do a BASICS assessment within his organization. He learns a lot about the individual, cultural, and systemic factors that maintain racism within the nonprofit, including racial group differences in performance evaluations. One thing he discovers is that although all employees are routinely asked to do extra community service (e.g., giving talks in predominantly BIPOC local schools) to fulfill the organization's anti-racism mission, these responsibilities are more often taken on by BIPOC employees. However, annual performance reviews are evaluated based on individuals' technical job descriptions, which do not include the community service tasks.

For example, technical analyst Toni's most recent evaluation was based on the number of reports they produced, and when they explained that they had done fewer reports because of all of the community work they did, their supervisor threw up his hands and said, "Sorry buddy, that's not what I'm evaluating you on." Toni expresses to Ned that this is a serious problem that is leading them to consider a job elsewhere. Ned tries to address the systemic issue of unrecognized labor by setting a goal of revamping the performance reviews to be more diversity focused. Ned then proceeds to go to the ACTION skill to evaluate his goal.

**Original Goal:** "Revamp performance reviews to be more diversity focused."

| ACTION Criterion | Response | Tweaked Goal |
|---|---|---|
| Anti-racist? | No, this goal is not about undoing racism. Although the goal mentions that the reviews should be more "diversity focused," the word *diversity* does not inherently mean anti-racism. Ned decides to change the focus to be more explicitly about anti-racism. | Revamp performance reviews <u>so they are informed by anti-racism.</u> |
| Concrete? | No. The goal isn't concrete for two reasons. First, what does "revamp" mean? Revamp how? What is the actual action being taken? Second, what does "informed by anti-racism" mean? It's unclear what it means to make something anti-racism informed. After a lot of soul-searching, consultation with employees, and self-education about racist policies, Ned further tweaks the goal to be more concrete. | <u>Within the next three months, create and implement a revised</u> performance review evaluation <u>that incorporates anti-racism as a specific criterion in which employees are evaluated.</u> |
| Thoughtful? | Yes, this goal is certainly thoughtful because it prioritizes BIPOC over Ned's own self-interest. It would be much easier for him to simply ignore the issue and expect additional labor from his BIPOC employees. Instead, this goal shows a clear commitment to centering his BIPOC employees' needs. | Within the next three months, create and implement a revised performance review evaluation that incorporates anti-racism as a specific criterion in which employees are evaluated. |
| Impactful? | Yes, this is impactful because in Ned's nonprofit, performance reviews determine whether someone gets a raise or promotion, so it is critical for the evaluation to be as equitable as possible. Making specific changes to make the processes fairer can significantly enhance BIPOC employees' success. | Within the next three months, create and implement a revised performance review evaluation that incorporates anti-racism as a specific criterion in which employees are evaluated. |
| Obtainable? | Yes. Although Ned may have to put in some additional labor to implement this change, such as presenting the idea to the nonprofit's board of directors, it is quite realistic. | Within the next three months, create and implement a revised performance review evaluation that incorporates anti-racism as a specific criterion in which employees are evaluated. |
| Necessary? | Not quite. Although this goal is necessary for progress toward a long-term commitment to change, Ned hasn't stated that in his goal. Stating that commitment upfront can help contextualize his goal and make sure it's part of a larger sustained effort. To do this, Ned reflects on what the broader purpose of this goal Is and Incorporates It Into the goal. | <u>As part of a long-term goal to listen to BIPOC employees' and volunteers' concerns,</u> within the next three months, create and implement a revised performance review evaluation that incorporates anti-racism as a specific criterion in which employees are evaluated. |

## REFLECTION

In the example, the goal morphed from "Revamp performance reviews to be more diversity focused" to "As part of a long-term goal to listen to BIPOC employees' and volunteers' concerns, within the next three months, create and implement a revised performance review evaluation that incorporates anti-racism as a specific criterion in which employees are evaluated." What do you think are the benefits of this transformation?

_____

_____

_____

_____

_____

_____

_____

# Why Use the ACTION Skill?

Without an ACTION plan, it can be very difficult to make sure that your goals are actually effective. Sometimes what feels like a helpful thing to do turns out to not be helpful, which is why it's valuable to always consult the ACTION skill. For example, in the heat of the moment, you might decide to participate in the latest social media trend to signal your social justice values, instead of reflecting on what that participation means and how it fits in with more effective goals. Without the ACTION skill, it is much harder to detect when your actions are performative rather than meaningful—and that information is critical for guiding your work as an ally.

Even worse than just being unhelpful, it is also possible for misguided goals to even cause harm. For example, you might have a lofty, unattainable goal that eventually depletes your organization's resources, takes away resources from other BIPOC-led efforts, and ultimately undermines your organization's commitment and willingness to invest in anti-racism efforts in the future. Just remember: It's okay for your initial goals to start out messy, vague, or superficial and become more refined after you go through the ACTION plan checklist!

## CHAPTER SUMMARY

At this point, you have overcome numerous cognitive, emotional, and interpersonal barriers to anti-racist work. All of that effort was to make sure that when you actually do the work, you are as effective as possible. In this chapter, we outlined the importance of goal setting and explained what it means to set effective goals. To help you develop anti-racist goals, we then moved through the ACTION skill, which helps you to determine whether the anti-racist goal you're setting meets certain criteria for being as effective as possible. This skill allows you to make tweaks to your goal as you go through each step—it's kind of like giving your anti-racist goals an effectiveness glow-up! With this knowledge in hand, it's time to learn how to apply all of the skills you have learned to the real world so you can keep moving toward your goals instead of getting stuck when faced with complex or overwhelming situations.

## CHAPTER 16

# Putting the Pieces Together: From Knowledge to Application

Although this book takes up one barrier and one skill at a time in each chapter, the real world is hardly ever this simple. The reality is that anti-racism work is complicated and messy, and often requires the use of more than one skill in a single situation. In fact, in the real world, there are lots of co-occurring barriers that require a tool*box* rather than just one specific tool to comprehensively address the issue. This is like tending to a garden; you would want to use a variety of tools even if you were addressing a single issue with one of your plants. You might need a garden trowel for digging up weeds and pruning shears for trimming plants. If you only came to the garden with a single tool, you might not be able to effectively tackle the problem. Similarly, in the anti-racist allyship world, if you only use one skill when you really need three, then you are not maximizing your effectiveness as an ally, and you are likely undermining your anti-racism efforts. Therefore, in this chapter, we briefly discuss difficulties in applying new skills in real time and in complex scenarios. We also introduce *one more* skill that can help you bring it all together so that you can do this work in the real world.

# What Gets in the Way of Applying New Skills?

Throughout this book, perhaps you have felt confident in your ability to implement the cognitive, emotional, and interpersonal skills the next time you encounter a situation that requires them. However, research shows that even if people demonstrate proficiency in simplified contexts, they have difficulty applying the same knowledge and skills in situations that impose added demands (Anderson et al., 1989). For instance, you may be masterful at multiplication, but doing so under time constraints may introduce added difficulty and require extra skills and practice.

We imagine the same is true in the context of anti-racism work—that applying anti-racism skills in complex, real-world scenarios is likely more challenging than completing this book's pop quizzes, exercises, and reflection prompts. Although you may be able to accurately identify cognitive distortions in a matching activity, you may struggle to identify *your* cognitive distortions in the heat of the moment after committing a racist misstep. In addition, you might be able to choose which skill to use in a straightforward situation but struggle to determine which set of skills is needed when the situation has many layers. This does not mean that your practice of the skills to date is not valuable but, rather, that learning how to apply these skills in tandem with other skills is necessary to ensure real-world success!

# APPLYing Your Anti-Racism Skills: Knowing How to Put It All Together

Now that you have been exposed to the various skills in this book, it is critical to seek out opportunities to apply these skills in the real world. Repeated practice in your everyday life will allow you to use these skills to face real-world challenges. Here, we outline steps for you to take to ensure you are putting it all together.

### "A" Is for Assess the Anti-Racist Thing to Do

The first step of APPLY is to figure out your anti-racist goal. Doing so allows you to take subsequent steps that are aligned with that goal. In order to determine what the anti-racist thing to do is in a given situation, you may need to go back to the definition of anti-racism we provided in chapter 2: "Anti-racism involves a commitment to actively identifying and fighting against policies, behaviors, beliefs, and perceptions that perpetuate racist ideas and actions. Therefore, *any* action that takes a step toward ending racial inequality is considered anti-racist." In other words, the anti-racist thing to do is the thing that is going to actively disrupt racism in the given scenario. Some other questions to help you identify the anti-racist action in a given context are:

- What action would oppose racial inequality at this moment?
- What action would challenge structures of power and privilege that maintain racism at this moment?
- What action would affirm multicultural diversity at this moment?

## "P" Is for Pinpoint the Barriers That Might Get in the Way

As we've mentioned throughout this book, there are several barriers that hinder anti-racist allyship. These barriers can include not truly understanding what racism is, interfering worldviews, inflexible thinking, difficulty tolerating unpleasant emotions, behavioral avoidance, and not knowing how to recover from a racist misstep. The barriers you encounter in the real world can consist of any number of these issues or others raised in the previous chapters. Therefore, this step of the APPLY skill requires you to familiarize yourself with these barriers so you can easily identify them when they arise. Regularly reviewing these barriers as outlined in the introductory chapter of this book may be a good way to keep them at the forefront of your mind when you encounter different scenarios. In addition, completing the reflection exercises throughout this book can help you to identify common barriers that tend to come up for you specifically.

## "P" Is for Pick Out the Appropriate *Beyond Fragility* Skills

Once you identify which barriers are interfering with your ability to be an anti-racist ally, the next step is to pick out the appropriate skills from this book to overcome those barriers. For example, let's say you are attending a class lecture and your instructor makes a racist misstep. If you know that the anti-racist thing to do is to speak out against the misstep, but you aren't sure what to say or how to say it, then the CALL OUT skill from chapter 12 would be most appropriate. If you're also worried that speaking out might jeopardize your relationship with the instructor, tackling your ambivalence via the CLEAR skill from chapter 6 would be appropriate as well. For a review of each skill and what barrier it aims to tackle, we encourage you to take full advantage of the chapter summaries at the end of each chapter and the skill summaries in the appendix.

## "L" Is for Look for an Effective Starting Point

Knowing where to start is tough! There isn't always a "right" answer because there are a lot of individual differences and contextual elements that dictate where it makes sense to start. For example, imagine someone is planning to confront a colleague who made a racist remark during a team meeting. If they are feeling really anxious about speaking out, it may make sense to start with the FEEL skill so they can reduce their anxiety enough to move forward with the CALL OUT skill. However, another person may decide to "rip the bandage off" and dive right into the CALL OUT skill despite their anxiety. They may then want to use the FEEL skill after the fact to deal with the emotional comedown from engaging in anxiety-inducing behavior.

Therefore, consider the first step you are willing to take and the skill that is best equipped to help you take that first step. It may also be helpful to start with the skill that feels the most motivating or practical for you. Either way, this step in APPLY encourages you to start *somewhere*, which can prevent you from spiraling and stagnating in your anti-racism journey.

## "Y" Is for Yield to Imperfection

One of the things we have said over and over since the beginning of this book is that there is no such thing as a perfect ally because the work of anti-racism is not clear-cut, simple, or straightforward with easy answers. Rather, it is ongoing, complex, and often difficult. This means missteps, mistakes, and imperfections will inevitably occur along the way. Therefore, along your allyship journey, it is important to let go of the need to be perfect and to be open to learning and growing, even when the process is uncomfortable and challenging. If you can accept that perfection is unattainable, you can also reframe your missteps, mistakes, and imperfections as areas for continued growth and offer yourself patience for these growing pains. You can always attempt to do better while letting go of perfection as the ultimate goal.

Yielding to imperfection can also mean accepting when you do not achieve your desired outcome. For example, if you call someone out and make a request for change and they retaliate, you will need to yield to imperfection by accepting the undesired outcome. The reality is that you cannot always change other people. This does not mean that you should opt out of anti-racism work altogether but, rather, still do the work to the best of your ability. Even though the "Y" comes at the end of the APPLY skill, we want to note that yielding to imperfection should occur throughout the process of implementing all of the *Beyond Fragility* skills.

# Using the APPLY Skill: Practicing How to Bring It Together

We know that the *Beyond Fragility* skills sometimes sound nice in theory, but it may be hard to picture what they actually look like in practice. That's why in the next part of this chapter, we offer you five detailed case examples that depict situations in which these skills would be needed. After each case example, we include questions for you to quiz yourself on each step of APPLY and provide recommended answers for each question. We then provide a description of how it might play out to implement the APPLY skill in a given scenario.

As you read through each example, we encourage you to really take the time to process the scenario and respond to each question carefully before reading our recommended answers. We admit there are a lot of skills in this book, and it will take time to master them all. We encourage you to use this exercise as a self-assessment for which parts of the book you may need to go back to and re-read. We also offer *recommended* (rather than "correct") answers. We use this language to reinforce the idea that there is no "one right way" to approach a situation. Instead, we hope to offer you one idea of how we think you can use the APPLY skill. If you find yourself coming up with a completely different configuration of skills, that's okay! We encourage you to process these differences with your peers and use them to spark discussion and growth.

## Case Study 1: Anti-Racism Education in Your Child's Elementary School

Imagine that you are a parent of a child who is in elementary school. One day, you read in the school's newsletter that the school is implementing a new, year-long module on anti-racism, which will involve your child learning about racism, White privilege, and empathy. To make room for this module, the principal plans to cut recess by 15 minutes. You are concerned and immediately look for information about the next parent-teacher town hall. Once the town hall rolls around, you attend and express your significant concerns about the new module. First, you note that even though you are "all about diversity," you worry your child is too young to learn about these concepts and feel like such discussions could make your child feel bad for being White. You think that until your child is older, it's better for them to "not see color" and to just treat everyone the same. Second, you express your disagreement about cutting recess, as you view unstructured play time as a critical activity that should be prioritized at this stage of your child's development.

After you express your concerns, other parents bring up research that challenges what you're saying. Parents mention that kids understand and notice race much earlier than expected and that using a "we don't see color" approach is more harmful in the long term because it actually perpetuates racism. After the other parents speak up, you still notice this lingering thought of "Yeah, but I still *feel* like my child is too young to deal with such mature content." You feel personally attacked, misunderstood, and as if you are being "bullied" into going along with the group consensus. The whole ordeal makes you worry that your actions have made you a failure as an ally and discredit any anti-racism efforts you might engage in moving forward.

It's time to use the APPLY skill! Take out your pen or pencil and work through the five steps of this skill for this example.

What is the anti-racist thing to do?

_____

_____

_____

_____

_____

What barriers might get in the way of your ability to do the anti-racist thing?

_____

_____

_____

_____

_____

What *Beyond Fragility* skills would help you overcome these barriers?

_____

_____

_____

_____

_____

What would be an effective starting point?

_____

_____

_____

_____

_____

What imperfections might you need to yield to?

_____

_____

_____

_____

_____

## Case Study 1 Recommended Answers

1.  The anti-racist thing to do is to support the implementation of the new, year-long module on racism. This action is the most likely to create change that benefits BIPOC.

2.  The following barriers might get in the way of your ability to do the anti-racist thing:

    ○ Cognitive barriers: Based on feedback from others, you notice that several of your concerns about the new racism module are rooted in inaccurate or problematic worldviews and beliefs, such as the belief that it's best not to see color. You also realize that you are having a rigid approach to what it means to be an ally.

- ○ Emotional barriers: After observing your emotional reaction and your thoughts, several cognitive distortions are apparent, especially emotional reasoning, which occurs when someone assumes that how they feel is an indicator of reality.

3. The following *Beyond Fragility* skills would help to overcome these barriers:
    - ○ ACCEPT to overcome the cognitive barrier of problematic worldviews
    - ○ FACTS to check whether the stories you are telling yourself are true
    - ○ AND to help you overcome the rigid approach to allyship

4. Given that your problematic worldviews seem to be particularly strong and getting in the way of your ability to engage in anti-racism, ACCEPT may be an effective place to start!

5. You might need to yield to the following imperfection:
    - ○ It is impossible to be a perfect ally.

## Putting It All Together for Case Study 1

As we noted in our recommended answers, the anti-racist thing to do in this scenario is to support the implementation of the new, year-long module on racism. One role of White allies is to leverage their White privilege to undo racism, and one way you can do this is by explicitly advocating for policies and programs that actively seek to dismantle racism. Next, you pinpoint the barriers that may prevent you from engaging in this anti-racist action. In terms of the cognitive barriers, you hold several inaccurate or problematic worldviews that have led to your concerns about the racism module. First, you believe that children of a certain age are "too young to learn about racism." Second, you believe that learning about racism will harm White children by making them "feel bad for being White." This belief also reveals an implicit assumption that we should care more about the possible harm experienced by White children when learning about racism than the actual harm that is done to BIPOC children when White children don't learn about racism. Third, you hold the worldview that "it is best not to see color," at least during this particular developmental period. Fourth, you believe that extended recess and play time are more developmentally important than learning about racism. Last, you are demonstrating some inflexible or rigid thinking in believing that one misstep will diminish your present and future anti-racism efforts.

There are also emotional barriers in the form of cognitive distortions, which are unhelpful and inaccurate ways of interpreting a situation. One type of cognitive distortion that is present is emotional reasoning, in which you assume that your feelings are an indicator of reality. In this case, you *feel* like your child is too young to learn about racism—even in the presence of information that contradicts this notion—and you continue to accept this feeling as truth. Additionally, you interpret other parents' counterpoints as "personal attacks" and *feel* like they are bullying you, all of which lead you to experience unpleasant emotions that linger the rest of the day.

At the next step of this skill, you pick out ACCEPT, FACTS, and AND as the most appropriate skills to use. In looking for an effective starting point, you realize that because your problematic worldviews seem to be particularly strong and are getting in the way of engaging in anti-racism, it makes sense to start with ACCEPT. You dive in and tackle the parts of this skill. For example, one step in this skill is to check in with reality. Let's take your belief that elementary-age children are too young to learn about racism. What truths or realities may you be rejecting with this belief? For one, this belief disregards the reality that BIPOC children don't get to opt out of knowing about racism and that shielding your child from racism is actually a byproduct of White privilege.

You then use FACTS to acknowledge the stories you are telling yourself and to determine whether they are indicative of cognitive distortions. Let's take the story that "my child will suffer if recess is shortened." Is this story true? Perhaps you are engaging in emotional reasoning by equating your feelings with reality. You may also be using a mental filter by only focusing on the negatives of the situation (e.g., your child will lose 15 minutes of recess time) and disregarding the positives (e.g., your child will gain information and skills that will better equip them to exist in a multiracial society). Last, you adopt the AND skill to help you embrace the dialectic that you did make a racist misstep by undermining the adoption of the anti-racism curriculum *and* you are continuing to learn and use new skills to undo racism moving forward.

Throughout this process, you yield to imperfection by recognizing that it is impossible to be a perfect ally who knows everything about anti-racism and who never makes a misstep. You notice that as you implement these skills, it becomes easier to see the importance of the anti-racism module and take steps to support it in your child's school. By using the APPLY skill and putting it all together, you realize that you are able to hold yourself accountable to your anti-racist allyship values and goals.

# Case Study 2: Racism in the Labor and Delivery Ward

Imagine that you are a labor and delivery nurse in a community hospital that serves mostly BIPOC patients. Your White coworker comes into the breakroom complaining about her Black patient who is "constantly asking for pain medication" because she "can't handle the leg cramps." Your coworker then says, "I'm not being a jerk. I just *know* she's not in real pain. Those people are always seeking drugs." You freeze and notice that you have the urge to change the subject immediately. You let out some nervous laughter and say you need to go check on a patient so you can leave the room as quickly as possible.

Although this is not the first time this coworker has made racist comments about patients of color, you never feel like you know what to say in response. You also feel torn because this coworker has done some really supportive things for you in the past, like covering your shifts with little notice when you've gotten sick or had emergencies. You worry that if you say something, she'll retaliate and this will ruin the relationship with one of the main people you get along with at work.

What is the anti-racist thing to do?

_____

_____

_____

_____

_____

What barriers might get in the way of your ability to do the anti-racist thing?

_____

_____

_____

_____

_____

What *Beyond Fragility* skills would help you overcome these barriers?

_____

_____

_____

_____

_____

What would be an effective starting point?

_____

_____

_____

_____

_____

What imperfections might you need to yield to?

_____

_____

_____

_____

_____

# Case Study 2 Recommended Answers

1.  The anti-racist thing to do in this scenario is to call out your coworker.

2.  The following barriers might get in the way of your ability to do the anti-racist thing:
    - Cognitive barriers: You are experiencing ambivalence because you desire to stand up for what you know is right *and* you also fear damaging a work relationship that benefits you in several ways.

- Emotional barriers: You aren't willing to sit with unpleasant or unwanted internal experiences (e.g., worry and anxiety about damaging the relationship), which leads you to take actions to avoid these experiences (e.g., exiting the situation ASAP).
- Interpersonal barriers: You are unsure about what to say and how to say it.

3. The following *Beyond Fragility* skills would help you overcome these barriers:
    - CLEAR to overcome the cognitive barrier of ambivalence
    - OPPOSE to do the opposite of what your avoidance urge is telling you to do
    - CALL OUT to determine what you can say to your colleague that communicates why her comment is inappropriate and that makes a clear request for change

4. The most effective starting point may be to address your ambivalence and behavioral avoidance before you implement the CALL OUT skill, since your ambivalence and avoidance could hinder your ability to call out your coworker's racist statement.

5. You might need to yield to the following imperfections:
    - Your coworker might get upset.
    - You might have missteps when using the CALL OUT skill, especially the first couple of times you use it.

## Putting It All Together for Case Study 2

For the first step in APPLY, you'd identify that the anti-racist thing to do is to call out your coworker because doing so will stop racism from continuing to fester in this way at your workplace. Then you pinpoint the barriers that are getting in the way of your ability to call out your coworker. Based on the information provided, it appears that the cognitive barrier of ambivalence is getting in the way. In particular, you desire to engage in actions that are aligned with anti-racism, such as challenging racist stereotypes about patients, *and* you fear damaging your work relationship with your colleague. There is also the emotional barrier of behavioral avoidance—you want to escape or distract yourself from feeling anxious, so you change the topic even though this behavior interferes with your anti-racist values. Finally, you notice an interpersonal barrier in that you lack the skills to call out your colleague effectively.

To overcome these barriers, you pick out CLEAR, OPPOSE, and CALL OUT as the best skills to use. You then look to start with either CLEAR or OPPOSE because you recognize that even if you *did* know how to call out your colleague effectively, you still may not do so if your ambivalence and behavioral avoidance go unaddressed. As you address your ambivalence, you may come to realize that you are really worried about how calling out your colleague will disrupt your relationship with her. One suggestion offered in the CLEAR skill is to problem solve: If you lose a friend in the workplace, can you seek community elsewhere where people have shared values around anti-racism? If things become awkward at work, can you reframe how you feel about the awkwardness? In other words, might it be easier to accept the awkwardness knowing that it is the result of you standing up for your values rather than the result of you allowing racism to persist? In using OPPOSE, you observe the urge to engage in behavioral avoidance, pinpoint your desire to avoid anxiety and fear, and pause to consider how giving in to your avoidance urge decreases your self-respect. You then identify that, rather than avoiding the situation, the effective thing to do is call out your coworker.

You then use the CALL OUT skill to plan what you will say to your colleague: "Earlier, you said that 'those people'—when referring to your Black patient—are always seeking drugs. When you say that a patient is not in real pain and just trying to get drugs, you may not mean any harm, but statements like those reify harmful stereotypes about Black patients—stereotypes that their pain isn't real or that they can tolerate more pain or that they are inherently dishonest and trying to take advantage of the system. Moving forward, it would be best to especially take Black patients' concerns to heart and provide them with whatever treatment and resources are available. And if you need support with this, I'd be willing to consult and provide a second opinion."

You then yield to imperfection in multiple ways. You wish you could deliver this script perfectly without any anxiety, but you accept that moments of anxiety will emerge and that you can still push through. After you deliver your request for change, your colleague expresses her resistance, so you hear her out and continue to assert your request gently. You remind yourself that although these skills will increase your alignment with your anti-racist values, boost your self-respect, and improve your ability to make change in your workplace, there is no way to control the actions of others. Your colleague may still get upset and accuse you of misunderstanding her motives and intentions. She may also become distant, leading to uncomfortable or awkward work interactions. As we have mentioned before, anti-racism is costly—it can cost you friends, relationships, status, and comfort. Yet we are confident that in using the APPLY skill and putting it all together, you have what it takes to recognize that preventing these losses is not more important than creating a just and anti-racist society!

## Case Study 3: Stereotyping During Ramadan

During the month of Ramadan, a holy month of fasting celebrated by many Muslims that involves abstaining from food and drink from sunrise to sunset, you decide you want to step up and be a supportive ally to your Arab employee, Layla. You read all about fasting and decide that because it seems hard to you, you want to find a way to make it easier for Layla. To this end, you send an email to all your employees mandating that everyone *only* eat their lunch privately in their offices and not in the public space (as they usually do) to not upset Layla. Layla immediately responds to your email saying that although she is Arab, she is not Muslim and therefore is not fasting for Ramadan. She notes that it is problematic for you to assume she is Muslim just because she is Arab. Further, Layla mentions that even if she were Muslim, making this request on her behalf without her feedback ignores her autonomy (and could lead to resentment from her coworkers). Layla expresses that she now feels singled out in the workplace.

While you feel weird about the fact that you assumed all Arabs were Muslim, you also aren't happy that Layla didn't see past the misstep to appreciate the gesture. Why couldn't she just give you credit for your good intentions as an ally? You worry that you are being misunderstood and that Layla will now view you as a racist, even though you know in your heart you are a good person. After reading the email from Layla, you feel activated—your heart rate is faster and your face feels flushed. While you aren't sure you want to respond, part of you also feels like you *should* do something in response.

What is the anti-racist thing to do?

_____

_____

_____

_____

_____

What barriers might get in the way of your ability to do the anti-racist thing?

_____

_____

_____

_____

_____

What *Beyond Fragility* skills would help you overcome these barriers?

_____

_____

_____

_____

_____

What would be an effective starting point?

_____

_____

_____

_____

_____

What imperfections might you need to yield to?

_____

_____

_____

_____

_____

# Case Study 3 Recommended Answers

1. The anti-racist thing to do is to repair the harm by sending a correction email to your employees and apologizing to Layla.

2. The following barriers might get in the way of your ability to do the anti-racist thing:
   - Emotional barriers: You notice you are experiencing discomfort but aren't sure what specific emotions you are feeling. You are also struggling to "sit" with this discomfort.
   - Interpersonal barriers: You are unsure how to repair the harm caused to Layla.

3. The following *Beyond Fragility* skills would help you overcome these barriers:
   - DETECT to better understand the emotions you are experiencing at this moment
   - FEEL to tolerate the unpleasant emotions you are experiencing
   - REPAIR to remedy the harm caused to Layla

4. It would be worthwhile to start with FEEL to make it easier for you to engage in the other two skills.

5. You might need to yield to the following imperfections:
   - You may continue to feel guilty or embarrassed about your misstep every time you see Layla (at least for a while).
   - Layla may not accept your apology.

## Putting It All Together for Case Study 3

The anti-racist thing to do is to repair the harm caused to Layla, which you can do by sending a correction email to all your employees and apologizing to Layla directly. Understandably, you might feel hesitant to act, as publicly apologizing can feel embarrassing given that you are the person in charge. So before you get started with this anti-racist action, you pinpoint the barriers, which you notice are mostly emotional and interpersonal. First, you have been feeling very uncomfortable and distressed since the moment Layla pointed out your misstep. You notice a strong urge to push these uncomfortable feelings and sensations away. Second, you want to make this up to

Layla, but you aren't sure how to do this, and you don't want to make Layla feel more put on the spot.

You decide to tackle these barriers and pick out the DETECT, FEEL, and REPAIR skills. You realize that it would make sense to begin with FEEL because you are physiologically activated. This skill will help you tolerate your distress so you can then use DETECT to dig more into what's going on with you emotionally. Perhaps as you move through the steps of DETECT, you notice feelings of guilt, anxiety, and defensiveness. Having this emotional clarity will allow you to better understand if your emotions are stirring up any thoughts that could be making your emotional experience more distressing. Perhaps your guilt is contributing to the thought "Layla now views me as racist!" Using the DETECT skill also allows you to create distance from your reactions, meaning that you can take a moment to consider whether or not you want to react to Layla in a defensive manner.

Once you use FEEL and DETECT to regulate your emotions, you feel like you are at a point where you can engage in REPAIR. In most scenarios that involve distress, it will make sense for REPAIR to come at the end because you need to be emotionally centered to implement the skill effectively. Otherwise, you run the risk of centering *your* emotions rather than the reparative action. Using the REPAIR skill, you apologize in a way that takes responsibility and communicate your plan to change your behavior to ensure that this kind of misstep does not happen again. You mention that one reason for the misstep is that you made assumptions based on stereotypes and insufficient information about Arab Americans. Aligned with the last two steps of REPAIR, you offer a plan to do more self-guided education about the history of Islam and Christianity in the Middle East and how it maps onto the current diversity of religion for Arab Americans. Still, you offer room for Layla to provide feedback about this plan and make other suggestions that she believes would be helpful.

You may continue to feel guilty or embarrassed even after you repair the situation. These feelings are imperfections you may have to yield to, reminding yourself that you have already righted this wrong and have committed to not making this misstep again. Also, just because you apologize and take responsibility does not mean Layla must accept your apology. Recognize that this possibility is a part of the allyship process and not a reflection of your inherent "goodness" as an ally. With that said, an apology delivered in a thoughtful manner will likely go a long away, especially when paired with changed behavior.

# Case Study 4: Basketball Courts in the Neighborhood

Imagine that you have bought your dream home in a wonderful, racially diverse neighborhood with an active homeowners association. After a few years in the neighborhood, you decide to run for a leadership position in the HOA. You have always wanted to be more involved, and after a surprisingly challenging election season, you win the seat to become the head of the HOA. Your first order of business in this new position is to review proposals filed by residents. The first proposal puts forth a mandate for there to be a 4 p.m. curfew for the basketball courts because residents "don't want kids walking around after dark" and "there have been way too many noise complaints." You notice that the signatures are all from White residents, whereas the basketball courts are most often used by Black youth in the neighborhood.

In a subsequent town hall meeting to discuss the proposed measure, several Black residents speak up strongly in opposition. They understandably express concern that no such measure has been proposed for other areas in the neighborhood (e.g., golf course, tennis courts, pool) and call out the racist undertones of the proposal given the racial demographics of the basketball court users. The Black residents share that if passed, this measure will undermine their sense of belonging and safety in the neighborhood. The White residents maintain that they, too, are simply concerned about their perceived safety. You feel conflicted—you want to make sure that the White residents feel heard, but you also want to support the Black residents and ensure you don't pass measures that are racially biased. Ultimately, you know you want to maintain harmony in the neighborhood, but you feel torn about your priorities. You also fear rocking the boat and are unsure if you have what it takes to hold your position if the White residents push back. You feel confused about what to do and what it even means to be an ally in this context.

What is the anti-racist thing to do?

_____

_____

_____

_____

_____

What barriers might get in the way of your ability to do the anti-racist thing?

_____

_____

_____

_____

_____

What *Beyond Fragility* skills would help you overcome these barriers?

_____

_____

_____

_____

_____

What would be an effective starting point?

_____

_____

_____

_____

_____

What imperfections might you need to yield to?

_____

_____

_____

_____

_____

# Case Study 4 Recommended Answers

1.  Based on this scenario, the anti-racist thing to do is to block the measure and support the Black residents.

2.  The following barriers might get in the way of your ability to do the anti-racist thing:
    - Cognitive barriers: You aren't sure what values are most important to you in this scenario.
    - Interpersonal barriers: You are unsure how to communicate your support for the position put forth by Black residents.
    - Other barriers: You notice that you feel some confusion about what it even means to be an ally, and you question whether you have the stamina to persist if the White residents push back.

3.  The following *Beyond Fragility* skills would help you overcome these barriers:
    - MIRROR to clarify your values
    - SUPPORT to communicate verbal support and validation for the BIPOC residents
    - DEAR ALLY to remind yourself of the traits of an effective anti-racist ally as well as to build your stamina as an ally

4.  DEAR ALLY will be an effective starting point to boost your clarity and stamina to persist in allyship.

5.  You might need to yield to the following imperfections:
    - The White residents may feel invalidated.
    - You may need to let go of any self-judgment that may arise during the MIRROR exercise.

# Putting It All Together for Case Study 4

The anti-racist thing to do is to block the measure and support the Black residents. In anti-racism work, all requests are not created equal. In other words, any action that seeks to dismantle or prevent racism from occurring should be emphatically prioritized over actions that could introduce or maintain racism. As you pinpoint the barriers that are most salient in this scenario, you realize there are several. First, there is a cognitive barrier—you aren't sure what values are most important to you. Second, there is an interpersonal barrier in that you know it's vital to support your Black residents, but you are unsure how to best do this. Third, you aren't 100 percent clear on what else it takes to be an ally in this situation, and you aren't sure you have what it takes to maintain your anti-racist position, especially if the White residents push back and accuse you of "taking sides."

To address these barriers, you pick out MIRROR, SUPPORT, and DEAR ALLY. You decide to first pump yourself up with affirmations from DEAR ALLY. You find that you are particularly drawn to the following affirmation: "I am dauntless in the face of resistance, and my consistent, courageous actions create change." This affirmation reminds you that anti-racist work requires meaningful advocacy and a sense of fearlessness and determination in the face of all forms of resistance. So even if your White residents *do* push back, you can imagine yourself meeting this resistance head-on with a fierce determination.

Once you are pumped up and ready to go, you decide to clarify your values with MIRROR. You understand that your values inform your decision-making when you are faced with dilemmas or opportunities; therefore, you take the time to get clear about which values you hold dear and the extent to which these values are congruent with anti-racism. As you go through the steps of MIRROR, you realize that you value maintaining harmony among residents and advocating for anti-racism. Although there are benefits to maintaining harmony, in this instance it may conflict with your anti-racism values if it means not blocking the measure. You rank these values and decide to prioritize advocating for anti-racism. Once you are clear that this value is most important to you at this moment, you can generate a supportive response to the Black residents from a genuine place.

As you move through the SUPPORT skill, you validate the Black residents' concern by saying, "I hear that you are concerned about this measure, particularly its racial undertone given that this mandate has only been proposed for the basketball courts and not other areas of the neighborhood. I also hear you saying that if passed, you would question if you were truly welcomed in this community. I understand how you would feel this way. There has been a long-standing history of Black youth having their normal actions interpreted as suspicious and inappropriately surveilled and policed. There is also a long-standing history of Black residents being racially profiled in their own neighborhoods. I just want to say I appreciate the courage it takes to share your concerns and perspectives, especially in a group forum. I am going to do everything in my power to block this measure because we must strive to create an equitable community. Is there any other action I can take to best support you right

232 · BEYOND FRAGILITY

now?" Such a response shows your concern because it reflects back what you heard the Black residents say, communicates that you understand the context of their concerns, and offers appreciation for their willingness to share their perspectives. It also tunes into their needs and does not challenge the validity of their concerns.

As is always the case with anti-racism work, you will have to yield to imperfections. In a perfect world, your values will always be compatible with each other and never be in conflict with anti-racism goals. Yet you'll need to let go of the desire for your values to always fit neatly together and let go of any self-judgment that emerges when you recognize that some of your values may conflict with anti-racism. Also in a perfect world, every White resident would support your position. However, it's more likely that you'll receive some pushback and be accused of taking sides, which may be particularly challenging to hear given your desire to maintain harmony. Yet trust that by using the APPLY skill and putting it all together, you did the best you could to align your actions with your anti-racism values.

## Case Study 5: Latinx Underrepresentation with the Organization

You recently began volunteering with a grassroots organization that provides pro bono legal services to people with limited socioeconomic resources in a densely populated city. Given that the organization relies on private donations, they must submit an annual impact report that summarizes their activities. In preparation for the impact report, an analyst in the company discovers that despite 55 percent of the legal service requests coming from Latinx community members, only 15 percent of clients served were Latinx individuals. In contrast, 60 percent of clients served were White individuals from rural communities. The organization's leaders share that they are alarmed by these disparities and express their utter confusion about what has been maintaining this racial inequity. Although they are embarrassed by the surprising findings, the organization decides to prioritize transparency and publishes the report in its entirety.

After the report comes out, community members speak out against the lack of representation of Latinx clients and the underwhelming effort exerted to identify the roots of the problem. After the story gets covered in the news, a local Latinx-owned firm tweets a link to the story, noting that they are disappointed. In subsequent tweets, the Latinx law firm also comments that "this is what happens when there are not enough BIPOC in executive leadership positions." Several staff members of the organization are alarmed by the response to the impact report. They also feel conflicted because while they are being called on to do anti-racism work, they are also being told that they are not equipped to do the work without outside consultation. Although this grassroots organization *wants* to take accountability, they have no idea where to start.

What is the anti-racist thing to do?

_____

_____

_____

_____

_____

What barriers might get in the way of the organization's ability to do the anti-racist thing?

_____

_____

_____

_____

_____

What *Beyond Fragility* skills would help the organization overcome these barriers?

_____

_____

_____

_____

_____

What would be an effective starting point?

_____

_____

_____

_____

_____

What imperfections might the organization need to yield to?

_____

_____

_____

_____

_____

## Case Study 5 Recommended Answers

1. You may note that up until now, this question has been presented with a focus on "what is the anti-racist thing to do" as an individual. However, in this final case we highlight that these skills are also applicable for troubleshooting barriers to anti-racist work at the organizational and institutional level. Therefore, in this case example, the anti-racist thing to do is for the organization to identify and tackle whatever processes and policies are maintaining racial inequity in the company.

2. The following barriers might get in the way of the organization's ability to do the anti-racist thing:
   - Interpersonal barriers: Based on the public's reaction to the report, members in the organization recognize that they need BIPOC support, but they aren't sure how to best ask for help.
   - Other barriers: The organization doesn't fully understand the multifaceted forces that contribute to and enable racism at the company, and they aren't sure how to determine whether their goal to fix the disparities is effective.

3.  The following *Beyond Fragility* skills would help the organization overcome these barriers:
    ◦  BASICS to identify the multifaceted elements that may be contributing to disparities in the company
    ◦  ACTION to create an effective anti-racism goal
    ◦  DEI CALCULATOR to determine how they should ask BIPOC for help

4.  Given that the organization does not even understand how such a major racial inequity occurred and has been maintained, it seems that BASICS would give the organization a great starting place.

5.  The organization might need to yield to the following imperfections:
    ◦  The organization is just starting to engage in a major DEI self-assessment, so things may not get done as quickly as the public wants.
    ◦  Conducting the BASICS skill to better understand racism within the organization might yield some uncomfortable truths that could be hard to face.

## Putting It All Together for Case Study 5

The pro bono law organization has identified a major racial inequity in that they underserved Latinx community members to an alarming degree. The anti-racist thing to do would be for the organization to identify and fix the problems so the disparities do not persist. In pinpointing the barriers, the organization recognizes that they don't fully understand how racism is operating within their organization or how the disparities even came to be. Even if they did have some information about potentially problematic processes in the organization, they have no clue what to do about them. They also suspect that in order to fix the barriers, they likely have to involve BIPOC consultants, but they don't want to overburden BIPOC with "cleaning up" the organization. They want to ask for help, but they don't want to use the request for help as a cop-out to keep them from doing the hard work of taking a cold hard look in the mirror.

To move past these barriers, the organization meets to discuss options for moving forward. They pick out BASICS, ACTION, and DEI CALCULATOR. They look for an effective place to start and decide it's in their best interest to get a full handle on the problem by using the BASICS skill to conduct a thorough DEI self-assessment. They start by asking themselves what background knowledge may be influencing these disparities. They do some research and discover that, in their town, most Latinx people live in areas that are far from the law office due to the legacies of redlining. Despite the fact that redlining is over "on paper," it still applies to the current geography of the town and influences access to the office for Latinx communities. They also note that prospective Latinx clients in their specific community deal with other systems of oppression, such as poverty and xenophobia, which may hinder their ability to access resources from the office. They next look at their data to determine if and how individual racism is being maintained in the company, and they discover that Spanish-sounding names receive fewer follow-up calls and that Latinx clients are more likely to be asked about documentation proof. Thus, implicit bias may be at play. Their assessment also uncovers cultural racism—for example, no materials are provided in languages other than English and the company does not automatically provide the option for a translator to prospective clients. They also discover that in terms of systemic racism, the company has a policy that all initial consultations must occur in person—an issue given their earlier discovery about Latinx individuals often living farther away from the office.

After completing the BASICS skill and learning more about how racism operates in their organization, they feel confident that they have done enough to now reach out for help. Thus, they create the following goal: "Hire an external consultant to help the organization make a change." Before implementing this goal, they put it through the ACTION test, which allows them to realize that this goal isn't concrete or impactful enough. With some tweaks, they revise their goal to be "Using a collaborative and non-exploitative approach, hire a long-term Latinx consultant to help revise the company's handbook to eliminate individual, cultural, and systemic racism within the organization." The goal became a mouthful, but it surely sounds more effective to us!

Given that part of the goal is to specifically utilize labor from BIPOC and that the organization wants to engage in this process collaboratively, they pull out the DEI CALCULATOR and start crunching the numbers. They realize that they only have 9 equity bucks, which puts them squarely in the yellow zone. This means they need to think very carefully and troubleshoot before making a request. They notice that although fair compensation is a high-ticket item on the calculator, they have $0 in this column because they do not typically have a budget for consultation, given that they rely on private donations. In response, the fundraising director begins applying for grants and talking with potential donors. After many failed attempts, the director is successful at obtaining the necessary funds to fairly compensate the external consultant.

They recalculate their balance and find they now have 11 equity bucks, which pushes them right into the green zone. The organization can now proceed with confidently making a request from a BIPOC consultant, while remembering that they must always take no for an answer. To maximize the effectiveness of their request and demonstrate their commitment to doing the work, they provide the consultant with the original impact report and the results of the BASICS skill. They also clearly lay out to the consultant all of the expectations and benefits of collaborating with them.

Throughout this process, there are several steps requiring the organization to yield to imperfection. First, after they used the BASICS skill to better understand racism within the organization, they uncovered some uncomfortable truths about the organization's institutional policies, which they needed to yield to in order to move on and ask for help. Second, the organization will need to continue yielding to imperfection on their collaborative journey with the consultant, especially if things do not change as quickly as the public (or the organization) prefers. They will need to remind themselves that they are taking their time to ensure that their commitment to anti-racism is impactful. They are overturning the bedrock of the organization and sowing seeds that will ideally promote long-term equity and, ultimately, align with their mission of serving their communities.

# Why Use the APPLY Skill?

Up until this point, you learned and practiced each skill by itself in relation to one specific barrier. However, in real-world scenarios, anti-racism situations are often complex, involving multiple barriers simultaneously. This complexity calls for the use of the APPLY skill in your anti-racist journey. Using this skill is critical because it can help you develop nuanced plans that align with the intricacies of the situation at hand. The APPLY skill is ideal for any anti-racism situation, regardless of its scale or the level at which racism is happening. Whether it involves rectifying a problematic email interaction at work or addressing systemic racism at an organizational level, the APPLY skill offers a versatile approach relevant across situations. It intentionally encourages the use of multiple *Beyond Fragility* skills so you can always keep going and try something else in the face of setbacks. This prevents you from getting stuck or overwhelmed when confronting situations that demand anti-racism action. Getting back up is so crucial because anti-racist work can be both rewarding and challenging. You might experience moments of pride that are juxtaposed with instances of wanting to quit. However, by using the APPLY skill, you will always be able to make a game plan that can drive meaningful anti-racist change.

## CHAPTER SUMMARY

In this final chapter, we started off by outlining why it can be hard to apply *Beyond Fragility* skills in the real world and explained the importance of expanding your metaphorical toolbelt. You know how each tool works, but now it's time to go out into the field and use the tools together with the APPLY skill. You can think of this skill as a way to guide your hand as it approaches your toolbelt, helping you ensure that you are pulling out the best tools to address the specific issue at hand and using those tools in the most effective way possible!

# CONCLUDING NOTE

• • • • •

As we noted at the start of this book, effective anti-racist allyship is not an innate essence, nor is it something you are born knowing how to do. Instead, moving from simply "not racist" to actively "anti-racist" requires a lot of skills—skills that up until now, you likely were not exposed to in your home, school, or workplace. Now, however, you know *what* you need to do and you know *how* to do it. In the words of Maya Angelou, "Do the best you can until you know better. Then when you know better, do better." We believe in you, and we hope that learning and practicing these skills helps you believe in yourself too. We look forward to the ways you will grow in your anti-racist allyship journey and, more importantly, we cannot wait to see the myriad of creative and impactful ways you dismantle White supremacy and promote racial equity in every space you occupy.

In solidarity,

Yara Mekawi, PhD

Natalie Watson-Singleton, PhD

Danyelle Dawson, MA

# APPENDIX

· · · · ·

# SKILL SUMMARIES

# BASICS of Racism: Understanding and Recognizing Racism

## Background

- How were BIPOC historically treated in this particular context or setting?
- What do we know about the history of segregation and rights within this context?

## Application

- In what ways does this historical background inform the current situation?
- How are BIPOC currently treated in this particular context as a result of historical racism?

## Systems of Oppression

- How do other systems of oppression, such as ableism, classism, sexism, heterosexism, genderism, and weight-based discrimination, worsen experiences of racism for BIPOC in this context?

## Individual Racism

- How often does discrimination occur in our organization?
- What types of racial discrimination do our BIPOC members experience?

## Cultural Racism

- How does White supremacy culture implicitly or explicitly affect the way we run this organization and view members' behavior?
- What values do we prioritize?
- What worldviews influence our assumptions and organizational processes?

## Systemic Racism

- What procedures might intentionally or unintentionally lead to the marginalization of BIPOC in this space?
- Who holds positions of power?
- How does power sharing occur in ways that amplify BIPOC voices?

# DEAR ALLY: The Qualities of Effective Anti-Racist Allyship

## Dauntless

- I am dauntless in the face of resistance, and my consistent, courageous actions create change.

## Engaged

- I am an engaged anti-racist ally and I take intentional actions to disrupt White supremacy.

## Attentive

- I am attentive to the needs of BIPOC and use their guidance as my North Star for anti-racist work.

## Reflexive

- My reflexive attitude makes me open to learning and being challenged.

## Adaptable

- I am adaptable and can meet the changing demands of anti-racism work.

## Lasting

- I participate in lasting anti-racism efforts that range from small, everyday actions to large, big-picture actions.

## Liberatory

- When I release my grip on White supremacy and privilege, I allow for collective liberation to occur.

## Yearslong

- My anti-racist journey is yearslong and not confined to arbitrary dates and holidays.

# ACCEPT: Overcoming the Denial of Racism

### Address Sources of Denial

- Which of your worldviews conflict with the reality of racism?

### Check in with Reality

- What are you telling yourself about racism?
- What truths or realities may you be rejecting?

### Create Community

- Reach out to other White anti-racist allies who can help you process your problematic worldviews and missteps.

### Embrace Discomfort

- Make room for all of your emotions and thoughts, however difficult it may be to experience them.

### Practice Self-Accountability

- Take responsibility for your actions without excuses and figure out ways to change your problematic worldviews.

### Tap into Your Best Self

- Remind yourself of your motivations for engaging in anti-racist work—your positive intentions, values, and goals.

# AND: Going from Rigidity to Flexibility

## Approach the Conflicting Messages

- What are the conflicting messages?
- Where are these messages coming from?
- What are the pros and cons of taking each message to the extreme?

## Notice the Kernels of Truth

- At the heart of each of these ideas, what part is true?
- Which parts of these messages are the most important?

## Determine a Dialectical Path Forward

- Combine and resolve the parts of the messages that initially seemed like a dilemma.
- Add language that tempers the extremity of the messages.
- Sit through difficult emotions and let go of the need for definiteness.

# Looking in the MIRROR: Clarifying Your Values

## <u>M</u>ap Your Values

- How do you wish that your closest family members, friends, and colleagues would describe you?
- What qualities do you seek in a romantic partner or friend?
- Describe someone you admire.

## <u>I</u>nterrogate the Meaning of Your Values

- Why do you think these values matter?
- In what way might the world be different if everybody embodied these values?
- What does it mean to live out these values?
- What specific behaviors would you say are associated with these values?

## <u>R</u>ank Your Values by Importance

- Rank your top five values.

## <u>R</u>elate Your Values to Anti-Racism-Congruent Values

- To what degree are your values compatible with anti-racist values?

## <u>O</u>bserve Whether Your Values Are Incongruent with Anti-Racism

- Which of your top five values conflict with anti-racist values?
- In what ways are they incongruent?

## <u>R</u>eassess Your Commitment

- Assess how much overlap there is between the three sets of values: your personal values, anti-racist values, and values that are incongruent with anti-racism.
- What barriers might you need to overcome in order to align your behavior with anti-racist values?
- Are you open to readjusting your values or prioritization?
- Review the chapters and skills that address the types of barriers that are keeping you stuck.

# CLEAR: Moving Beyond Ambivalence

### Challenging Your Assumptions and Worldviews

- Is your ambivalence rooted in your attachment to assumptions and worldviews that perpetuate White supremacy?
- Are you feeling defensive about your own identity and self-worth?

### Losing Relationships

- Is your ambivalence related to fears that you will lose personal or professional relationships?
- What steps can you take to minimize the effects of retaliation and to build other relationships?

### Enduring Emotional Distress

- Is your ambivalence related to a desire to avoid emotional discomfort?
- Use distress tolerance skills to combat avoidance and manage emotional discomfort.

### Accepting Changes to the Status Quo

- Is your ambivalence fueled by a resistance to change the status quo?
- Do you fear losing your status and privilege?
- Do you fully acknowledge the degree to which the status quo harms BIPOC and reinforces White supremacy?

### Resolving Internal Conflicts

- What internal conflicts do you need to resolve to feel ready and able to challenge your assumptions, potentially lose relationships and opportunities, endure emotional distress, and challenge the status quo—all to ensure equity and justice for all?
- Do you know what your values are and which values are most salient in this situation?
- Are you willing to act *in spite of* these conflicts in order to persist in anti-racist action?

# DETECT Your Emotions: Noticing and Labeling Your Emotions

## <u>D</u>escribe the Precipitating Event

- Identify the event that prompted this emotion (e.g., something that happened in your environment, something you thought about).

## <u>E</u>xamine Bodily Sensations

- Notice your current physical sensations and consider which emotions may be causing them.

## <u>T</u>une into Your Thoughts

- Notice the thoughts that are going through your mind and consider which emotions may be connected to them (whether as a cause or an effect).
- Notice whether you are having thoughts related to your experience as a White person.

## <u>E</u>xplore Behavioral Urges

- Notice any physical or verbal actions you feel an urge to take and consider which emotions may be causing them.
- Consider whether your behavioral urges are related to your experiences as a White person.

## <u>C</u>onsult the Feelings Wheel

- Identify the core emotion you are feeling, then move to the outer rings of the wheel to see if a more specific emotion better describes your current experience.
- Also label any secondary emotions that you are experiencing.

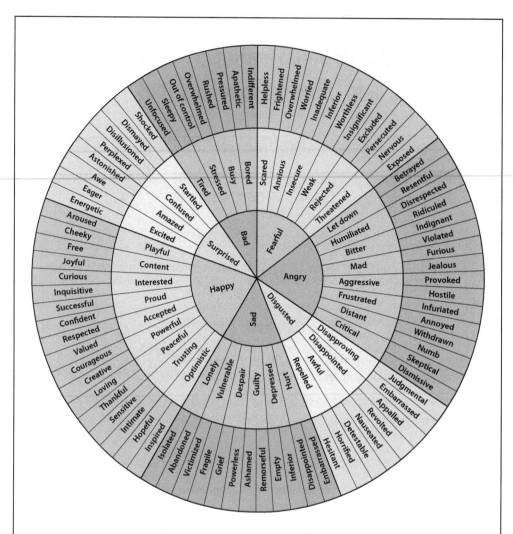

## <u>T</u>ie Your Emotional Experience to Your Racialized Identity

- Are you having this emotion as a result of your racialized identity as a White person?

- Is this emotion the result of a personal situation unique to you, a situation that made you aware of your White identity, or both?

- Does this emotion motivate you to protect your racial group or to prioritize the wants and needs of BIPOC?

# FEEL: Tolerating Unpleasant Emotions

## Find Your Center

- Find a quiet space with no distractions.
- Turn your attention toward the place in your body where you feel your physical and energetic strength comes from.
- Observe the feeling of being centered and at peace.
- Connect to your inner goodness and selfless desire to bring justice to the world.

## Embody Nonjudgment

- Reframe any evaluative thoughts you find yourself having about the emotion, yourself, or the world, replacing them with dialectical thinking and acceptance.
- Remind yourself, "The emotion cannot hurt me. The emotion is what it is. It is neither good nor bad."

## Embrace Difficult Emotions as a Human Experience

- Sit with the difficult emotion, observing it with compassion and without judgment.
- You can also sit with the urge to change the emotion until you are ready to sit with the emotion itself.

## Let Your Senses Ground You

- Notice what you perceive through any or all of your senses (sight, hearing, touch, smell, and taste) to help you feel more centered and present in the current moment.

# Checking the FACTS: A Solution to Cognitive Distortions

### <u>F</u>igure Out the Emotion

- What emotion am I feeling? (Use the DETECT skill as needed.)

### <u>A</u>cknowledge the Stories You Are Telling Yourself

- What do I believe just happened?
- What do I think are the implications, in terms of how I am perceived, of what just happened?

### <u>C</u>heck for Cognitive Distortions or Racist Worldviews

- Are the stories I am telling myself true?
- What is the evidence for and against these stories?
- Are they rooted in any racist worldviews?
- Do my emotions fit the facts (skip to "S"), or are they cognitive distortions (continue to "T")?

### <u>T</u>ackle the Distortions or Racist Worldviews

- Challenge racist worldviews using ACCEPT, DETECT, FEEL, and AND.
- Fact-check cognitive distortions.
- Replace inaccurate, unhelpful thoughts with dialectical thinking that is realistic, compassionate, and supportive of your growth.

### <u>S</u>elect an Appropriate Path Forward

- Use what you have learned to take the most effective step forward.
- This may involve changing unhelpful behaviors, rectifying harm you have caused, using distress tolerance skills to manage overwhelming emotions, and so on.

# OPPOSE Behavioral Avoidance: Engaging in Effective Anti-Racism Action

## <u>O</u>bserve the Urge to Engage in Behavioral Avoidance

- Notice the urge as it arises, without judgment and without acting on it.

## <u>P</u>inpoint the Emotion You Are Trying to Avoid

- Identify the emotion you are trying to avoid or disengage from (using the DETECT skill).

## <u>P</u>ause to Consider the Consequences of Your Behavioral Avoidance

- Determine whether following this avoidance urge would be beneficial or detrimental to the goal of undoing racism.

## <u>O</u>rganize a List of Effective Actions

- Identify all of the possible opposite actions you could take that would be consistent with your values.

## <u>S</u>elect the Most Effective Action

- Determine which opposite action would be the most effective and feasible.

## <u>E</u>nact a Specific Plan to Implement the Effective Action

- Make a concrete plan to engage in the action you've selected—and follow through!

# The REPAIR Process: Managing the Aftermath of a Racist Misstep

## <u>R</u>ecognize What Caused the Misstep

- Identify the type of racial misstep you made and the factors that contributed to it (e.g., your feelings, a lack of knowledge, skills you need to improve).

## <u>E</u>valuate Your Emotional Reactions

- Label your feelings, sit with them, and consider whether they fit the facts of the situation (using the DETECT, FEEL, and FACTS skills).

## <u>P</u>ay Attention to Your Motives

- Ask yourself, "What is driving my desire to repair?"
- If you are motivated by a sense of obligation or worries about negative consequences, use other skills (such as ACCEPT or CLEAR) to overcome your resistance to making a genuine apology.

## <u>A</u>pologize in a Way That Takes Responsibility

- When apologizing, clearly state what the misstep was and *why* it was a misstep.
- Do not sugarcoat or minimize the impact of your actions.

## <u>I</u>nvite Feedback, Not Forgiveness

- Do *not* ask for forgiveness, which would center you and put pressure on the person you harmed.
- Do consider asking for feedback about whether you have correctly understood the issue.
- You can also ask the person you have harmed whether there are specific actions they would like you to take, beyond the reparative actions you have already identified for yourself.

## <u>R</u>esolve to Change Your Behavior

- Create a plan to change your behavior so that you can make repair and avoid similar missteps in the future. Then follow through!

# CALL OUT: Effectively Confronting Racism

### Clarify What Happened

- State the facts of the situation—the specific language or behaviors that were racist.
- Do *not* express your feelings, opinions, perspectives, or requests at this stage.

### Acknowledge Possible Intentions

- Explain that someone can have good intentions and still say or do something racist.
- Maintain focus on the impact, not the intention.

### Lay Out the Reasons It's Racist

- Provide concrete feedback on why the language or behavior was racist.
- Identify the underlying biases and prejudices that may have contributed to it.

### List Possible Solutions

- Propose clear, specific, behaviorally oriented actions the person could take to repair the harm they have caused and avoid future missteps.

### Observe Your Internal Reactions

- Pay attention to your own feelings and urges during this process to help yourself stay emotionally regulated and intentional in your responses.

### Use Humility

- Be direct and respectful; consider how *you* would want to be approached.
- Remind yourself—and perhaps share with the other person—that you have also made missteps and are continually learning and growing.

### Tolerate Resistance

- Expect resistance and remain clear, firm, and persistent.
- If the other person wants to argue, deflect, or stray off topic, repeat your request for change like a "broken record."
- If they remain unwilling to follow your request, disengage from the conversation.

# Offering SUPPORT: Providing Compassionate Verbal Responses to BIPOC

## Show Genuine Concern

- Show that you are listening and that you consider the person's experience to be meaningful by reflecting back what they say, subtly mirroring their body language, nodding, or similar behaviors.

## Understand the Context

- Educate yourself about historical and contemporary racism, and use the BASICS skill to recognize racism in specific situations.
- Express to the person you are listening to how their reaction makes sense given the situation.

## Process Your Own Internal Reactions

- Notice and manage your own emotional reactions using BASICS, ACCEPT, DETECT, FEEL, and OPPOSE.

## Prioritize the Experiences of BIPOC Over Your Own Experience

- Keep the focus on the other person and their experience with racism.
- Do *not* bring up your own experiences, marginalized identities, contributions as a White ally, or White guilt.

## Offer Appreciation

- Express your gratitude that this person has chosen to share their experience with you (especially given that you are a White person).
- You can also let them know that you will continue to make space for them in the future whenever they would like to share with you.

## Resist the Urge to Give Advice or Challenge Them

- Do *not* challenge or question a BIPOC's experience with racism.
- Do *not* give advice or start problem-solving if they have not asked you to do so.

# Tune into the Person's Needs

- Remember that each situation—and each person—is different.
- Ask the person how *they* would like you to support them in this moment (e.g., simply listen, give them space, help them problem solve, take a particular action).

# The DEI CALCULATOR: Prioritizing Equitable Collaboration with BIPOC

| DEI CALCULATOR Component | Question | Value | Your Equity Bucks |
|---|---|---|---|
| Demonstrated collaboration | As part of your request, will you communicate that this initiative will be collaborative and that you will provide support as needed? | $0.50 | |
| Equity | Is there an equitable power balance where you make it clear to the person that there will be no consequences if they decline your request? | $2.00 | |
| Interest | Has this person expressed interest in this kind of DEI or anti-racism work? | $1.00 | |
| Capability | Does this person have relevant DEI or anti-racism experience (i.e., you're not just asking because they are a BIPOC)? | $1.00 | |
| Appropriate | Is it the person's literal job (i.e., it's in their job or role description)? | $1.50 | |
| Limited | Is this a limited task, rather than a recurring one? | $0.50 | |
| Compensation | Is the person going to be fairly compensated (e.g., pay increase, adjustment in their usual workload to create time)? | $2.00 | |
| Useful | Is there some clear benefit to them for doing this work (e.g., networking opportunities, resume building)? | $1.50 | |
| Long-term goals | Is the endeavor meaningful and part of a long-term anti-racism goal? | $1.50 | |
| Authority | Will their position in this initiative give them the power or authority to contribute to change? | $1.00 | |
| Timing | Is this a good time to ask (e.g., not after a major incident has happened)? Does the person have enough time to consider your request? | $0.50 | |
| Other resources | Have you checked for other related efforts and resources to avoid redundant work and to not overburden this specific person? | $1.00 | |
| Relationship | Is your request appropriate for this relationship (i.e., is it a reasonably close, positive, reciprocal relationship)? | $1.00 | |
| | **Total Equity Bucks:** | | |

### Less Than $5: Don't Ask! (The Red Zone)

You absolutely should *not* make this request for collaboration. There is a high potential to cause harm due to the inequities inherent in your request. However, all is not lost! Review the areas where you had a score of $0, especially those that have a higher potential equity value. What can be done to change those areas so you can move into the yellow or green zone? If you are not able to do so, you'll have to either change your request or find other White folks who might be able to contribute.

### $5 to $10: Proceed with Caution (The Yellow Zone)

You need to think very carefully and troubleshoot (as described in the red zone) to see if you can move your total to the green zone. Then decide whether it feels fair to make the request. If you choose to proceed, ask tentatively. You may even acknowledge the ways in which the request is flawed. Additionally, if the person agrees, keep the equitable collaboration strategies in mind so as to avoid exploitation and harm. If the person does not agree, continue to problem solve so that you can get to the green zone.

### More Than $10: Ask with Some Confidence (The Green Zone)

Congratulations! You have thoughtfully considered and taken meaningful steps to ensure equity and to minimize harm to your BIPOC collaborator. We encourage you to make your request confidently while also knowing that it will always be important for you to take no for an answer. To maximize the effectiveness of your request, provide as much information as possible and clearly lay out all of the expectations and benefits. If the person agrees, use all of your *Beyond Fragility* skills to make sure it's as smooth and impactful of a collaboration as possible.

# Ready, Set, ACTION: Evaluating Your Anti-Racism Goals

## <u>A</u>nti-Racist

- Does my goal *explicitly* seek to dismantle racism?

## <u>C</u>oncrete

- Is my goal specific and action-oriented versus vague and aspirational?

## <u>T</u>houghtful

- Is my goal thoughtful in prioritizing BIPOC over my own self-interest?

## <u>I</u>mpactful

- Will achieving this anti-racism goal lead to measurable change?

## <u>O</u>btainable

- Is this goal obtainable (i.e., realistic and within my control)?

## <u>N</u>ecessary

- Is this goal something that's necessary for progress toward a long-term commitment to change?

# APPLYing Your Anti-Racism Skills: Knowing How to Put It All Together

## Assess the Anti-Racist Thing to Do

- What action would oppose racial inequality at this moment?
- What action would challenge structures of power and privilege that maintain racism at this moment?
- What action would affirm multicultural diversity at this moment?

## Pinpoint the Barriers That Might Get in the Way

- Which of the common barriers to anti-racist allyship might be arising in this scenario?
- Which of the barriers tend to come up for you specifically?

## Pick Out the Appropriate Beyond Fragility Skills

- Which skills will help you to address the barriers you're facing?

## Look for an Effective Starting Point

- Which step are you willing to take first, and which skill is best suited to help you take that first step?
- Which skill feels the most motivating or practical for you to use first?

## Yield to Imperfection

- Accept that perfection is unattainable (and that you cannot always change other people).
- Reframe your missteps, mistakes, and imperfections as areas for continued growth and offer yourself patience for these growing pains.

# REFERENCES

Accapadi, M. M. (2007). When White women cry: How White women's tears oppress women of color. *The College Student Affairs Journal, 26*(2), 208–215.

Allport, G. W. (1954). *The nature of prejudice.* Longman Higher Education.

Anderson, C. (2016). *White rage: The unspoken truth of our racial divide.* Bloomsbury Publishing USA.

Anderson, J. R., Conrad, F. G., & Corbett, A. T. (1989). Skill acquisition and the LISP tutor. *Cognitive Science, 13*(4), 467–505. https://doi.org/10.1207/s15516709cog1304_1

Baker-Bell, A. (2020). *Linguistic justice: Black language, literacy, identity, and pedagogy.* Routledge.

Beck, A. T. (1967). *Depression: Clinical, experimental, and theoretical aspects.* Harper and Row.

Bezrukova, K., Spell, C. S., Perry, J. L., & Jehn, K. A. (2016). A meta-analytical integration of over 40 years of research on diversity training evaluation. *Psychological Bulletin, 142*(11), 1227–1274. https://doi.org/10.1037/bul0000067

Blanchard, F. A., Crandall, C. S., Brigham, J. C., & Vaughn, L. A. (1994). Condemning and condoning racism: A social context approach to interracial settings. *Journal of Applied Psychology, 79*(6), 993–997. https://doi.org/10.1037/0021-9010.79.6.993

Blitz, L. V., & Kohl, B. G. (2012). Addressing racism in the organization: The role of White racial affinity groups in creating change. *Administration in Social Work, 36*(5), 479–498. https://doi.org/10.1080/03643107.2011.624261

Blum, L. A. (1992). *Antiracism, multiculturalism, and interracial community: Three educational values for a multicultural society* [Lecture]. Distinguished Lecture Series, 1991–1992, Office of Graduate Studies and Research, University of Massachusetts at Boston.

Bryant, T., & Arrington, E.G. (2022). *The antiracism handbook: Practical tools to shift your mindset and uproot racism in your life and community.* New Harbinger Publications.

Bryant-Davis, T., & Ocampo, C. (2006). A therapeutic approach to the treatment of racist-incident-based trauma. *Journal of Emotional Abuse, 6*(4), 1–22. https://doi.org/10.1300/J135v06n04_01

Burns, D. D. (1980). *Feeling good: The new mood therapy.* William Morrow.

Cascio, C. N., O'Donnell, M. B., Tinney, F. J., Lieberman, M. D., Taylor, S. E., Strecher, V. J., & Falk, E. B. (2016). Self-affirmation activates brain systems associated with self-related processing and reward and is reinforced by future orientation. *Social Cognitive and Affective Neuroscience, 11*(4), 621–629. https://doi.org/10.1093/scan/nsv136

Chapman-Hilliard, C., & Adams-Bass, V. (2016). A conceptual framework for utilizing Black history knowledge as a path to psychological liberation for Black youth. *Journal of Black Psychology*, *42*(6), 479–507. https://doi.org/10.1177/0095798415597840

The Combahee River Collective. (1978). *The Combahee River Collective statement.* https://americanstudies.yale.edu/sites/default/files/files/Keyword%20Coalition_Readings.pdf

Crenshaw, K. W. (2017). *On intersectionality: Essential writings.* The New Press.

Czopp, A. M., & Monteith, M. J. (2003). Confronting prejudice (literally): Reactions to confrontations of racial and gender bias. *Personality and Social Psychology Bulletin*, *29*(4), 532–544. https://doi.org/10.1177/0146167202250923

Desmond, M., & Emirbayer, M. (2009). What is racial domination? *Du Bois Review: Social Science Research on Race*, *6*(2), 335–355. https://doi.org/10.1017/S1742058X09990166

DiAngelo, R. (2018). *White fragility: Why it's so hard for White people to talk about racism.* Beacon Press.

Doan, J. M., & Kennedy, R. B. (2022). Diversity fatigue: Acknowledging and moving beyond repetitious emotional labor. In A. Brissett & D. Moronta (Eds.), *Practicing Social Justice in Libraries* (pp. 145–153). Routledge.

Erskine, S. E., & Bilimoria, D. (2019). White allyship of Afro-Diasporic women in the workplace: A transformative strategy for organizational change. *Journal of Leadership & Organizational Studies*, *26*(3), 319–338. https://doi.org/10.1177/1548051819848993

Fischer, R., & Boer, D. (2016). Values: The dynamic nexus between biology, ecology and culture. *Current Opinion in Psychology*, *8*, 155–160. https://doi.org/10.1016/j.copsyc.2015.12.009

Fischer, R., & Smith, P. B. (2006). Who cares about justice? The moderating effect of values on the link between organisational justice and work behaviour. *Applied Psychology*, *55*(4), 541–562. https://doi.org/10.1111/j.1464-0597.2006.00243.x

Ford, B. Q., Green, D. J., & Gross, J. J. (2022). White fragility: An emotion regulation perspective. *American Psychologist*, *77*(4), 510–524. http://dx.doi.org/10.1037/amp0000968

Frankenberg, R. (1993). *White women, race matters: The social construction of Whiteness.* University of Minnesota Press.

Frantz, C. M., & Bennigson, C. (2005). Better late than early: The influence of timing on apology effectiveness. *Journal of Experimental Social Psychology*, *41*(2), 201–207. https://doi.org/10.1016/j.jesp.2004.07.007

Gelfand, M. J., Raver, J. L., Nishii, L., Leslie, L. M., Lun, J., Lim, B. C., Duan, L., Almaliach, A., Ang, S., Arnadottir, J., Aycan, Z., Boehnke, K., Boski, P., Cabecinhas, R., Chan, D., Chhokar, J., D'Amato, A., Subirats, M., Fischlmayr, I. C., … Yamaguchi, S. (2011). Differences between tight and loose cultures: A 33-nation study. *Science*, *332*(6033), 1100–1104. http://dx.doi.org/10.1126/science.1197754

Goff, P. A., Jackson, M. C., Nichols, A. H., & Di Leone, B. A. L. (2013). Anything but race: Avoiding racial discourse to avoid hurting you or me. *Psychology*, *4*(3A), 335–339. https://doi.org/10.4236/psych.2013.43A048

Goldenberg, A., Garcia, D., Halperin, E., & Gross, J. J. (2020). Collective emotions. *Current Directions in Psychological Science, 29*(2), 154–160. https://doi.org/10.1177/0963721420901574

Gu, R., Yang, J., Yang, Z., Huang, Z., Wu, M., & Cai, H. (2019). Self-affirmation enhances the processing of uncertainty: An event-related potential study.

*Cognitive, Affective, & Behavioral Neuroscience, 19,* 327–337. https://doi.org/10.3758/s13415-018-00673-0

Haeny, A. M., Holmes, S. C., & Williams, M. T. (2021). The need for shared nomenclature on racism and related terminology in psychology. *Perspectives on Psychological Science, 16*(5), 886–892. https://doi.org/10.1177/17456916211000760

Hamed, S., Bradby, H., Ahlberg, B. M., & Thapar-Björkert, S. (2022). Racism in healthcare: A scoping review. *BMC Public Health 22,* Article 988. https://doi.org/10.1186/s12889-022-13122-y

Han, S. (2018). Neurocognitive basis of racial ingroup bias in empathy. *Trends in Cognitive Sciences, 22*(5), 400–421. https://doi.org/10.1016/j.tics.2018.02.013

Hayes, S. C., Wilson, K. G., Gifford, E. V., Follette, V. M., & Strosahl, K. (1996). Experimental avoidance and behavioral disorders: A functional dimensional approach to diagnosis and treatment. *Journal of Consulting and Clinical Psychology, 64*(6), 1152–1168. https://doi.org/10.1037//0022-006x.64.6.1152

Hayes-Skelton, S. A., & Eustis, E. H. (2020). Experiential avoidance. In J. S. Abramowitz & S. M. Blakey (Eds.), *Clinical handbook of fear and anxiety: Maintenance processes and treatment mechanisms* (pp. 115–131). American Psychological Association. https://doi.org/10.1037/0000150-007

Helms, J. E. (2017). The challenge of making Whiteness visible: Reactions to four Whiteness articles. *The Counseling Psychologist, 45*(5), 717–726. https://doi.org/10.1177/0011000017718943

Ho, A. K., Sidanius, J., Pratto, F., Levin, S., Thomsen, L., Kteily, N., & Sheehy-Skeffington, J. (2012). Social dominance orientation: Revisiting the structure and function of a variable predicting social and political attitudes. *Personality and Social Psychology Bulletin, 38,* 583–606. https://doi.org/10.1177/0146167211432765

Hochman, A. L., & Suyemoto, K. L. (2020). Evaluating and dismantling an intervention aimed at increasing White people's knowledge and understanding of racial justice issues. *American Journal of Orthopsychiatry, 90*(6), 733–750. https://doi.org/10.1037/ort0000506

Howell, J. L., Collisson, B., Crysel, L., Garrido, C. O., Newell, S. M., Cottrell, C. A., Smith, C. T., & Shepperd, J. A. (2013). Managing the threat of impending implicit attitude feedback. *Social Psychological and Personality Science, 4*(6), 714–720. https://doi.org/10.1177/1948550613479803

Jones, J., & Mosher, W. D. (2013, December 20). *Fathers' involvement with their children: United States, 2006–2010.* (National Health Statistics Report No. 71). U.S. Department of Health and Human Services, Centers for Disease Control and Prevention, National Center for Health Statistics. https://www.cdc.gov/nchs/data/nhsr/nhsr071.pdf

Jost, J. T., & Thompson, E. P. (2000). Group-based dominance and opposition to equality as independent predictors of self-esteem, ethnocentrism, and social policy attitudes among African Americans and European Americans. *Journal of Experimental Social Psychology, 36*(3), 209–232. https://doi.org/10.1006/jesp.1999.1403

Kaiser, C. R., & Miller, C. T. (2003). Derogating the victim: The interpersonal consequences of blaming events on discrimination. *Group Processes & Intergroup Relations, 6*(3), 227–237. https://doi.org/10.1177/13684302030063001

Kutlaca, M., & Radke, H. R. M. (2023). Towards an understanding of performative allyship: Definition, antecedents and consequences. *Social and Personality Psychology Compass, 17*(2), Article e12724. https://doi.org/10.1111/spc3.12724

Levine-Rasky, C. (2000). The practice of Whiteness among teacher candidates. *International Studies in Sociology of Education, 10*(3), 263–284. https://doi.org/10.1080/09620210000200060

Lewan, T., & Barclay, D. (2001, December 2). When they steal your land, they steal your future. *Los Angeles Times.* https://www.latimes.com/archives/la-xpm-2001-dec-02-mn-10514-story.html

Lewicki, R. J., Polin, B., & Lount, R. B. (2016). An exploration of the structure of effective apologies. *Negotiation and Conflict Management Research, 9*(2), 177–196. https://doi.org/10.1111/ncmr.12073

Lewis, J. A., & Neville, H. A. (2015). Construction and initial validation of the Gendered Racial Microaggressions Scale for Black women. *Journal of Counseling Psychology, 62*(2), 289–302. https://doi.org/10.1037/cou0000062

Locke, E. A., & Latham, G. P. (2002). Building a practically useful theory of goal setting and task motivation: A 35-year odyssey. *American Psychologist, 57*(9), 705–717. https://doi.org/10.1037/0003-066X.57.9.705

Mackie, D. M., Maitner, A. T., & Smith, E. R. (2016). Intergroup emotions theory. In T. D. Nelson (Ed.), *Handbook of prejudice, stereotyping, and discrimination* (2nd ed., pp. 149–174). Psychology Press.

Mai, T., & Whitlock, J. (2022, November 28). *How to respond with compassion when someone is hurt by racism.* Accelerate Learning Community, University of Utah Health. https://accelerate.uofuhealth.utah.edu/equity/how-to-respond-with-compassion-when-someone-is-hurt-by-racism

Maio, G. R., & Haddock, G., & (2004). Theories of attitude. Creating a witches' brew. In G. Haddock & G. R. Maio (Eds.), *Contemporary perspectives on the psychology of attitudes* (pp. 425–453). Psychology Press.

Malott, K. M., Schaefle, S., Paone, T. R., Cates, J., & Haizlip, B. (2019). Challenges and coping mechanisms of Whites committed to antiracism. *Journal of Counseling & Development, 97*(1), 86–97. https://doi.org/10.1002/jcad.12238

Marshburn, C. K., & Knowles, E. D. (2018). White out of mind: Identity suppression as a coping strategy among Whites anticipating racially charged interactions. *Group Processes & Intergroup Relations, 21*(6), 874–892. https://doi.org/10.1177/1368430216681178

Mekawi, Y., Bresin, K., & Hunter, C. D. (2017). Who is more likely to "not see race"? Individual differences in racial colorblindness. *Race and Social Problems, 9*(3), 207–217. https://doi.org/10.1007/s12552-017-9211-3

Mekawi, Y., Todd, N. R., Yi, J., & Blevins, E. J. (2020). Distinguishing "I don't see color" from "Racism is a thing of the past": Psychological correlates of avoiding race and denying racism. *Journal of Counseling Psychology, 67*(3), 288–302. https://doi.org/10.1037/cou0000427

McIntosh, K., Moss, E., Nunn, R., & Shambaugh, J. (2020, February 27). *Examining the Black-White wealth gap.* The Brookings Institute. https://www.brookings.edu/blog/up-front/2020/02/27/examining-the-black-white-wealth-gap/

McIntosh, P. (2020). White privilege and male privilege: A personal account of coming to see correspondences through work in women's studies. In P. McIntosh (Ed.), *On privilege, fraudulence, and teaching as learning: Selected essays 1981–2019* (pp. 17–28). Routledge.

Mu, F., & Bobocel, D. R. (2019). Why did I say sorry? Apology motives and transgressor perceptions of reconciliation. *Journal of Organizational Behavior, 40*(8), 912–930. https://doi.org/10.1002/job.2376

Nadal, K. L. (2023). *Dismantling everyday discrimination: Microaggressions toward LGBTQ people.* American Psychological Association.

Nelson, J. K., Dunn, K. M., & Paradies, Y. (2011). Bystander anti-racism: A review of the literature. *Analyses of Social Issues and Public Policy, 11*(1), 263–284. https://doi.org/10.1111/j.1530-2415.2011.01274.x

Neville, H. A., Awad, G. H., Brooks, J. E., Flores, M. P., & Bluemel, J. (2013). Color-blind racial ideology: Theory, training, and measurement implications in psychology. *American Psychologist, 68*(6), 455–466. https://doi.org/10.1037/a0033282

Nunes, J. C., & Ordanini, A. (2014). I like the way it sounds: The influence of instrumentation on a pop song's place in the charts. *Musicae Scientiae, 18*(4), 392–409. https://doi.org/10.1177/1029864914548528

Oluo, I. (2019, March 28). Confronting racism is not about the needs and feelings of White people. *The Guardian.* https://www.theguardian.com/commentisfree/2019/mar/28/confronting-racism-is-not-about-the-needs-and-feelings-of-white-people

Paluck, E. L. (2011). Peer pressure against prejudice: A high school field experiment examining social network change. *Journal of Experimental Social Psychology, 47*(2), 350–358. https://doi.org/10.1016/j.jesp.2010.11.017

Patallo, B. J. (2019). The multicultural guidelines in practice: Cultural humility in clinical training and supervision. *Training and Education in Professional Psychology, 13*(3), 227–232. https://doi.org/10.1037/tep0000253

Picower, B. (2009). The unexamined Whiteness of teaching: How White teachers maintain and enact dominant racial ideologies. *Race Ethnicity and Education, 12*(2), 197–215. https://doi.org/10.1080/13613320902995475

Pratto, F., Sidanius, J., Stallworth, L. M., & Malle, B. F. (1994). Social dominance orientation: A personality variable predicting social and political attitudes. *Journal of Personality and Social Psychology, 67*(4), 741–763. https://doi.org/10.1037/0022-3514.67.4.741

Reichelmann, A. V., & Hunt, M. O. (2022). White Americans' attitudes toward reparations for slavery: Definitions and determinants. *Race and Social Problems, 14*, 269–281. https://doi.org/10.1007/s12552-021-09348-x

Rosette, A. S., Leonardelli, G. J., & Phillips, K. W. (2008). The White standard: Racial bias in leader categorization. *Journal of Applied Psychology, 93*(4), 758–777. https://doi.org/10.1037/0021-9010.93.4.758

Saad, L. F. (2020). *Me and White supremacy: How to recognise your privilege, combat racism and change the world.* Quercus.

Sampson, D., & Garrison-Wade, D. F. (2011). Cultural vibrancy: Exploring the preferences of African American children toward culturally relevant and non-culturally relevant lessons. *The Urban Review, 43*(2), 279–309. https://doi.org/10.1007/s11256-010-0170-x

Schwartz, S. H. (1992). Universals in the content and structure of values: Theoretical advances and empirical tests in 20 countries. *Advances in Experimental Social Psychology 25*, 1–65.

Schwartz, S. H. (2012). An overview of the Schwartz theory of basic values. *Online Readings in Psychology and Culture, 2*(1). https://doi.org/10.9707/2307-0919.1116

Schwartz, S. H., Caprara, G. V., & Vecchione, M. (2010). Basic personal values, core political values, and voting: A longitudinal analysis. *Political Psychology, 31*(3), 421–452. https://doi.org/10.1111/j.1467-9221.2010.00764.x

Spanierman, L. B., & Smith, L. (2017). Roles and responsibilities of White allies: Implications for research, teaching, and practice. *The Counseling Psychologist, 45*(5), 606–617. https://doi.org/10.1177/0011000017717712

Sue, D. W. (2015). *Race talk and the conspiracy of silence: Understanding and facilitating difficult dialogues on race.* Wiley.

Sue, D. W. (2017). The challenges of becoming a White ally. *The Counseling Psychologist, 45*(5), 706–716. https://doi.org/10.1177/0011000017719323

Sue, D. W., Capodilupo, C. M., Torino, G. C., Bucceri, J. M., Holder, A. M. B., Nadal, K. L., & Esquilin, M. (2007). Racial microaggressions in everyday life: Implications for clinical practice. *American Psychologist, 62*(4), 271–286. https://doi.org/10.1037/0003-066X.62.4.271

Tajfel, H. (1974). Social identity and intergroup behaviour. *Trends and Developments, 13*(2), 65–93. https://doi.org/10.1177/053901847401300204

Tesler, M. (2020, August 19). Support for Black Lives Matter surged during protests, but is waning among White Americans. *FiveThirtyEight*. https://fivethirtyeight.com/features/support-for-black-lives-matter-surged-during-protests-but-is-waning-among-white-americans/

Todd, N. R., & Abrams, E. M. (2011). White dialectics: A new framework for theory, research, and practice with White students. *The Counseling Psychologist, 39*(3), 353–395. https://doi.org/10.1177/0011000010377665

Trawalter, S., Hoffman, K. M., & Waytz, A. (2016). Racial bias in perceptions of others' pain. *PLOS ONE, 11*(3), Article e0152334. https://doi.org/10.1371/journal.pone.0152334

Van Dijk, D., Seger-Guttmann, T., & Heller, D. (2013). Life-threatening event reduces subjective well-being through activating avoidance motivation: A longitudinal study. *Emotion, 13*(2), 216–225. https://doi.org/10.1037/a0029973

van Harreveld, F., Nohlen, H. U., & Schneider, I. K. (2015). The ABC of ambivalence: Affective, behavioral, and cognitive consequences of attitudinal conflict. *Advances in Experimental Social Psychology, 52*, 285–324. https://doi.org/10.1016/bs.aesp.2015.01.002

van Harreveld, F., van der Pligt, J., & de Liver, Y. N. (2009). The agony of ambivalence and ways to resolve it: Introducing the MAID model. *Personality and Social Psychology Review, 13*(1), 45–61. https://doi.org/10.1177/1088868308324518

Verkuyten, M., Adelman, L., & Yogeeswaran, K. (2020). The psychology of intolerance: Unpacking diverse understandings of intolerance. *Current Directions in Psychological Science, 29*(5), 467–472. https://doi.org/10.1177/0963721420924763

Watanabe, S., & Laurent, S. M. (2021). Volition speaks louder than action: Offender atonement, forgivability, and victim valuation in the minds of perceivers. *Personality and Social Psychology Bulletin, 47*(6), 1020–1036. https://doi.org/10.1177/0146167220953996

Williams, M. T., Faber, S., Nepton, A., & Ching, T. H. W. (2023). Racial justice allyship requires civil courage: A behavioral prescription for moral growth and change. *American Psychologist, 78*(1), 1–19. https://psycnet.apa.org/doi/10.1037/amp0000940

Womick, J., Rothmund, T., Azevedo, F., King, L. A., & Jost, J. T. (2019). Group-based dominance and authoritarian aggression predict support for Donald Trump in the 2016 U.S. presidential election. *Social Psychological and Personality Science, 10*(5), 643–652. https://doi.org/10.1177/1948550618778290

Yi, J., Neville, H. A., Todd, N. R., & Mekawi, Y. (2022). Ignoring race and denying racism: A meta-analysis of the associations between colorblind racial ideology, anti-Blackness, and other variables antithetical to racial justice. *Journal of Counseling Psychology*. Advance online publication. https://doi.org/10.1037/cou0000618

# ABOUT THE AUTHORS

**Yara Mekawi, PhD,** is a licensed psychologist, co-founder of the DEAR Project, and assistant professor at the University of Louisville. She earned her bachelor's degree in applied psychology at the University of Illinois Chicago and her PhD in clinical-community psychology at the University of Illinois Urbana-Champaign. Her work focuses on understanding how racism is maintained and how it affects the mental health of BIPOC. Dr. Mekawi has published over 50 empirical research papers on topics like dehumanization, denial of racism, and racial microaggressions. Dr. Mekawi's clinical work emphasizes culturally informed assessment, contextually driven hypothesis generation, collaborative goal setting, and implementation of evidence-based, culturally informed intervention. Administratively, Dr. Mekawi is interested in the assessment and integration of anti-racism and social justice oriented practices within organizations and the implementation of interventions designed to effectively dismantle White supremacy at individual, cultural, and systemic levels.

**Natalie Watson-Singleton, PhD,** is a licensed clinical psychologist, co-founder of the DEAR Project, and associate professor at Spelman College in Atlanta, Georgia. She received her PhD in clinical-community psychology at the University of Illinois Urbana-Champaign and completed her predoctoral internship and postdoctoral fellowship at Emory University Department of Psychiatry and Behavioral Sciences. Dr. Watson-Singleton strongly identifies as a clinical-community psychologist, which is reflected in her scholarship, teaching, and clinical-community work. Her research focuses on two lines of inquiry: (1) understanding how racism influences African Americans' health disparities, with special attention to African American women and (2) modifying interventions to meet the cultural needs of African Americans. Overall, Dr. Watson-Singleton aims to produce research that can bridge science and practice to improve the lives of marginalized communities.

**Danyelle Dawson, MA,** is a doctoral candidate in clinical-community psychology at the University of Illinois Urbana-Champaign and co-founder of the DEAR Project. She received her bachelor's degree in psychology and social and economic justice from the University of North Carolina at Chapel Hill and her master's degree in psychology from North Carolina Central University. Ms. Dawson's program of research focuses on (1) the mental and physical impacts of racism and discrimination on marginalized populations and (2) individual- and community-level engagement in resistance and healing (e.g., radical healing, anti-racism advocacy, sociopolitical action, community building). As a researcher trained in both clinical and community psychology, her research and applied work aims to enhance both individual- and systems-level capacity to resist and challenge oppressive contexts and realities. Ms. Dawson has published numerous papers related to these topics and has won several awards recognizing her commitment to diversity and anti-racist endeavors in her work. She has worked with university counseling centers, local mental health boards, and community organizations to build their evaluation capacity and facilitate their intentional work to continuously create and sustain organizational processes consistent with their organizational goals.